Controversies in Second Language Writing

Michigan Series on Teaching Multilingual Writers

Series Editors
Diane Belcher (Georgia State University) and
Jun Liu (University of Arizona)

Available titles in the series

Peer Response in Second Language Writing Classrooms
   Jun Liu & Jette G. Hansen

Treatment of Error in Second Language Student Writing
   Dana R. Ferris

Critical Academic Writing and Multilingual Students
   A. Suresh Canagarajah

Controversies in Second Language Writing:
Dilemmas and Decisions in Research and Instruction
   Christine Pearson Casanave

Controversies in Second Language Writing

Dilemmas and Decisions in Research and Instruction

Christine Pearson Casanave

Teachers College Columbia University
Tokyo, Japan

Michigan Series on Teaching Multilingual Writers

Ann Arbor
THE UNIVERSITY OF MICHIGAN PRESS

Copyright © by the University of Michigan 2004
All rights reserved
Published in the United States of America by
The University of Michigan Press
Manufactured in the United States of America
∞ Printed on acid-free paper

2007   2006   2005   2004   4   3   2   1

A CIP catalog record for this book is available from the British Library.

Library of Congress Cataloging-in-Publication Data

Casanave, Christine Pearson, 1944–
    Controversies in second language writing : dilemmas and decisions
in research and instruction / Christine Pearson Casanave.
        p.   cm. — (Michigan series on teaching multilingual writers)
    Includes bibliographical references and index.
    ISBN 0-472-08979-X (pbk. : alk. paper)
    1. English language—Study and teaching—Foreign speakers.
2. English language—Composition and exercises—Study and
teaching—Foreign speakers.   3. English language—Rhetoric—
Study and teaching—Foreign speakers.   4. Report writing—
Study and teaching.   5. Second language acquisition.   I. Title
II. Series.

PE1404.C3495 2004
808'.042'071—dc22   2003016342

Contents

Series Foreword

More than a decade ago Tony Silva (1990) observed that the "merry-go-round of approaches" in the field of second language writing "generates more heat than light and does not encourage consensus on important issues" (p. 18). Silva noted further that "such a situation engenders a great deal of confusion and insecurity among ESL composition teachers" (p. 18). A number of helpful teacher reference books on L2 writing pedagogical methods have appeared since Silva's observations, for example, Ferris and Hedgcock's (1998) *Teaching ESL Composition* and Hyland's (2002) *Teaching and Researching Writing,* to name just two. However, while such introductory overviews of the teaching of L2 writing help pre- and in-service teachers become aware of competing approaches to L2 writing pedagogy, none of them, given their broader goals, focuses so explicitly and extensively on a wide range of methodological controversies as does Christine Casanave's *Controversies in Second Language Writing: Dilemmas and Decisions in Research and Instruction.* In her characteristically engaging and highly accessible prose style, Casanave evenhandedly foregrounds and backgrounds what are arguably among the most compelling and complex areas of interest in the field of L2 writing—topics that have long attracted well-deserved attention but also provoked protracted debate. Casanave clearly recognizes how crucial it is for classroom practitioners to take control of their decision making, for while questions about, for instance, what helps or hinders L2 writing improvement or how L2 writing is best evaluated may be of abiding intellectual interest to many, they are far more than academic to those who also actually teach L2 writing.

Practitioners, after all, are faced on a daily basis with the need to either make decisions about such questions for themselves in their classrooms or cede decision-making power to the textbooks, syllabi, or program policies already decided upon by others.

It is difficult to think of a key L2 writing controversy, or decision-making challenge, that Casanave does not cover in her volume. The range of topics impressively extends from some of the most fundamental nuts-and-bolts issues—for example, fluency versus accuracy, process versus product, various types of response and their debatable relationship with improvement—to those that are more ideological and theoretical but no less important for classroom practitioner decision making—for example, situatedness and genre theory (i.e., direct instruction vs. learning in situ), the ethics of assessment, accommodation versus resistance to established discourse expectations. Obviously, however, in the six chapters of this book, Casanave does not attempt to provide exhaustive coverage of any single topic (other, single-topic books in this series do delve more deeply into their areas of focus). What Casanave does do for the reader is clearly and succinctly highlight the main arguments involved in each L2 writing controversy, with expertly selected reviews of the literature and easy-to-relate-to personal accounts of the author's own grappling with the issues as a writer and writing teacher. One may justifiably wonder, though, considering how rapidly the methodological scene changes, if history won't eventually take care of currently unresolved controversies for us, sorting out the faddish chaff from what is more pedagogically valuable. The reality is, of course, that one can easily still find teachers and textbooks utilizing approaches, such as controlled composition and current-traditional rhetoric, that L2 writing researchers and theorists long ago lost interest in but that practitioners may still cling to, and perhaps with good reason, based on the day-to-day action research data they have gathered themselves. Certainly no one knows the contexts within individual classrooms better than the teachers whose classrooms they are. Casanave argues, however, that reflection on ongoing issues in the field in addition to one's own class-room experience can lead to "a vision that gives direction to the daily grind" as well as benefit L2 writing students. Far from being a source of further confusion, as many of the conflicting findings of the research literature can initially be, Casanave's guided tour through the seemingly never-ending debates of our profession will likely encourage readers to read more widely, purposefully, and critically in the field and ul-timately to make their own thoughtful, informed decisions about the challenging everyday classroom dilemmas all L2 writing teachers face.

References

Ferris, D., & Hedgcock, J. (1998). *Teaching ESL composition: Purpose, pro-cess, and practice.* Mahwah, NJ: Lawrence Erlbaum.

Hyland, K. (2002). *Teaching and researching writing.* London: Pearson Education.

Silva, T. (1990). Second language composition instruction: Developments, issues, and directions in ESL. In B. Kroll (Ed.), *Second language writing: Research insights for the classroom* (pp. 11–23). Cambridge: Cambridge University Press.

Introduction

Controversies in Second Language Writing: Dilemmas and Decisions in Research and Instruction (henceforth *Controversies*) is a book designed to help L2 writing teachers make informed decisions in their writing classes and build a knowledge base for conducting research on L2 writing. It is not a "how-to-teach" book but a book about thinking, reading, and reflecting.

In both the broad field of education and the specific field of second language education, there is great interest in how novice and experienced teachers make decisions in their classrooms. This question can be approached in many ways, and in this book I focus on just one of these: *that of how teachers in L2 writing can be helped to make reasoned decisions by understanding some of the key issues and conflicting opinions about L2 writing research and pedagogy.* By reviewing some of the controversies that have influenced how we conceptualize and teach writing to multilingual learners in school contexts, I hope in this book to help current and future L2 writing teachers make informed decisions in their own ESL/EFL classrooms.

The controversies pertain to both L1 and L2 writing and include questions about the incompatibility of fluency and accuracy, the contrastive rhetoric debate, the process-product debate, ways to assess improvement, the purpose and value of different kinds of feedback and error correction on writing, the argument about the value of explicit teaching of genres versus situated practice, issues of audience and plagiarism, and the dilemma of helping marginalized or disempowered writers accommodate or resist the way language is used in dominant cultures. Many of these debates among writing scholars remain unresolved or unresolvable. Still, because they deal with issues that L2 writing instructors face on a daily basis, novices as well as seasoned professionals in both foreign and second language settings must act on them in some way. Reviewing the scholarly arguments will help teachers take a reasoned position on them within the realities of their own classrooms and in light of their own underlying beliefs and assumptions about teaching and learning. The discussions in this book, in short, are intended to help writing teachers become both more knowledgeable and more reflective about the decisions they make in their teaching as well as more aware of their agency as decision makers in their own settings.

The stance I take in this book is that some of the debates that have characterized our field set up false dichotomies but that they should not be dismissed for this reason. The process-product debate is a clear example of such a false dichotomy that still merits thoughtful discussion by L2 writing teachers. There can be no product without a process for getting there, and there can be no process without some kind of resulting product, even if that product is a shopping list or an application form. Teachers, therefore, in good conscience, cannot ignore either but can choose to focus more on one than the other for pedagogical purposes (or may be forced to do so by curricular mandates) and can help students understand that the two sides of this particular coin cannot be separated. Reviewing this particular debate will also help teachers recognize that other aspects of writing, such as social and political factors, complicate the apparent dichotomy of process and product (see the 2003 special issue of the *Journal of Second Language Writing* [*12*(1)], "L2 Writing in the Post-process Era").

Another example comes from genre studies and contrastive rhetoric. Here arguments persist about whether genres are most usefully seen as primarily formal and textual regularities that are specific to particular cultures or as social and disciplinary phenomena enacted in texts and whether students benefit from explicit teaching of genres as opposed to learning them in situ.

The picture is not black-and-white, nor is the argument fully resolvable, given the legitimacy of multiple views and goals.

A third example of false dichotomies can be seen in the debate between pragmatist and critical approaches to EAP (English for Academic Purposes). This debate pits teachers who believe their main job is to teach L2 students functional writing skills against those who hope to encourage students to develop a critical awareness of the political and ideological aspects of their writing tasks and possibly contribute to social change. Other controversies in the field have been similarly falsely dichotomized, giving novice teachers in particular the message that they should make either-or decisions in their teaching, that clear decisions are in fact possible, and that the latest fad surely must be the best. In this book I hope to counter these misunderstandings, not only through summaries of the key arguments themselves, but also through examples of how teachers have dealt with them in their own classrooms.

A thread running through the entire book, and framing the book in chapter 1, will be that writing teachers benefit from being aware of, and openly discussing with others, the criteria they use to make the countless decisions that they need to make every day in the classroom. The criteria fall into three broad areas: philosophy of teaching and learning; knowledge of relevant issues; and the practical constraints of local teaching and learning settings. These decision-making criteria apply across the board, to ESL, EFL, and FL settings and across the topics I discuss in *Controversies.*

Writing teachers who are new to the field of L2 writing will find this book particularly valuable in that from the first day of class they will be faced with the questions raised in the book in their daily practice of teaching. Although the book does not provide novice teachers with immutable answers, it lays out issues, presents reasoned opinions and guidelines, and poses questions for ongoing discussion and reflection. Seasoned teachers as well will find the discussion and question-oriented approach of the book valuable in that it encourages knowledge building and reflection by all teachers. The presumption is that teachers' knowledge changes and grows throughout a career and that ongoing knowledge-based reflection helps prevent teaching practices and attitudes toward teaching from becoming stale and routinized. Debate, controversy, and informed discussion contribute to this growth. Teachers are likewise encouraged to recognize that a book like this can provide only an introduction to key controversies in the field and that to become fully informed about and engaged in the debates, they need to delve into the literature where the issues are discussed in more depth and detail. Reference lists and selected bibliographies of relevant resources are provided at the end of each chapter to encourage teachers to read further.

Controversies consists of an introductory chapter and five main chapters, each of which is divided into several sections. The first part of each main chapter begins with thought-provoking quotations from the literature and initial decision-oriented questions for readers to consider, after which an introduction lays out the issues or controversies to be reviewed. The second section, "Discussions in the Literature," reviews some of the important literature that has addressed the issues, focusing in some depth on the arguments of a few key people. The third section, "Classroom Perspectives," presents descriptive and research data from the author's classroom experiences or from the classroom research and pedagogy of others. The following short section, "Ongoing Questions," sums up the ongoing and unresolved issues. A final section, "Beliefs and Practices," can usefully be used as either a starting or a concluding point for each chapter. This section of direct questions to readers encourages personal reflection on teaching beliefs and practices in the specific contexts of their own teaching and learning. Each chapter is followed by a combined reference list and list of other relevant readings. These resources are provided at the end of each chapter rather than at the end of the book so as to cluster them according to the themes in the chapters. The extensive lists are designed to encourage readers to consult original source readings and to continue their explorations as part of graduate course work, classroom teaching, or research projects in L2 writing.

Chapter 1, "Beliefs and Realities: A Framework for Decision Making," introduces readers to the roles played in their decision making by a carefully thought-out belief system, in conjunction with a realistic assessment of the practical constraints of local contexts of teaching.

Chapter 2, "Contrastive Rhetoric," reviews some of the arguments surrounding the contrastive rhetoric field since the appearance of Robert Kaplan's triggering article in 1966. Some of the arguments involve methodological issues in contrastive rhetoric research, the dangers of cultural stereotyping, and the textual, as opposed to social, focus of the field.

Chapter 3, "Paths to Improvement," examines only three controversies that concern ways that students might improve their writing. One is the fluency-accuracy dilemma, another is the process-product debate, and the third is the role of response with a particular focus on error correction.

Chapter 4, "Assessment," reviews some of the difficult issues surrounding the methods and purposes of assessing L2 students' writing. These issues include questions about objectivity and subjectivity, rater reliability, and ethical dilemmas in assessment.

Chapter 5, "Interaction," deals with only two controversial issues connected with the concept of interaction in L2 writing practices, those of audience (writers' interaction with readers) and plagiarism (writers' interaction with the published words of others).

Finally, chapter 6, "Politics and Ideology," covers three difficult areas of controversy: the debate in EAP between those favoring accommodationist pragmatism and those favoring critical pedagogy; the cultural politics of critical thinking; and the politics of Internet technology.

Some issues inevitably overlap in different chapters of this book and may be covered more thoroughly in other books in the Michigan Series on Teaching Multilingual Writers, but I see this as a strength rather than a weakness in that it reinforces the idea that L2 writing is a complex interweaving of practices that can be studied at several levels of detail. The book offers readers few solutions and no prescriptions but draws them into some of the complex issues about which L2 writing teachers need to make decisions every day.

Acknowledgments

Writing a professional book is far from a solitary endeavor, in spite of the fact that writers log in thousands of solitary hours behind a computer screen and in libraries and in coffee shops. During the two-year period of planning and drafting this book, I was employed at Keio University in Fujisawa, Japan, and I am deeply grateful for the resources made available to me there. Yasuko Kanno and David Shea discussed the idea for this book with me at its earliest stages and helped me realize that the idea for it was worth pursuing. I am particularly grateful to Paul Kei Matsuda and his students for their detailed comments on and suggestions for the chapter on contrastive rhetoric and to Kathi Bailey for her expert advice on the chapter on assessment. In a more general sense, I owe a great deal to the M.A. students at Teachers College Columbia University in Japan for providing a forum in which I could organize and share my evolving ideas and knowledge about L2 writing. Special thanks go to several of the Starbucks Japan coffee shops I frequented around Fujisawa, Japan, in particular the one in Shonandai, for providing me with smiling faces and a smoke-free environment in which to work when I could not face the computer. Finally, a project like this could not have been completed without support from superb editors like Diane Belcher and Jun Liu, from the reviewers who initially provided helpful comments at the earliest stage of this project, and from Kelly Sippell, Christina Milton, and the other professional production staff at the University of Michigan Press.

I dedicate this book to the many wonderful students who "suffered" through my labor-intensive writing classes over the 12 years that I taught in Japan, and who—when the experience was over—returned to thank me. I thank them, for helping me realize that L2 writers, like everyone else I suppose, live up to the challenge of high expectations.

Chapter 1

Beliefs and Realities:
A Framework for Decision Making

"How do teachers decide what to teach, how to represent it, how to question students about it and how to deal with problems of misunderstanding?" (Shulman, 1986)

"[T]eacher education needs to engage teachers not merely in the mastery of rules of practice but in an exploration of the knowledge, beliefs, attitudes, and thinking that inform such practice." (Richards, 1998)

LEADING QUESTIONS

- What roles do teacher beliefs, assumptions, and philosophies of learning and teaching play in the decision-making process in L2 writing classes?
- How can knowledge of relevant issues in L2 writing inform teachers' decisions?
- To what extent do belief systems and practical realities of the classroom support or work against each other?

Introduction to the Issues

Teachers make hundreds of decisions in their classrooms every day. Some decisions involve planning. With greater or lesser degrees of control over their decisions, teachers decide what content to teach, what materials to use, what sequences to present content in, what pedagogical activities to set up using different participation structures, what kinds of homework and in-class work to assign, and what kinds of assessments and grading criteria to use. Other decisions need to be made on the spot: how to respond to students' questions, how to explain an activity if students misunderstand the initial set of instructions, how to handle recalcitrant or overly silent or talkative students on a particular day, how to switch gears midclass either to take advantage of opportunities that arise unexpectedly or to adjust a lesson plan that cannot be finished in the allotted time, how to respond to a piece of writing that contains disturbing personal information, and generally how to manage and negotiate the countless unforeseen contingencies that arise every teaching day. These decisions are based on teachers' current goals for and beliefs about teaching and learning, on their current knowledge of their subject matter and relevant content-based issues, and on constraints of the immediate teaching context.

If asked, teachers can often explain that they are using certain materials in a particular way because they believe, for example, that students will be motivated by this approach and therefore learn more, or that this or that approach has been shown to be effective through research on writing and second language acquisition (SLA), or that the adaptations they make in an approach stem in part from classroom factors such as class size, time constraints, and curricular mandates at the departmental level. Of course, there are unarticulated default beliefs—unexamined assumptions about teaching and learning—that may seem not like beliefs at all but more like routines and patterns, developed and followed through habit and through teachers' own experiences with learning in their pasts rather than through systematic reflection and conscious choice. Teachers may also choose, or be given, materials, lessons, and assessment tools without reflecting on the assumptions about teaching and learning that underlie those materials and tools. If the materials look good, if they are written by reputable authors and published by good publishers, and if they have been approved by the department, they must be good. Many teachers, moreover, pressed for time and short of energy, just hope to get through another day. Reflection on beliefs and issues, which requires some intellectual and emotional investment, may not be high on their lists of daily or weekly activities.

Nevertheless, examined or unexamined, within awareness or not, teacher choices and behaviors in the classroom reflect underlying beliefs and assumptions. One of my own strong beliefs is that teachers benefit from bringing underlying beliefs into conscious awareness by articulating those beliefs, reflecting on them, and modifying them as needed (Burns, 1992; Calderhead, 1989; Casanave & Schecter, 1997; Day, Calderhead, & Denicolo, 1993; Freeman & Richards, 1996; Gebhard & Oprandy, 1999; Richards, 1998; Richards & Lockhart, 1994; Ross, 1989; Schön, 1983, 1987; Valli, 1992). Our teaching can thus become more principled, less random, perhaps more experimental and innovative, more connected to the learning of particular students, and more subject to our own critical evaluation of techniques, methods, successes, and failures. With sets of articulated beliefs, we become more able to ask and respond to the important questions, Why am I choosing to teach in this way? and What effect is my teaching having on my students? and Given the practical constraints in my teaching situation, how can I best implement what I feel to be good decisions?

In this introductory chapter, I lay out several foundational areas for decision making in the L2 writing class. The areas fall into three broad categories that apply to teaching of any kind: **philosophy of teaching and learning; knowledge of relevant issues;** and the **practical realities of local teaching and learning settings.** First, being able to articulate a set of beliefs and assumptions about the teaching and learning of writing will help teachers evolve a consistent philosophy and match their decisions with those beliefs to the extent possible. Second, knowing what the relevant issues are will help teachers make principled decisions in conjunction with what we know to date about the teaching and learning of writing (including decisions that reject current trends). Finally, recognizing the

reality of practical constraints, such as bureaucratic requirements and structural realities, the unique characteristics of
particular classes, and classroom management factors, will
help writing teachers make the best decisions possible when
perhaps none are optimal.

Building a Philosophy of Teaching and Learning

Getting Started: Literacy Autobiographies

A good place to begin considering beliefs about teaching and
learning L2 writing is with a literacy autobiography. A **literacy
autobiography** recounts the history of one's key literacy experiences throughout a lifetime: memories of learning to read
and write, influential moments and people that contributed to
one's sense of self as a reader-writer, memorable pieces of
writing, breakthroughs and blocks, struggles with and joys
of writing. For those involved in L2 writing, a literacy autobiography crucially includes one's experiences learning to read
and write in an L2 oneself. It is likely that our own L2 learning experiences influence choices we make today about teaching L2 writing. That L2 may be English, not just the stereotypical "foreign languages" that predominantly monolingual
English speakers think of when they hear the term *second/
foreign language.* Some of the most influential published literacy autobiographies in the L2 writing field have been written by scholars for whom English was not a mother tongue (see
Belcher & Connor, 2001; Braine, 1999; several of the pieces in
Casanave & Vandrick, 2003; Pavlenko, 1998, 2001). These literacy autobiographies reveal issues and challenges faced by
the authors as they developed a professional level of L2 literacy and provide clues about where their beliefs and assumptions about L2 literacy originated. In the broader field of SLA,
diary studies achieve a similar purpose (Bailey, 1983, 1990;
Bailey et al., 1996).

The polished form of a published literacy autobiography or
of a finished autobiography written as a class assignment in a

graduate applied linguistics or composition studies program lends the impression that once written, the literacy autobiography is finished. However, as a piece of writing that can both reveal underlying beliefs and assumptions about writing and contribute to their further development and to the development of a philosophy of teaching and learning, a literacy autobiography can productively be revised many times over a teaching career. In revising and rethinking their own literacy experiences, authors can add new experiences and insights and reinterpret ones from the past, just as they can from a life story (Bell, 1997; Giddens, 1991; Linde, 1993; Polkinghorne, 1991). The literacy autobiography is thus a piece of writing in perpetual draft form, ready to be revisited, restoried, and reinterpreted in light of new experiences and of responses of self and others with whom it is shared. It provides the initial airing of beliefs about teaching and learning that can be linked later to decisions in the classroom.

Examining the Sources of Beliefs from the Inside Out

In further articulating a philosophy of L2 teaching and learning, we can also consider sometimes intangible "internal" factors that may or may not have been addressed in a literacy autobiography. I am thinking here of the rather amorphous factors of personality, cognitive style, preferences in learning strategies, and even influences of upbringing as to what behaviors and attitudes are considered efficient, productive, and even moral in leading to future goals for self and students. Whether we realize it or not at the time, these intangible internal factors influence decisions we make in the classroom. Understanding these influences can help us sort the reasoned decisions from knee-jerk responses in the classroom or from strongly felt emotional beliefs that appear so normal that they cloud other ways of seeing.

For example, it is possible that a teacher who is fundamentally outgoing, social, and confident will tend to set up class activities that differ from those set up by a teacher who is shy, inward, and solitary by nature. I have sometimes found myself questioning my decisions in the classroom: Should I ask students to do what I could not do at their age or what I still dislike doing today? A second example, more directly connected to writing, concerns the extent to which a writing teacher is by nature a "radical outliner" or a "radical brainstormer" (Reid, 1984). I have never been able to outline before I write, at least according to the textbook rules, so for years I never asked my students to do outlines either. But by turning my own predisposition into an unreflective belief about how to teach, I was probably limiting students' choices in unfair ways, in that some people benefit greatly from making very detailed outlines. My beliefs about how people plan their writing needed to expand and to become more accessible to self-analysis and critique, and as they did, my messages to students in the writing classroom changed.

The point is that our internal beliefs and predispositions tend to be less clearly visible and articulatable than those we can trace to external influences. They thus merit careful attention through self-observation, interaction with colleagues, reflective journal writing, and open discussion with students. Once articulated, beliefs that develop from the inside out can be acted upon, or not, as teachers decide how to construct and respond to teaching and learning situations in the L2 writing class.

Examining the Sources of Beliefs from the Outside In

Adding further to the development of an articulated philosophy of teaching and learning, we can point to the influence of external factors on our belief systems and concomitant classroom decision-making behaviors (see also the discussion in the following section "The Reality of Practical Constraints"). For example, teachers may have first learned to teach primarily by using certain textbooks and not others. Textbooks embody (often inconsistent) philosophies of teaching and learning in the kinds of exercises they ask students to do, the sequences of those exercises, and the implicit or suggested roles of teachers. Teachers who are required to use certain textbooks and not others, or who have favorite textbooks, methods, or tasks, or who have free rein to choose and develop materials can profit from examining the assumptions about teaching and learning inherent in those materials and tasks. The assumptions may or may not accord with teachers' own articulated beliefs and may or may not contribute to the development of those beliefs.

Another external influence on teachers' beliefs includes the lessons learned from mentors, master teachers, or colleagues. These influential people may be part of a graduate school program as one's professors and peers, they may be charismatic and inspiring presenters at conferences, or they may be other teachers or even students with whom one is working. As an example, I recall one of my first encounters with second language educator John Fanselow at a conference many years ago, where he was speaking to a hall of enthusiastic admirers. Through his presentation, and later through collegial contact (see Casanave, 2002, chap. 6; Fanselow, 1997), I learned from him to *see* in a different, more open way, even though my teaching style was not modeled on his.

A third external influence on teachers' beliefs comes from books and articles available in the field, through self-study or schooling, that express views about approaches to teaching, often regrettably to the exclusion of currently unpopular or "old-fashioned" approaches. For example, strong and persuasive voices in the field can intimidate teachers into believing that attention to grammar is wrong or right, that communication is or is not the central goal of language education, or that students either should or need not learn to express themselves personally in their writing. However, strong and persuasive voices can also advocate openness, flexibility, and change. By attending to and comparing many voices in the field, teachers discover consistencies and conflicts, allies and enemies, inspiration and trivia, and they can selectively merge and adapt the views of others as they build their own belief systems.

As an example of some of the early external influences on my beliefs and practices in second language education, when

I first began teaching ESL many years ago, my only qualification was that I was a native speaker of English. I had not yet studied anything in applied linguistics or education, and I relied heavily on the textbook that I was assigned to teach, Robert Lado's now classic audiolingual text series, *English 900*. I "learned" to believe in the primacy of speech, the importance of habit formation and pattern drills, and the need for students to practice, repeat, and practice some more. In the several years that followed I worked as a part-timer with only one other teacher, and she was thoroughly schooled in the same audiolingual behaviorist camp. My teaching and materials development followed in her footsteps. My beliefs in the audiolingual approach began to erode thanks to another external influence, a publisher's review of the draft of a grammar textbook this colleague and I had submitted. Although two of the three reviews had been quite positive, the third claimed in no uncertain terms that our approach was dated, that attention to grammar was passé, and that we needed to go back to the drawing board and familiarize ourselves with the new communicative approach to language teaching. Like many others, I jumped on the communicative language teaching and process writing bandwagon, read all the right books, didn't talk about grammar for a number of years, and rethought my whole approach to teaching and learning. When I eventually recognized the bandwagon I had jumped on, I once mentioned the importance of grammar in communicative approaches to language teaching at a conference talk I was giving, before it became fashionable to do so. I was publicly put down by an assertive-voiced male in the audience who walked out of the room when I countered *his* strongly held belief that grammar did not belong in communicative approaches. Although several members of the audience later expressed support for my then controversial view, the experience of not being on the bandwagon was difficult for me as a relatively new scholar in the ESL field.

I am embarrassed today about my earlier bandwagon escapades but realize that as an inexperienced teacher without a strong graduate education at the time, I developed my beliefs and practices in quite normal ways. Now, many years later, I continue to study and to learn from external sources such as published literature, colleagues, and even students, but I hope I am not deceiving myself into thinking that I am impervious to fads. They lurk around every corner waiting to capture my attention. Nevertheless, by becoming close observers of the influences on and characteristics of our own belief systems, I and other teachers become able to render these systems into the flexible, dynamic, growing philosophies of teaching and learning that they deserve to be and that can contribute to reasoned decision making in the classroom. The challenges involve developing a coherent and internally consistent belief system in the first place, then recognizing it not as dogma, fixed in stone (or print, as the case is more likely to be), but as a dynamic evolving system that continues to grow over a lifetime.

Knowledge of Relevant Issues

It is not enough to know thyself. Teachers must also know the content of their fields and which issues are historically important and currently unresolved. In the field of language teacher education in general, teachers need to build a knowledge base that includes theories of teaching, knowledge of teaching and communication skills, subject matter knowledge, pedagogical reasoning and decision-making skills, and knowledge of the contexts of teaching (Hedgcock, 2002; Richards, 1998). In the broader field of education, Shulman (1987) adds curricular knowledge, knowledge of educational purposes and philosophies, and (Shulman, 1986) case knowledge (understanding of specific cases in teaching) to the knowledge base of effective teachers. In the field of L2 writing, this expertise is based on thorough knowledge about the target language, including knowledge of the conventions of writing and rhetoric in the target language, and some knowledge about the languages, cultures, and writing conventions pertinent to the students they are teaching. It includes as well knowledge about theories of L2 writing, such as they are (Silva, 1990, 1993), about methods and processes of teaching writing, and about key issues in writing research and practice. In this section, I discuss primarily the need for teachers to build knowledge of relevant content and issues in L2 writing, many of which are taken up in other books in this series and are dealt with in the remaining chapters of this book. With the help of such knowledge, teachers are in a position to make principled and informed decisions in the face of sometimes conflicting ideas in the field or dilemmas that arise in the classroom itself. Questions that integrate such information with teaching methods and processes are taken up as well in general books on teaching ESL writing (e.g., Ferris & Hedgcock, 1998; Reid, 1993).

Where does writing teachers' knowledge come from? One essential source is intuitions—about writing processes, products, and problems—that teachers develop over a lifetime of their own experiences with writing. Intuitions about writing can be considered a kind of felt knowledge and may or may not be fully accessible to conscious reflection. (This is one reason why teachers can benefit from writing a literacy autobiography, discussed earlier.) Many of us, for example, can state unequivocally that we find it difficult to write in our first languages, to say nothing of our second (or third) languages. (It is not just our students who find writing difficult.) However, it is more challenging to try to explain to someone, or to ourselves, just why it is difficult to write. In attempting such an explanation, both teachers and students may identify some of the relevant issues in writing: I worry so much about getting every word and phrase right that I lose the forest for the trees, become stuck, and can't move on (a problem of fluency and accuracy); I fear being judged (critiqued, assessed, graded) (a problem of assessment); I don't know what is expected of me in terms of content or rhetorical structure in a particular piece of writing (a problem of genre and explicitness of instruction); I don't know who I am really writing for or how to incorporate the voices of others in my writing without plagiarizing (problems of interaction); I don't know whether I should take a stand or innovate in a piece of writing or just paraphrase the ideas and formal conventions of others (a problem of accommodation and resistance). The more experience L2 writing teachers have as writers themselves, the more likely it is that they will be able to articulate issues such as these and to help their students identify them as well. But these issues have all been researched in the L2 writing field, so teachers do not need to rely solely on their intuitions and experiences. The books in this series on teaching multilingual writers, *Controversies* in particular, are designed to help writing teachers and their students identify, bring under conscious control, and put to good use relevant issues in L2 writing.

Perhaps the best way to begin accruing already researched knowledge of the fundamental issues that characterize the field of L2 writing is through a good graduate-level education. Writing teachers and future writing teachers become acquainted with central ideas, issues, and theories through books, journal articles, and lectures and discussions. By learning *about* relevant content and issues, teachers can then integrate this knowledge with the intuitive and experiential knowledge they have gained throughout their lifetimes. Important conflicts and contradictions will no doubt surface, providing teachers with the opportunity to wrestle with issues at deep levels of analysis and reflection. Reflective journals and learning logs are especially useful for this purpose (Richards & Ho, 1998).

Although a good graduate-level education can start novice teachers on the road to a life of study of relevant content and issues, equally important is a commitment to ongoing study after graduate education ends. By continuing to read key books and journals, attending occasional conferences, discussing issues with colleagues, and perhaps writing for publication, teachers build relevant content knowledge over the lifetime of their careers and keep up with current issues and controversies. This knowledge in turn contributes to their evolving intuitions, philosophies, and ability to make reasoned decisions in their classrooms.

Knowledge of relevant issues and content will rarely provide teachers with clear answers, however. As I will suggest in this book, there are enough debates and controversies in the L2 writing field to keep L2 writing teachers thinking, studying, learning, and reflecting for many years to come. Building knowledge over our professional lifetimes will complicate, not simplify, our teaching lives. But it will enable us to see, understand, and, where practically feasible, act on choices that were once invisible.

The Reality of Practical Constraints

Fortunate teachers are able to integrate their beliefs and assumptions about teaching and learning L2 writing, their knowledge of relevant content and issues, and the practical realities of their teaching situations. However, it is often the case that practical realities get in the way of what we believe and know, with the result that teaching materials and practices conflict with deeply held philosophies. Graduate language teacher education programs that have a substantial practicum in actual teaching as part of their requirements can begin to deal with this integration in that novice teachers soon discover that their energies are often taken up more with practical concerns than with content and theory they learned from course work. For instance, teaching journals and follow-up discussions in the practicum class might focus less on the benefits of small-group peer reading in a writing class than on how to get students efficiently into groups and interacting productively with each other in the first place. The problem is exacerbated if there are no movable desks in the classroom. Wonderful ideas learned in course work and readings, in other words, may be difficult to implement in specific teaching settings.

Structural and systemic constraints that have plagued my own teaching include writing classes that meet only once a week for 90 minutes, just 13 times a semester; large classes that prevent my being able to work with student writers as closely as I would like; and schedules so heavy for students in the Japanese university system that they do not have time or focus to read or write regularly. These constraints clash with my beliefs that learning to write requires years of practice, not weeks; that writing is a social practice requiring deep engagement with readings and with other writers; and that focused, rather than fragmented, time is needed if writers are to move their writing forward. I have myself tried to write a paper along with students within the one-semester time period and find that the term-paper assignment when applied to myself brings out many of these structural and systemic constraints. Weeks go by when I do not or cannot make time to write; colleagues who are my potential peer readers are busy; other obligations in my life interfere with my ability to concentrate. What gets turned in at the end is as much an artificially concluded and incomplete draft as are those drafts that my students turn in, and I have a great advantage over them in that I choose topics about which I already have a great deal of organized knowledge. At the same time, the artificial deadlines imposed by the realities of the classroom situation ensure that we all get something written.

Other institutional realities may require that teachers use materials that have been selected by others, such as administrators or committees of teachers, or that have been selected from a limited pool of choices approved by a government or educational board. Teachers' choices are also severely constrained when there is an institutional mandate to cover a certain amount of material within a semester or a school year or to work in lockstep with other teachers who are forced to use the same material. A pervasive problem in many settings that further undermines the good ideas and intentions of teachers is institutional (and cultural and parental) concern with students' standardized examination scores rather than with their learning to write. In my own experience working with high school teachers in Japan, for example, I find that frustrated teachers may be able to squeeze in just 10 minutes a class session for real writing activities. The rest of the time they follow a mandated, exam-oriented curriculum.

Another practical reality of every classroom concerns classroom management and the ways that interactions with individual students and groups of students influence how teachers' decisions play out and how their beliefs and knowledge are enacted. By listening to teachers talk around the lunch table, it is possible to get a sense of how pervasive these concerns are. I seldom hear teachers talking about their beliefs, about current issues in the field, about relevant books or articles they are reading, or about ways to enact their beliefs and knowledge in their classes. It is more likely that teachers focus on problem situations that impinge in very real ways on what happens on a day-to-day basis in their classes. How can I get students to stop chatting and to listen to me when I am giving them important information or instructions? What do I do with the disruptive student who refuses to cooperate and who damages the whole atmosphere of the class? How do I get quiet students to participate actively? What if students show no interest in revising their writing, believing perhaps that what they need is grammar lessons, and so do not turn in required drafts? How do I handle the student who communicates to me or to other students (orally, electronically, or in print) in ways that seem disrespectful? What do I do with the small group of students in the back that insists on chatting rather than on completing in-class writing activities? These concerns and others can consume the time and energy of well-meaning teachers who really want to be spending every possible precious moment helping their students learn to write in their second language.

In sum, teachers who are forced to follow imposed materials and practices may inevitably find that materials and decisions imposed by others clash, in ways that range from frustrating to enraging, with their own evolving philosophies about how their students can best learn to write (or speak or read) in their second language. Additionally, structural constraints such as large class size, immovable student desks, and minimal time available for writing instruction and practice can easily take precedence over teachers' belief systems and knowledge of their field. Finally, the daily grind of classroom management can subvert teachers' enactment of what they believe and know about learning to write in a second language. This picture may sound bleak, but it does not necessarily have to be so. I have found that some teachers working under constraints that make me want to escape the field are able to find clever, inspiring, and forward-looking ways to work with and around the realities of practical constraints. These teachers have developed a strong sense of what they believe about teaching and learning L2 writing, and their beliefs and knowledge help provide them with a vision that gives direction to the daily grind. Their students—in the long run, at any rate—benefit.

Ongoing Questions

This chapter has laid out some of the basic factors that influence the decisions that teachers make in their L2 writing classes. It urges that teachers consider not only what they do on a daily basis but what they believe and know about teaching and learning. Such reflection is part of an ongoing lifetime effort to develop a consistent and coherent belief system that can help guide teachers through the practical realities and constraints they face in each classroom setting and provide a sense of vision when the daily grind seems to want to swallow us up. However, the controversies in L2 writing that I discuss in this book and around which I pose ongoing questions have no easy resolution—hence the word *dilemmas,* rather than *problems,* appears in my subtitle. Dilemmas, Cuban (1992, p. 6) points out, are "often intractable to routine solutions." Dilemmas, therefore, involve decisions and choices that may lead to "good-enough" compromises rather than ideal outcomes (p. 7). Whatever the outcomes, if teachers' decisions are based on thoughtful reflection and a solid knowledge base, L2 writing students stand to benefit.

Many specific questions remain, and I hope readers will approach each chapter in this book, and each book in this series, with questions about their own beliefs and practices: Why am I teaching in the way I do? Why do I believe that this or that kind of exercise will improve my students' writing? Why am I using the particular materials that I have and why in the particular way I am adapting them? Whose voices in the field make most sense to me? Whose agendas am I following, should I resist or accommodate, and should I encourage my students to resist or accommodate? Perhaps one of the most important questions of all is, How do all of my questions pertain to me as a writer, in my first and second languages? What teachers believe about themselves as writers influences their decisions as teachers of writing in ways that can be enlightening and inspiring.

References and Relevant Readings

Almarza, G. (1996). Student foreign language teachers' knowledge growth. In D. Freeman & J. C. Richards (Eds.), *Teacher learning in language teaching* (pp. 50–78). Cambridge: Cambridge University Press.

Bailey, K. M. (1983). Competitiveness and anxiety in adult second language learning: Looking at and through the diary studies. In H. W. Seliger & M. H. Long (Eds.), *Classroom oriented research in second language acquisition* (pp. 67–102). Rowley, MA: Newbury House.

Bailey, K. M. (1990). The use of diary studies in teacher education programs. In J. C. Richards & D. Nunan (Eds.), *Second language teacher education* (pp. 46–61). New York: Cambridge University Press.

Bailey, K. M., Bergthold, B., Braunstein, B., Fleischman, N. J., Holbrook, M. P., Truman, J., Waissbluth, X., & Zambo, L. J. (1996). The language learner's autobiography: Examining the "apprenticeship of observation." In D. Freeman & J. C. Richards (Eds.), *Teacher learning in language teaching* (pp. 11–29). New York: Cambridge University Press.

Belcher, D., & Connor, U. (Eds.). (2001). *Reflections on multiliterate lives.* Clevedon: Multilingual Matters.

Bell, J. (1997). Shifting frames, shifting stories. In C. P. Casanave & S. R. Schecter (Eds.), *On becoming a language educator: Personal essays on professional development* (pp. 133–143). Mahwah, NJ: Lawrence Erlbaum.

Braine, G. (Ed.). (1999). *Non-native educators in English language teaching.* Mahwah, NJ: Lawrence Erlbaum.

Burns, A. (1992). Teacher beliefs and their influence on classroom practice. *Prospect, 7*(3), 56–66.

Calderhead, J. (1989). Reflective teaching and teacher education. *Teaching & Teacher Education, 5*(1), 43–51.

Casanave, C. P. (2002). *Writing games: Multicultural case studies of academic literacy practices in higher education.* Mahwah, NJ: Lawrence Erlbaum.

Casanave, C. P., & Schecter, S. R. (Eds.). (1997). *On becoming a language educator: Personal essays on professional development.* Mahwah, NJ: Lawrence Erlbaum.

Casanave, C. P., & Vandrick, S. (Eds.). (2003). *Writing for scholarly publication: Behind the scenes in language education.* Mahwah, NJ: Lawrence Erlbaum.

Clandinin, D. J., & Connelly, F. M. (1995). *Teachers' professional knowledge landscapes.* New York: Teachers College Press.

Clandinin, D. J., & Connelly, F. M. (2000). *Narrative inquiry: Experience and story in qualitative research.* San Francisco: Jossey-Bass.

Cuban, L. (1992). Managing dilemmas while building professional communities. *Educational Researcher, 21*(1), 4–11.

Day, C., Calderhead, J., & Denicolo, P. (Eds.). (1993). *Research on teacher thinking: Understanding professional development.* London: Falmer Press.

Fanselow, J. (1997). Postcard realities. In C. P. Casanave & S. R. Schecter (Eds.), *On becoming a language educator: Personal essays on professional development* (pp. 157–172). Mahwah, NJ: Lawrence Erlbaum.

Ferris, D., & Hedgcock, J. (1998). *Teaching ESL composition: Purpose, process, and practice.* Mahwah, NJ: Lawrence Erlbaum.

Freeman, D. (1989). Teacher training, development, and decision-making. *TESOL Quarterly, 23,* 27–45.

Freeman, D., & Richards, J. C. (Eds.). (1996). *Teacher learning in language teaching.* Cambridge: Cambridge University Press.

Gebhard, J. G., & Oprandy, R. (1999). *Language teaching awareness: A guide to exploring beliefs and practices.* Cambridge: Cambridge University Press.

Giddens, A. (1991). *Modernity and self-identity: Self and society in the late modern age.* Stanford, CA: Stanford University Press.

Hedgcock, J. (2002). Toward a socioliterate approach to second language teacher education. *Modern Language Journal, 86,* 299–317.

Johnson, K. E. (1992). Learning to teach: Instructional actions and decisions of preservice ESL teachers. *TESOL Quarterly, 26,* 507–535.

Linde, C. (1993). *Life stories: The creation of coherence.* New York: Oxford University Press.

Pavlenko, A. (1998). Second language learning by adults: Testimonies of bilingual writers. *Issues in Applied Linguistics, 9*, 3–19.

Pavlenko, A. (2001). "In the world of the tradition, I was unimagined": Negotiation of identities in cross-cultural autobiographies. *International Journal of Bilingualism, 5*, 317–344.

Peacock, M. (1999). Beliefs about language learning and their relationship to proficiency. *International Journal of Applied Linguistics, 9*, 247–265.

Peacock, M. (2001). Pre-service ESL teachers' beliefs about second language learning: A longitudinal study. *System, 29*, 177–195.

Polkinghorne, D. E. (1988). *Narrative knowing and the human sciences.* Albany: State University of New York Press.

Polkinghorne, D. E. (1991). Narrative and self-concept. *Journal of Narrative and Life History, 12*(2 & 3), 135–153.

Reid, J. (1984). The radical outliner and the radical brainstormer. *TESOL Quarterly, 18*, 529–533.

Reid, J. M. (1993). *Teaching ESL writing.* Englewood Cliffs, NJ: Prentice-Hall.

Richards, J. C. (1998). *Beyond training.* Cambridge: Cambridge University Press.

Richards, J. C., & Ho, B. (1998). Reflective thinking through journal writing. In J. C. Richards, *Beyond training* (pp. 153–170). Cambridge: Cambridge University Press.

Richards, J. C., & Lockhart, C. (1994). *Reflective teaching in second language classrooms.* Cambridge: Cambridge University Press.

Ross, D. D. (1989). First steps in developing a reflective approach. *Journal of Teacher Education, 40*(2), 22–30.

Schön, D. (1983). *The reflective practitioner: How professionals think in action.* New York: Basic Books.

Schön, D. (1987). *Educating the reflective practitioner: Toward a new design for teaching and learning in the professions.* San Francisco: Jossey-Bass.

Shulman, L. (1986). Those who understand: Knowledge growth in teaching. *Educational Researcher, 15*(2), 4–14.

Shulman, L. (1987). Knowledge and teaching: Foundations of the new reform. *Harvard Educational Review, 57*, 1–22.

Silva, T. (1990). Second language composition instruction: Developments, issues, and directions in ESL. In B. Kroll (Ed.), *Second language writing:*

Research insights for the classroom (pp. 11–23). Cambridge: Cambridge University Press.

Silva, T. (1993). Toward an understanding of the distinct nature of L2 writing: The ESL research and its implications. *TESOL Quarterly, 27,* 657–677.

Smith, D. (1996). Teacher decision-making in the adult ESL classroom. In D. Freeman & J. C. Richards (Eds.), *Teacher learning in language teaching* (pp. 197–216). Cambridge: Cambridge University Press.

Valli, L. (Ed.). (1992). *Reflective teacher education: Cases and critiques.* Albany: State University of New York Press.

Chapter 2
Contrastive Rhetoric

"[A] group of languages need not in the least correspond to a racial group or a culture area." (Sapir, 1921/1949)

"The study of language . . . shows that the forms of a person's thought are controlled by inexorable laws of pattern of which he is unconscious. . . . And every language is a vast pattern system, different from others, in which are culturally ordained the forms and categories by which the personality not only communicates, but also analyzes nature, notices or neglects types of relationship and phenomena, channels his reasons, and builds the house of his consciousness." (Whorf, 1956)

"Logic (in the popular, rather than the logician's sense of the word) which is the basis of rhetoric, is evolved out of a culture; it is not universal. Rhetoric, then, is not universal either, but varies from culture to culture and even from time to time within a given culture." (Kaplan, 1966)

"The thought patterns which speakers and readers of English appear to expect as an integral part of their communication is a sequence that is dominantly linear in its development." (Kaplan, 1966)

"[Q]uite a few Japanese intellectuals believe that the language they use and the texts they create are not logically organized. Obviously, these claims defy common sense. Japanese texts cannot be a sum of mutually unrelated semantic fragments. They must have a logical structure which prevents the text from disintegrating." (Nanri, 2001).

LEADING QUESTIONS

- What are the main arguments in the contrastive rhetoric debate?
- How might aspects of contrastive rhetoric continue to inform our views of writing from different cultures?
- What are the implications of contrastive rhetoric for the teaching of writing?

Introduction to the Issues

Contrastive rhetoric (CR) as a field of study began with the publication of Robert Kaplan's 1966 article in *Language Learning*. Kaplan assumed a kind of linguistic relativity, specifically that the rhetorical aspects of each language are unique to each language and culture. In second and foreign language education, this assumption implies that differences between the discourse-level features of a learner's first and second language cause difficulties for L2 learners who are trying to acquire discourse-level patterns in their second languages. In other words, inherent in the CR project is the assumption of negative transfer from L1 to L2. Understanding such differences, so the claim goes, can help scholars and teachers explain some of the problems that L2 learners have in organizing their writing in ways that seem acceptable to native speakers.

In the applied linguistics literature, "rhetoric" usually refers to discourse-level organizational patterns rather than, as Aristotle defined it, to a constellation of techniques for persuasion. Beginning with Kaplan's early article, Aristotle's five elements (invention, memory, arrangement, style, and delivery) were reduced to "arrangement" (Liebman, 1992, p. 142). In Kaplan's work CR is also tied to "modes of thinking," however, in the sense that what is considered logical in one culture may not be in another.

Kaplan's motivation in looking at rhetorics contrastively was pedagogical and, according to Connor (1998), continues to be so. The project, moreover, has been descriptive rather than predictive (Kaplan, 1988, pp. 275–276). As Kaplan pointed out, "the interest was primarily in finding solutions to an immediate pedagogical problem" (Kaplan, 1988, p. 277), one that L2 writing teachers continue to struggle with. He had observed many nonnative-like patterns (e.g., nonlinearity) in the English-language essays of undergraduates at his U.S. university and wished to help teachers design content and instructional materials that would help students write according to expected conventions, especially at the paragraph level. Since that time Kaplan's descriptions of several different culturally based rhetorical patterns, and the accompanying "doodles" of straight lines, circles, and zigzags, have been widely cited for their intuitively compelling "truths" and equally criticized for overgeneralizing a highly complex idea. Others, and Kaplan himself, later expanded Kaplan's original pedagogical project to one of research in which scholars investigated rhetorical features of writing across many languages (see, e.g., the collections in Connor & Kaplan, 1987, and Purves, 1988, and reviews in Connor, 1996, and Grabe & Kaplan, 1996).

Kaplan (1988) noted that the linguistic roots of CR stem from the Prague school of linguistics, but he did not discuss the philosophical underpinnings of linguistic relativity in the most widely read of his articles and book chapters. Matsuda (2001, p. 260) quotes from his personal communication with Kaplan that Kaplan was "really into Whorf-Sapir at the time." However, Kaplan cites Edward Sapir only twice in the (1966) original article and does not cite Sapir's student Benjamin Whorf at all, either in the original article or in "Cultural Thought Patterns Revisited" (Kaplan, 1987), so these underpinnings are unclear from Kaplan's writings. It may be that Kaplan has been more interested in the textual and pedagogical aspects of CR than in the philosophical connections among language, mind, and reality. Further speculation about the influences on Kaplan were made by Kowal (1998), who discussed some of Kaplan's work on Chinese counterfactuals.

Kowal suggested that by the mid-1980s Kaplan was familiar with the work of Alfred Bloom (1981) on the linguistic shaping of thought in the context of Chinese and English. However, Matsuda (1995, 2001) has pointed out that another very strong influence on Kaplan's ideas, including Kaplan's original focus on paragraph structure in students' writing, came from his teacher Francis Christensen at the University of Southern California. Christensen (1963, 1965) had authored two influential papers on sentence and paragraph rhetoric that Kaplan applied to the writing of nonnative English-speaking undergraduate students at USC. According to Matsuda, Kaplan hoped to show that L2 students were not suffering from cognitive deficits but revealing the influence of different rhetorical traditions in their L1s (Matsuda, email communication, February 1, 2002).

Most summaries of CR, however, claim that CR assumes the validity of the so-called Sapir-Whorf hypothesis of linguistic relativity or linguistic determinism (Connor, 1996; Kowal, 1998). As taken up by applied linguistics, the basic idea of this principle is that each language is characterized by a set of rhetorical conventions unique to it and that these rhetorical conventions influence (control? determine? shape?) how people in those cultures think and write. As reviewed in much literature post–Kaplan 1966, there is a strong version of the Whorfian principle that claims that language determines our perceptions and thoughts. This version, it is generally agreed, is too extreme as well as unprovable. The weaker version, that language influences thought, is more accepted and is considered testable by some (Hunt & Agnoli, 1991). Even though its status as a research program is somewhat uncertain (but see Connor, 2002), the Whorfian principle remains a comfortable, but vague, truism.

Regardless of our views on the Sapir-Whorf principle, if we look primarily at structural and organizational features of comparable texts written in different languages, differences are regularly found (e.g., Bickner & Peysantiwong, 1988; Clyne, 1987; Connor, 1987, 2000; Connor & Lauer, 1988; Eggington, 1987; Jenkins & Hinds, 1987; Kachru, 1988; Kamimura & Oi,

1997; Ostler, 1987; Régent, 1985; Söter, 1988; Taylor & Ting-guang, 1991), but the discussions in this work tend to avoid the difficult philosophical and ideological questions. In L2 educational circles, we are perhaps more interested in these structural aspects of our students' writing than in the intractable speculations about the connections among language, culture, mind, and reality. But even at the structural level, questions arise as to the sources of differences among languages. The assumption of CR enthusiasts has always been that cultural patterns inherent in the rhetorics of different languages cause L2 students to write in ways that are not native-like.

But what is a "cultural" pattern of rhetorical organization in writing? Is this aspect of culture something inside our heads or bodies? Is it something taught in schools? Is it something modeled in certain kinds of literature within cultures? How can we identify a "cultural pattern" when multiple cultures and subcultures, languages, dialects, and text types coexist within most countries of the world? ("Countries" themselves are national and political entities, not necessarily cultural or even linguistic ones.) What, additionally, does it mean to say that there is a "logic" peculiar to English? Does this refer to the language itself or to the users of the language and the text types they create? On the other hand, to what extent are problems that nonnative speakers have in writing the result of cultural influences, low L2 proficiency, schooling, inexperience in writing (a serious problem that L1 writers have), or something else?

In the next section of this chapter, I review some of the arguments that have persisted about CR, but I urge readers to go to some of the original sources, including Whorf, the original Kaplan (1966) article, and some of the subsequent published critiques and research in order to deepen their understanding of how complex the issues are. In TESOL graduate programs, for example, the Sapir-Whorf principle and the basic tenets of CR can be presented in a paragraph and demonstrated graphically by Kaplan's doodles. These doodles simply will not go away: They even showed up in a short Japanese newspaper article in 1999 (*Asahi Weekly,* October 3) as a taken-for-granted truth. It is tempting, with such clarity and simplicity, to assume we understand the issues and then to either accept or reject them in toto. I urge teachers not to do this. Within the walls of the classroom, given teacher and student goals and purposes, these questions need to feed into teachers' decisions about how and what to teach. I return to these decision-making issues in the last two sections of the chapter.

Discussions in the Literature

Kaplan and Early Contrastive Rhetoric

To begin at the beginning of the CR controversy, we need to go back to Robert Kaplan's (1966) original CR article, which these days is still often cited but less often read. I found this article to be a very strange piece of writing. I don't know if I am the only reader who reacted this way, but in spite of the fact that Kaplan discussed the linear nature of English expository prose (or more broadly, "English communication"), I did not find the piece to be particularly linear. Kowal (1998) analyzed the article in some detail, noting that it has three main sections (theoretical position, empirical data, and pedagogical implications) that reveal a "well-orchestrated and engaging argument" (p. 107) and that it is carefully hedged in places, but he did not comment further on its coherence or linearity (or lack thereof) as an example (or counterexample) of Kaplan's message. True, Kaplan starts and ends with comments about teaching. What follows is a collection of long quotes from philosophy and rhetoric (without his commentary), the promise of research (analysis of 600 student essays) that is not fulfilled, and a conclusion consisting of textbook-like exercises. Even though his main evidence rests on the analysis of hundreds of essays, there is no sign of any analysis at all, beyond the statement that these essays were "examined." Moreover, a number of his text samples are not from the student essays but from the Bible or from published texts.

That being said, Kaplan's point was that nonnative English speakers who write in English violate the norms of English rhetoric, that "each language and each culture has a paragraph order unique to itself, and that part of the learning of a particular language is the mastering of its logical system" (Kaplan, 1966, p. 14). In one of the reprints of this article (Kaplan, 1980), Kaplan included an addendum in which he admitted that some of his claims about the uniqueness of paragraph orders in different cultures were both naive and too strong. He also asserted that "the basic notion remains valid; that is, there is a preferred order in discourse blocs" (p. 416). In a later article still (Kaplan, 1988), he explained and defended the early article, emphasizing that the original goal of CR was pedagogical. He put it this way.

> What was being sought . . . was some clear-cut unambiguous difference between English and any other given language, the notion being that such a clear-cut difference might provide the basis for pedagogical approaches that would solve—within the normative academic space of one or two semesters—the writing problems of speakers of other languages trying to learn to function in written English in the peculiar constraints of tertiary-level education in the United States. (p. 278)

Although the goal of finding such unambiguous difference between English and other languages now seems elusive and misguided, in this article as elsewhere, Kaplan's CR project is mainly focused on form—how paragraphs or longer texts in English and other languages are organized and how textual conventions such as punctuation and indentation make them look. In later work, in response to criticisms, Kaplan has been more likely to mention audience, shared knowledge, genre, coherence, function, and so on, in addition to culture, as important factors that influence how people write (Grabe & Kaplan, 1996; Kaplan, 1987, 1988).

In spite of CR's pedagogical goals, Kaplan and his colleagues are careful to point out that notions of CR cannot be applied directly to instructional decisions, partly because too little research has been done (some of the original CR ideas are not testable) and partly because there is no strong theoretical base for CR, which has always been a *descriptive* project. Nevertheless, Grabe and Kaplan (1996) defend CR as follows.

> What is clear is that there are rhetorical differences in the written discourses of various languages, and that those differences need to be brought to consciousness before a writer can begin to understand what he or she must do in order to write in a more native-like manner (or in a manner that is more acceptable to native speakers of the target language). (p. 198)

This view, as "true" and uncontestable as it may seem, avoids some of the difficult issues associated with the CR project, which have been pointed out by various scholars in the debate over many years.

The Critics' Responses

John Hinds (1983) was one of the first to point out some of the flaws in Kaplan's original CR article. In particular, Hinds felt that it was essential to examine the rhetoric of writers' first languages if we wish to make statements about culturally influenced rhetoric. Looking at essays written in English by foreign students simply cannot guarantee that the problems we see result from L1 negative transfer. Audiences may differ and developmental problems may wrongly be assumed to be cultural. Hinds also pointed out that Kaplan (1966) grouped his languages in odd ways (inexplicably excluding Japanese from his "Oriental" category even though they constituted the largest group of students in his study) and that he mistakenly overgeneralized the term *Oriental* to include four different language families (Hinds, 1983, p. 186). Finally, Hinds (1983) criticized Kaplan for ethnocentrically representing English prose as a straight line. Unlike Kaplan's early article, Hinds's work was restricted to structural features of languages and did not include philosophical or cognitive speculations about writers' thinking or logical abilities.

To correct some of these methodological problems, Hinds looked at texts in Japanese, the most well-known studies using a specific popular column from a Japanese newspaper (the *tensei jingo* from the *Asahi Shimbun*). In the Japanese and English translations of those columns, Hinds identified what he saw as a typically Japanese digressive element in the structure of the writing (the *ten* of the *ki-shoo-ten-ketsu* arrangement), in which the writer first begins an argument *(ki)*, then develops it *(shoo)*, digresses *(ten)*, and concludes *(ketsu)*. Hinds generalized from this type of newspaper column to "expository prose in Japanese." He further noted that these popular-opinion columns demonstrated the reader-responsible nature of Japanese writing (Hinds, 1987), in contrast to English (and modern Chinese), which he described as writer-responsible. In Japanese, he claimed, it is the responsibility of the reader to construct meaning, whereas in English the responsibility lies with the writer to ensure clarity. Japanese writers provide fewer landmarks and transition markers, leaving it to the reader to surmise the connections. Writers of English create unity more overtly, providing "appropriate transition statements so that the reader can piece together the thread of the writer's logic which binds the composition together" (Hinds, 1987, p. 146). In a later article, Hinds (1990) again examined the structure of the *tensei jingo* newspaper column from Japan's *Asahi Shimbun* (along with several texts written by Chinese, Korean, and Thai writers) and identified in all the texts what he called a "delayed introduction of purpose," or a "quasi-inductive" style. In these texts the conclusions do not seem to follow logically, in the way a reader of English would expect, from the previous statements. He noted that native English-speaking readers expect a deductive style and, not finding this style, will automatically assume the organization is inductive and thus be baffled at the odd conclusions. Hinds's point in this article is that contrastive rhetoric is in large part about reader expectations. I return to this point in the third section of this chapter.

In short, Hinds followed a CR tradition begun by Kaplan but looked at samples of writing in L1 and translations into L2 in order to generalize about how writers create, and readers understand, coherence and unity in their native languages. ESL writers from a Japanese language background might need to be taught that they should not necessarily assume that there is a "sympathetic reader who believes that a reader's task is to ferret out whatever meaning the author has intended" (Hinds, 1987, p. 152). These kinds of ESL learners, says Hinds, need to learn that "effective written communication in English is the sole provenience of the writer" (p. 152).

Peter McCagg (1996) added to the CR debate by challenging Hinds's (1987) assertion that Japanese is a reader-responsible language and English a writer-responsible one. McCagg used his own translation, as well as that by Hinds, of the same popular newspaper column article from Hinds 1987, one on the topic of disposable chopsticks. McCagg argued that readers of this text who are deeply familiar with Japanese culture and traditions will not find it necessary to do more work at comprehending than would readers of the English version, as long as both sets of readers share background knowledge. He also argued that the text is not circular and indirect, as CR would predict, but that it quite directly gets to the point and lays out a variety of reasons and explanations. "Writers in every language," noted McCagg, "expect their audiences to contribute to the communicative act according to the conventions of the genre and their shared cultural experiences" (p. 248). This point will hold even if we perceive Japan to be a relatively homogeneous culture (itself a debatable notion) where readers share more background knowledge than they might in a more diverse culture.

Another participant in the debate about CR is Ryuko Kubota, a native-born Japanese who received her Ph.D. in Canada and then entered university work in the United States. As a native speaker of Japanese, she is able to bring in a great many resources in Japanese to add to the literature, such as the advice from Japanese writing experts in published books on how to write in Japanese. In her critique of Hinds, for example,

Kubota (1997) revealed that even Japanese scholars do not agree on precisely what the *ki-shoo-ten-ketsu* structure of Japanese prose consists of and that numerous writing books advise students to write clearly and directly. Perhaps more important, she asserted that Hinds wrongly implied that the *tensei jingo* newspaper column used for much of his research represents Japanese expository prose, which in reality is as diverse as one might expect within any culture and which certainly does not characterize typical academic writing in Japanese schools. (My own M.A. TESOL students from Japan expressed a wide range of opinions and experiences, some saying they had never been taught, or used, the *ki-shoo-ten-ketsu* structure in school, others saying they learned about it quite early in school. All recognized it as typical of this particular *Asahi Shimbun* newspaper column but did not find it typical of school writing. See also Cahill, 2003; Matsuda, 2003.)

Kubota (1998) further explored and critiqued the assumptions of CR in her study of 46 Japanese students, approximately half of whom wrote expository essays in both English and in Japanese and the other half persuasive topics. Where CR would have predicted some uniformity in the structure of students' essays as well as transfer of a typically Japanese structure (characterized by indirectness or digression), she found no strong evidence that culturally unique patterns either existed or were transferred to students' English writing. Some of the students followed the CR stereotype, but many did not. Some of the students also believed that Japanese essays should be organized inductively, but interestingly her Japanese raters preferred the more deductive (and equally stereotypical?) English organizational style. Kubota speculated that students' poor writing abilities in L1, their L2 language proficiency, their beliefs about their own writing and about the presumed homogeneity of Japanese culture, and their experience composing in their second language all contributed to the very diverse findings in her study.

These speculations parallel those of other scholars, such as Mohan and Lo (1985). These authors attributed some of the rhetorical difficulties that Chinese students in their study had when writing in English to normal developmental problems that inexperienced writers have even in their first language. However, Ostler (2002) claimed that this argument has been debunked by subsequent research, a strong assertion that we should take with caution. Mohan and Lo (1985) pointed to other factors as well that might cause difficulty for Chinese students writing in English, such as topic knowledge, language proficiency, and knowledge of writing conventions that are learned in school. They also noted that writing traditions in Chinese are very diverse and that they include both inductive and deductive styles even in classical works such as the *Analects* of Confucius. The famous eight-legged Chinese essay, they claimed, is no longer an influential genre (see also Cahill, 2003). Péry-Woodley (1990), too, focused her critiques of Kaplan's (1966) groundbreaking article on the lack of attention to a number of important variables other than L1 rhetorical traditions that could influence students' writing problems, some of which were pointed out by Kubota. Kaplan's early views, stated Péry-Woodley (1990), were done "outside of any question of awareness of projected audience, writer-reader interaction, communication situation, text-type, or . . . sociolinguistic factors" (p. 148). More recent work by Kaplan and his followers (e.g., Connor, 1996, 2002; Grabe & Kaplan, 1996; Purves, 1988) attempts to correct some of these deficiencies.

One reason that critiques of Kaplan's early work keep surfacing is that his original, seductively simple ideas and the notion of the "Sapir-Whorf hypothesis" of linguistic relativity continue to capture people's attention and to help them see their own writing and that of L2 speakers in new ways. Simple treatments and interpretations of complex issues always invite critique, particularly if they also contain elements of truth. In his book-length treatise, Kowal (1998) presented a critique of Kaplan's position on linguistic relativity and a critique of simplistic interpretations of the Whorfian principle, in addition to the detailed analysis of the original Kaplan (1996) article, mentioned earlier. (Interestingly, Kowal noted [1998, p. 41] that Whorf did not use the term *hypothesis*. It was J. B. Carroll who did so in his introduction to Whorf's [1956]

Language, Thought, and Reality. The term *Sapir-Whorf hy-pothesis* is thus a misnomer, picked up by others and used ever since.)

Kowal (1998) reviewed the work of Whorf and several other philosophers, anthropologists, and linguists, then presented specific critiques of some of Kaplan's underlying assumptions (critiques that can be applied to Hinds as well), such as that of the "native speaker" and of the myth of clearly demarcated linguistic and cultural groups. He argued that these are complex notions, characterized in reality by heteroglossia and great diversity, crosslinguistic and cultural influence, and change. Work in CR that refers to "English," "native" speakers and writers of English, "the West," "China," and so on and that reduces cultural influences to classical "Aristotelian" or "Buddhist" logic misses this diversity and therefore misleads in any conclusions it might make. Kowal believes that these assumptions reflect essentialist thinking, and he suggested that Kaplan's views of English and Oriental (and so on) rhetoric come from Kaplan's own prescriptive expectations as a U.S. scholar within a very particular kind of educational system rather than from an understanding of world Englishes. Kaplan's native speaker, Kowal claims, is Kaplan himself (a speculation refuted by Matsuda, personal communication and 2001; see the following section). Additionally, for Kaplan's original ideas of "unique paragraph orders" to be plausible, we need to presume that languages must be self-contained systems, "untinctured by influence from other languages" (Kowal, 1998, p. 126). Kaplan seems to have presumed this but, as Kowal pointed out (p. 131), also conflated language, nationality, and geography in his odd grouping of languages in his early CR work. It is impossible to establish such linguistic purity, of course, given the natural heteroglossia exhibited by every language.

Kowal also criticized Kaplan's exclusive focus on written products, and specific grammatical constructions in them, because it led to Kaplan's bypassing the pragmatic intent of writers and the creative ways they can convey meaning. Kowal demonstrated the importance of pragmatic intent in the main part of his book. Here he evaluated claims by Kaplan (conference papers cited in Kowal, 1998) and Bloom (1981) that Chinese has no overt counterfactual grammatical structure *(If I had . . . -ed, I would have . . . -ed),* making it difficult for Chinese speakers to reason counterfactually. Kowal's Taiwanese students, in oral debates and essays in English, rarely used the grammatical counterfactual structure but found many imaginative ways to express counterfactuality (Kowal, 1998, p. 203). According to Kowal, Kaplan would not have counted these as examples of counterfactual thinking, even though the pragmatic intent was clear. In an earlier critique, Hunt and Agnoli (1991) asserted that the point is not whether Chinese speakers can reason counterfactually or understand a counterfactual but "whether the relative cost of such reasoning is greater in Chinese than in English" (p. 386). They suggest that further research would be needed to answer this question. (See the debate between Bloom [1981, 1984] and Au [1983, 1984].)

In short, Kowal (1998) acknowledges, as do other applied linguists, the contribution of Kaplan in starting the entire field of CR and in pursuing questions related to it for most of his career. He also finds, however, that Kaplan reduces complex notions in ways that do not reflect the diversity, change, and heteroglossia that are normal in any group of speakers and writers and that he overlooks the pragmatic intent of writers if they do not use specific grammatical forms. Kowal claims as well that most of us vastly oversimplify the complex thinking of Whorf. He urges us to read the original(s).

The Defenders Strike Back

On the less critical side of the CR controversy is Ulla Connor, perhaps one of the applied linguistics field's most ardent CR supporters. She has devoted much of her professional life to the exploration of various aspects of CR, the study of which she began under the tutelage of Robert Kaplan. More steadily than other scholars, she has noted the weaknesses of some of the early CR work and attempted to correct them (Connor, 1996, 2002). For one thing, she has helped expand the field of

CR to include different languages, text types, genres, and research methodologies and thus has helped to overcome one of the serious problems of CR research, that of comparability. As many have pointed out, it does not make sense to make assertions about L1 rhetoric or thought processes based on the L2 essays of student writers, as Kaplan did, or to analyze a popular newspaper column in Japanese and presume that the features of this column parallel those in Japanese expository writing in general, as Hinds did. Bilingual in Finnish and English, Connor has been able to analyze texts such as grant proposals prepared by English and Finnish scholars (Connor, 2000; Connor & Mauranen, 1999); describe how students from different countries tackle the same writing assignment, such as preparation of a case report in business management (Connor & Kramer, 1995); and compare the argumentative patterns of students from four countries who participated in the IEA (International Association for the Evaluation of Education Achievement) project (Connor, 1987) (see also the collected essays in Purves, 1988). Unlike Kaplan and Hinds, she also adds interview data to some of her studies.

Because Connor is more interested in text analysis than in the philosophical and cognitive assumptions underpinning CR, she is able to point out differences in linguistic, structural, and topical aspects of writing within different genres without getting embroiled in philosophical controversy. This same interest, however, leads Connor to neglect attention to important sociolinguistic, developmental, or ideological factors that influence how, why, and what people write. She recognizes that differences in written products of native English speakers and ESL students "result from many factors besides linguistic, rhetorical, and cognitive ones, such as schooling and writing instruction" (Connor, 1997, p. 202), but her own work does not explore these factors deeply. Looking ahead to future CR studies, she affirms that as a research method CR "is embracing research-situated reflexivity and is becoming more sensitive to the social context and the local situatedness and particularity of writing activity" (Connor, 2002, p. 506). Important questions remain about the extent to which we can understand textual features without examining closely the extratextual influences on written texts.

Perhaps Connor's most important contribution has been her ongoing effort to move CR out of the quagmire in which it has been lodged for so long (Connor, 1998, 2001, 2002). She recognizes the value of comparative and contrastive text analyses for both research and pedagogy and has enlisted colleagues in the United States, Finland, and Europe in multilingual research projects, often outside the classroom context. In publications and presentations since the mid-1980s, Connor has stressed that research has consistently found differences in how L1 and L2 speakers organize their texts and achieve different rhetorical purposes. She argues that in spite of weaknesses, CR is a field still in its infancy that has great potential and so deserves the attention of L2 writing scholars. As Connor and others increasingly point out, many new directions in CR can help move it away from accusations of ethnocentricity and reductionism, thus helping teachers of L2 writing understand the many sources of difficulty that students have in learning to write in a second language. These include contrastive text linguistics (e.g, Enkvist, 1987), translation studies, classroom studies, studies that take local contexts and comparable genres into account, contributions from psychology and anthropology as well as linguistics, and studies of first language literacy in different languages.

To wrap up this summary of the CR debate, I turn to the thoughts of Ilona Leki and Paul Kei Matsuda. These scholars desire, as do Connor (1996, 2002) and others, to help CR move forward. Leki (1997) and Matsuda (1997) both note that in spite of the original pedagogical intention of CR, "the insights gained by research have not been effectively translated into the practice of teaching organizational structures" (Matsuda, 1997, p. 45). Matsuda has shown that CR has tended to look at L2 writing problems mainly as a problem of negative transfer of L1 rhetorical patterns to L2 writing. The result is a static model of L2 writing, in which the only context for and influence on writing are the writer's and reader's linguistic, educational, and cultural background. The writer's agency is denied, as is the dynamic complexity of decision-making processes that occur in the actual context of writing. In pedagogical applications of CR, the concept of background needs to be expanded, argues Matsuda, to include writers' and readers' dialect variation, socioeconomic class, knowledge of topic, past writing experiences, and memberships in multiple L1 and L2 discourse communities (p. 53).

For her part, Leki (1997) has explained that the contributions of CR to writing instruction have advanced little since 1966, primarily because scholars have paid such scant attention to the ideological implications of their work (p. 244). Rhetorical choices are not linked to thought patterns, she asserts, but "are made in response to social, political, and rhetorical contexts and histories" (p. 236). What would we be ready to conclude about native English speakers' writing and reasoning, she asks, from a sample of essays that these students write in a foreign language (p. 236)? She hopes not much. She has further noted, as have others, that in studies of CR we need to distinguish between CR problems and problems of low L2 language proficiency and to determine as well whether L2 students are doing satisfactory work in their subject matter courses. Some evidence shows that students manage fairly well in their subject matter courses and are held back by ESL requirements (see Johns, 1991; Leki & Carson, 1997; Schneider & Fujishima, 1995). Leki reminds us as well that some elegant academic writing is not necessarily linear (S. J. Gould). Finally, she has pointed out that CR's primary focus on differences rather than similarities "has a distancing and exoticizing effect" (Leki, 1997, p. 242) that contributes little to our understanding of the complexities of writing in L1 and L2.

As is the case for other controversies that I describe in this book, the CR debate continues to interest L2 writing scholars because it remains unresolved and because the ideas on which it is based continue to be meaningful for teachers and students of L2 writing. It also continues to interest us because CR itself, stuck for so long in oversimplified assumptions, interpretations, and research methodologies, is now being viewed by some scholars in more complex, more contextually situated, and more politically relevant ways. Even though uncritical and oversimplified treatments still surface (e.g., Dyer & Friederich, 2002), CR contains enough promise and leaves us with enough unanswered questions to keep scholars and teachers studying and wondering about it for many years to come. All writing teachers, however, should exercise caution in uncritically applying principles from it in their classrooms.

Classroom Perspectives

Although the principles of CR cannot be applied directly to classroom writing instruction, they can alert teachers to a number of important issues that will help them make decisions in their own classrooms.

First, Grabe and Kaplan (1989, 1996) alert us to some of the kinds of knowledge which CR focuses on that will help teachers and students in the L2 writing class. Teachers and students need to be familiar with

1. Knowledge of rhetorical patterns of arrangement and the relative frequency of various patterns (e.g., exposition/ argument, classification, definition, etc.)
2. Knowledge of composing conventions and strategies needed to generate text (e.g., prewriting, data collection, revision, etc.)
3. Knowledge of the morphosyntax of the target language, particularly as it applies at the intersentential level
4. Knowledge of the coherence-creating mechanisms of the target language
5. Knowledge of the writing conventions of the target language in the sense of both frequency and distribution of types and text appearance (e.g., letter, essay, report)
6. Knowledge of the audience characteristics and expectations in the target culture

7. Knowledge of the subject to be discussed, including both "what everyone knows" in the target culture and specialist knowledge.

(Grabe & Kaplan, 1996, p. 200)

The authors point out that they intend not to prescribe a method for instruction based on CR but to suggest the body of knowledge required in the teaching and learning of reading and writing (Grabe & Kaplan, 1989, p. 271) and to suggest as well some pedagogical objectives (Kaplan, 1988). These objectives include making composition teachers aware that different conventions for writing exist in different cultures, that discourse-level and coherence features of text production may differ across languages, and that readers and writers may take on different responsibilities in different cultures. They include helping L2 writers learn that it is important to define an audience before writing; that writing types, tasks, and organizational and other conventions may differ in L1 and L2; and that writers need subject matter knowledge and knowledge of the interactive and social nature of writing (Kaplan, 1988, pp. 296–297; Grabe & Kaplan, 1989, pp. 276–277).

Leki (1991) noted, as have others, that CR has a textual orientation, appearing to be concerned primarily with form. However, she clarified that "the true or ultimate focus of a textual orientation, and of contrastive rhetoric studies, and an appropriate pedagogical agenda of a textual orientation in a writing class, is a focus not on form but on audience" (p. 135). Here she concurs with Hinds (1990) on the central importance of reader expectations. However, she cautions that as novice L2 writers, students are clearly not participants in the construction of knowledge, making it difficult for them to assess social aspects of writing, such as knowledge of audience. Concluding that students must be taught to write in ways that fit audience expectations within the cultures they are learning to write in, she emphasizes how important it is for teachers and students to build awareness of the existence, if not the details, of different rhetorics. Awareness does not necessarily lead to improvement, but it can help students realize that their writing problems do not stem from personal failures (Leki, 1991, p. 138).

When it comes to applying some of these ideas to the L2 writing classroom, however, we lack precise guidelines, mostly because CR research has not provided us with clear answers to pedagogical questions. There are some well-established techniques in reorganizing scrambled sentences, identifying topic sentences and supports, and other general writing tasks (see Ferris & Hedgcock, 1998; Grabe & Kaplan, 1989, 1996; Reid, 1993). But if we accept the idea that CR deals mainly with questions of what readers expect with regard to organizational and coherence features of different text types in different languages, a sensible place to begin seems to be with carefully planned awareness-building activities of audience expectations of rhetorical features. Of course, even though many scholars recommend consciousness-raising activities in the L2 writing class (Connor, 1996, Leki, 1991), Kubota urges teachers to be cautious in "constructing and reinforcing the notion of cultural uniqueness" (Kubota, 1998, p. 90). In the L2 writing class, when we ask students to consider rhetorical features of different kinds of writing within their own cultures, we may perpetuate stereotypes if students themselves, as Kubota found, hold overly simple beliefs about their L1 cultures and rhetorics. Teachers, too, may not know enough about rhetorical conventions in students' own languages to counter these stereotypes effectively. Additionally, we misapply findings from CR only when we presume it has provided us with Kaplan's impossible dream (1988, p. 278): "clear-cut unambiguous difference between English and any other given language." I suggest in the next section an investigative pedagogical approach.

Taking an Investigative Pedagogical Approach in the Classroom

Deciding what to compare and contrast in the L2 writing class depends upon a number of factors. For example, L2 writing teachers should ask first what students need to do with their

L2 writing. Decisions also depend on whether we believe that it is easier to learn to write for particular purposes if we have a deep understanding, rather than just a formulaic knowledge, of rhetorical conventions. They may further depend on practical considerations such as how much time students and teachers have. Students who need to pass a onetime exit test, for example, and who do not need to write in their L2 beyond this, probably do not need to develop a deep understanding of rhetorical differences. Students who need to write regularly in settings outside the L2 writing class—in other subject matter classes, in the workplace, or professionally for publication—will probably benefit from an approach that asks them to carefully consider reader expectations and to observe closely how different texts use organizational and linguistic features to fit those expectations. This kind of investigation may involve breaking down students' stereotypes of their L1 and L2 and helping them come to a more complex understanding of how their L1 rhetoric creates meaning. (See, e.g., the discussion by Nanri [2001] on the stereotypical belief held by some Japanese scholars that Japanese texts lack logic—and her analysis of several texts to counter this fallacy.)

If teachers choose not to take the quick route of applying simplistic formulae to students' L2 writing, it makes sense to take an investigative, questioning approach to CR issues in the L2 writing class. Because CR deals with paragraph- and discourse-level features, teachers would be wise to introduce CR issues to intermediate and advanced learners rather than to beginners. Teachers and students can investigate L1 and L2 texts, the kinds of writing instruction students received, and the expectations that readers have in L1 and L2. The investigations can be set up as discussions, simple or complex discourse analyses of comparable texts, mini–research projects involving surveys and interviews, and practice writing from models. Existing research on CR can be used as models for class activities.

In comparing L1 and L2 texts, teachers can first look to Kaplan, who began by comparing paragraphs written in English by students from different language backgrounds. In my previous discussions I noted the dangers of looking only at L2 writing to make inferences about L1 rhetoric. Therefore, if teachers and students wish to investigate how paragraph features in L2 and different L1s differ, it is important to look at samples in students' L1s. In doing so, it is tempting to assume that the concept of "paragraph" is similar across languages. However, Régent (1985) found that even in another Western language the concept of "paragraph" was not shared. He compared 60 articles from medical journals in English and French and found that the French paragraphs were distinguished not by topic sentences that led readers through an argument but by loose collections of data. Similarly, Clyne (1987) compared 52 articles in English and German from linguistics and sociology and found as well that the German writers tended to present their data in loosely organized chunks rather than integrated into an argument the way the L1 English and English-educated German writers did. He found as well that the texts written by German scholars were more digressive. They were less likely than the English writers to place topic sentences early in a paragraph or to define terms. The question to ask is, Does the concept of "paragraph" exist in students' L1s? Discussion and examination of writing samples from students' L1s can help clarify this. The point is that in making comparisons and contrasts, teachers and students should not impose a rhetorical feature from one language directly onto another without investigating whether the feature is comparable.

Students who need to read and write academic articles within specific fields can conduct their own mini-surveys, at the paragraph and the whole-text levels, of published articles in their fields. In an EFL setting, students will have access to articles published in their own languages as well as in English, making it relatively easy to secure materials for comparison, but comparisons in English only, across disciplines, can be equally revealing. The work of John Swales (1990a, 1990b; Swales & Feak, 1994, 2000; Swales & Najjar, 1987) can provide teachers with a great deal of information on structural features of academic and research genres, such as the "moves" within research article introductions or other sections of research

articles and features of other genres such as grant proposals
(see also Connor, 2000; Connor & Mauranen, 1999). In my own
writing classes in a Japanese university, some students needed
to write theses, conference proposals and presentations, or articles for publication. By comparing readings they did across
their various disciplines, primarily in English, according to
some of the structural features identified by Swales and others,
they developed a text-level sense of what kinds of information typically belong in different sections of academic articles
and a sense as well (important!) that not all academic texts
follow the observations made by Swales. At this point the
students were able to take control of some of their own decisions, notice similarities and differences within their own
disciplines, compare their observations of published English
language materials with those in Japanese, and make informed
choices in their own writing.

Not all students need to learn to write academic essays or
research articles. Students who are interested in journalism
could model an investigation of newspaper articles on Ron
Scollon's (2000) study of parallel news stories in Chinese and
English editions of the same newspaper. Scollon looked at
five consecutive days of stories in parallel editions of Chinese
and English newspapers and discovered that different genres
coexisted within the same papers and that parallel stories
in English and Chinese editions differed in significant ways.
Scollon cautions scholars, and by extension, teachers of L2
writing who look to CR for classroom applications, against
making conclusions about genres and about characteristics of
writers and of discourse communities (e.g., of journalists) without carefully controlling for genre. But given that many newspapers from different language and culture groups are now
available on the Internet as well as in libraries, students could
use some of Scollon's categories of comparison to do their
own investigations of journalistic texts in their L1 and L2.

In short, it is important to compare and contrast *comparable* texts, and portions of texts, both across and within languages and across and within disciplines. In the L2 writing
class, such comparisons and contrasts need to be carried out

according to what students need and want to learn, and they need as well to avoid succumbing to stereotypes.

Another investigative activity that can be conducted in L2 writing classes asks what the students' previous instruction in L1 and L2 writing has been and what their beliefs are about what "good writing" consists of. Liebman (1988, 1992; Liebman-Kleine, 1987) recommends that L2 writing students become "ethnographers" of their own writing and that teachers at the very least learn something about their students' previous writing experiences and engage students in discussion about writing in their L1s. For example, Liebman (1992) asked her Japanese- and Arabic-speaking students about the writing instruction they received in their home countries, using a variety of question types (Likert, open-ended, checklist, ranking). She discovered interesting differences in students' previous writing experiences, ones that would be valuable for writing teachers to know as they plan class activities. Although Liebman's questionnaire was used for research purposes, adaptations of it would function wonderfully as the basis for students' mini–research projects and class discussion. It is likely that students will find as much diversity of beliefs and experiences as Liebman found in her research.

A third area of investigation that teachers can pursue in their L2 writing classes, perhaps the most important application of CR to writing classrooms, concerns reader (audience) expectations. Such investigations can involve students in learning how teachers of writing in different cultures respond to writing or how they themselves respond. In her ethnographic study, Xiaoming Li (1996) compared the responses of four U.S. and mainland Chinese teachers' to six student essays (personal narratives) written by students in the United States and China, a genre she noted is widely used in both countries. (She notes that the research paper is not taught in China [p. 7].) The essays themselves were not compared, but the teachers' evaluations of them were. The criteria for "good writing," Li found, were somewhat different for the American and Chinese teachers, the former appreciating logic and a clear opening and the latter appreciating an essay that expressed sentiment, natural scenes, and a moral message. In addition to finding some differences in reader response that could be attributed to culture, she also speculated that responses to writing are deeply personal and individual. Her project involved interviews of teachers in the United States and China—an investigative project that could be adapted by students in ESL and EFL settings to be conducted in person, by letter, or by email.

Li (1996) interviewed teachers about their responses to student essays in English and Chinese. It is also possible to investigate students' own responses as peer readers to essays by students like themselves. For example, in a revealing study of Japanese undergraduates' perceptions of different features of two compositions written by Japanese students in English, Rinnert and Kobayashi (2001) compared the responses of four groups of readers to different versions of the two compositions, altered to reflect typically American English and Japanese rhetorical patterns (based on some of the literature that I reviewed in this chapter). They found that the responses of the four groups (inexperienced L2 writers, experienced L2 writers, Japanese teachers of writing, and native English-speaking teachers of writing in Japan) differed significantly in a number of ways. The inexperienced writers paid more attention to the content of the different versions of the essays than to the organization, logical connections, or language. The more experience the readers had in L2 writing, the more likely they were to respond positively to the typically "American" features of the essays. This study is important for CR because it demonstrates what many scholars have suggested, namely, that reader expectations and audience analysis are where we need to begin in many L2 writing classes. Whether they are L1 or L2 speakers, if writers misjudge their readers, their writing will not communicate or will be judged faulty. Teachers can help students design mini–research projects like that of Rinnert and Kobayashi (2001; see also Kobayashi & Rinnert, 1996) to see how peer readers respond to different kinds of L1 and L2 essays.

Even without doing a mini–research project, teachers and

students can explore facets of reader expectations across cultures. In discussion, some of my students in Japan have echoed what Clyne (1987) observed about writers of academic texts in German and what Connor (1999) observed about Finnish writers: A writer who is too clear and too redundant insults the intelligence of readers or, as Hinds (1990) implied, does not allow readers to do their own thinking. Readers of academic English, however, usually do not wish to struggle to understand a writer's message. Whether the reader is a teacher-evaluator of an important essay test, a graduate advisor reading a thesis, or a manuscript reviewer reading an article for publication, readers of academic English tend to want to get through the material fast and yet still have their thinking provoked. Friends of mine who read TOEFL essays by students from all over the world for the Educational Testing Service sometimes read well over 200 essays at a sitting. If readers have to struggle to find a point, students will surely receive a lower score than if the evaluators can sail through a clearly introduced and structurally coherent essay. On the other hand, the student who gets the structure "right" (following the stereotype of the linear English essay) but fills in formulaic slots with boring content will also probably not receive the maximum possible points. Teachers and students in the L2 writing class can therefore profit greatly by investigating what the expectations of readers are across and within languages and text types and by bringing those expectations explicitly to the surface. In other words, in addition to comparing texts and portions of texts, teachers and students can compare and contrast the responses of different readers to the same material.

In the L2 writing class, then, it is important to ask students, and ourselves, a great many questions. If students have no idea what their readers expect, then it is the job of teachers to help make these expectations explicit and to help students learn to ask appropriate questions of the texts they are reading and modeling their own writing on. If students have stereotypical ideas of what readers expect, it is our job to complicate their understanding and help them recognize that they have choices and therefore agency. Both within and across cultures, as readers change, so must our writing. Students who are new to a culture or to a discipline need our help in analyzing the many possible audiences for the many possible types of writing they may need to do. Our goal is to provide students with this help without perpetuating stereotypes.

I have suggested in this section that teachers and students interested in CR take an investigative pedagogical approach to differences in L1 and L2 texts, writers' instructional backgrounds, and reader expectations. This approach involves awareness building rather than actual writing. Of course, in setting up teaching activities, L2 writing teachers need to decide how simple or complex to make CR issues in their own classrooms, depending not just on their knowledge of CR but also on the constraints in their own settings and the local needs of their own students. Does a one-size-fits-all approach make sense even if it does perpetuate stereotypes? It may, if students need only to pass a particular kind of writing test. Does a more complex approach make sense, perhaps involving students in actual analyses of different kinds of texts and readers from their L1 and L2? In such cases, teachers can turn to some of the studies that have been conducted in CR and adopt some of the survey, analysis, and interview methods as techniques in their own classrooms for helping students investigate writing from a CR perspective.

Ongoing Questions

Teachers of L2 writing, within both English-medium settings and foreign language contexts, may be disappointed that clearer conclusions did not result from the discussions in this chapter. Throughout this book, however, a primary message is that many of the issues are in fact unresolved and that teachers therefore need to consider them not in isolation as problems to be resolved but as dilemmas to be dealt with in the context of their own teaching. In this section, I review the key issues and questions and urge teachers to consider them within the realities of their own classrooms.

First, I think it is important to look closely at the language with which we discuss CR issues. Throughout the CR literature, from 1966 until the present, we see phrases such as "language or culture X prefers such and such rhetorical pattern" or "Japanese is more indirect than English." However, it simply does not make sense to say that "English prefers . . . " or "Japanese prefers . . . " Languages and cultures cannot prefer anything, nor is it languages that are inherently direct or indirect. It is people who prefer things, with language, used directly or indirectly, as a vehicle for our preferences. A more accurate and productive question, therefore, is where do our preferences come from, as people, as writers, as readers, and, importantly, as members not just of one homogeneous culture but of multiple and often fuzzily defined subcultures?

Second, with regard to the long-debated issue of possible connections between the rhetorical patterns people use in their writing and the cognitive abilities or patterns in people's thinking, it seems clear that it makes little sense to speculate that our students cannot think "logically" (for example) based on a sample of their L2 writing. It behooves us to ask what we as teachers would want anyone to conclude about our own thinking from a sample of our less-than-proficient foreign language writing. What factors do influence the thinking patterns of students and teachers? To what extent might those factors be culturally shared, individual and idiosyncratic, or educationally shaped?

Third, much of the literature on CR points to interesting differences in L1 and L2 texts, but questions remain as to the sources of those differences. What are the roles of readers in different cultures, and do these roles change according to text type, genre, and purpose for reading? How do cross-cultural influences, such as international audiences in business, Internet communication, and research, affect the rhetorical choices that writers make? Studies have also pointed to important similarities across particular types of L1 and L2 texts. Should we be paying more attention to these similarities in our teaching of L2 writing?

Fourth, what are the educational backgrounds and writing experiences of our students? What have they been taught directly or indirectly about writing in their L1, as well as in their L2? Where do their beliefs about "good writing" come from? As pointed out in the CR literature, many of the problems that L2 students have with writing parallel those that inexperienced L1 writers have. Whether L1 or L2, students who have no experience writing a certain genre will struggle to recognize what the appropriate pieces are and how to fit them together.

Fifth, how are teachers to distinguish among problems of low language proficiency, CR problems, and thinking problems?

Finally, what role do stereotypical beliefs and formulae for writing play in particular writing classes? How much complexity can a particular group of students deal with, given their particular needs and purposes for learning to write? Without undermining our goal of helping students become better writers, how can we help them understand that when someone says, "Americans write and think directly," we need to ask: "What Americans? Writing what, and writing for what purposes?" If we choose to offer our students rhetorical formulae, how can we help them understand that these formulae may not reflect English in general, or even academic English in general, but are linked to particular types of writing written for particular audiences and purposes?

CR assumes differences but necessarily presumes some uniformity within cultures and languages. Otherwise, comparisons and contrasts cannot be made. It is up to teachers and students, not just to researchers, to inject diversity and dynamism into their own explorations of rhetorical choices in writing and not fall prey to quick and easy answers.

Beliefs and Practices

Beliefs

1. What are your own beliefs about the connections among language, culture, and thought?
2. What kind of project do you believe CR is: textual analysis or textual analysis augmented by other factors?

If the latter, what do you believe some of the extra-textual factors are?

3. CR began as a pedagogical project. Do you believe that a viable research agenda should also be vigorously pursued? What should that agenda consist of?
4. To what extent can pedagogical applications be devised from incomplete or inconclusive research?
5. After reading some of the CR debates in this chapter, and reading as well some of the original articles, what are your views on the different opinions and evidence that different scholars have presented?

Practices

1. In your own experiences writing in your L1 and L2 (and L3 etc.) what CR issues have arisen for you? Have you been consciously aware of your rhetorical decisions? Where did your awareness come from?
2. In your teaching experiences, have you noticed any rhetorical features of your students' writing that would lend credence to the claims of CR? If so, describe these, making sure to describe the kinds and purposes of the writing.
3. In your teaching, what kinds of implicit or explicit instruction do you, or might you, provide students about the rhetorical features of the kinds of writing you would like students to practice?
4. What do you know about your students' writing practices in L1, including any instruction they have received and features of different kinds of L1 writing that they believe are typical?
5. To what extent do your students have a clear sense of what the audiences for their L1 and L2 writing expect?

References and Relevant Readings

Au, T. K. F. (1983). Chinese and English counterfactuals: The Sapir-Whorf hypothesis revisited. *Cognition, 15,* 155–187.

Au, T. K. F. (1984). Counterfactuals: In reply to Alfred Bloom. *Cognition, 17,* 289–302.

Bickner, R., & Peyasantiwong, P. (1988). Cultural variation in reflective writing. In A. C. Purves (Ed.), *Writing across language and cultures: Issues in contrastive rhetoric* (pp. 160–174). Newbury Park, CA: Sage.

Birdsong, D., & Odlin, T. (1983). If Whorf was on the right track [Review of the book *The linguistic shaping of thought: A study in the impact of language and thinking in China and the West*]. *Language Learning, 33,* 401–412.

Bloom, A. H. (1981). *The linguistic shaping of thought: A study in the impact of language on thinking in China and the West.* Hillsdale, NJ: Lawrence Erlbaum.

Bloom, A. H. (1984). Caution—the words you use may affect what you say: A response to Au. *Cognition, 17,* 275–287.

Cahill, D. (2003). The myth of the "turn" in contrastive rhetoric. *Written Communication, 20,* 170–194.

Cai, G. (1999). Texts in contexts: Understanding Chinese students' English compositions. In C. R. Cooper & L. Odell (Eds.), *Evaluating writing: The role of teachers' knowledge about text, learning, and culture* (pp. 279–297). Urbana, IL: National Council of Teachers of English.

Carson, J. G., & Nelson, G. L. (1994). Writing groups: Cross-cultural issues. *Journal of Second Language Writing, 3,* 17–30.

Choi, Y. H. (1988). Text structure of Korean speakers' argumentative essays in English. *World Englishes, 7,* 129–142.

Christensen, F. (1963). A generative rhetoric of the sentence. *College Composition and Communication, 14,* 155–161.

Christensen, F. (1965). A generative rhetoric of the paragraph. *College Composition and Communication, 16,* 144–156.

Clyne, M. G. (1987). Cultural differences in the organization of academic texts: English and German. *Journal of Pragmatics, 11,* 211–247.

Connor, U. (1987). Argumentative patterns in student essays: Cross-cultural differences. In U. Connor & R. B. Kaplan (Eds.), *Writing across languages: Analysis of L2 text* (pp. 57–71). Reading, MA: Addison-Wesley.

Connor, U. (1996). *Contrastive rhetoric: Cross-cultural aspects of second-language writing.* Cambridge: Cambridge University Press.

Connor, U. (1997). Contrastive rhetoric: Implications for teachers of writing in multicultural classrooms. In C. Severino, J. C. Guerra, & J. E. Butler (Eds.), *Writing in multicultural settings* (pp. 198–208). New York: Modern Language Association.

Connor, U. (1998). Contrastive rhetoric: Developments and challenges. *Studia Anglica Posnaniensia, 33,* 105–116.

Connor, U. (1999). Learning to write academic prose in a second language: A literacy autobiography. In G. Braine (Ed.), *Non-native educators in English language teaching* (pp. 29–42). Mahwah, NJ: Lawrence Erlbaum.

Connor, U. (2000). Variation in rhetorical moves in grant proposals of U.S. humanists and scientists. *Text, 20,* 1–28.

Connor, U. (2001, February). *Contrastive rhetoric: New directions in cross-cultural writing.* Paper presented at the International Conference of Teachers of English to Speakers of Other Languages, St. Louis, Missouri.

Connor, U. (2002). New directions in contrastive rhetoric. *TESOL Quarterly, 36,* 493–510.

Connor, U., Davis, K., & De Rycker, T. (1995). Correctness and clarity in applying for overseas jobs: A cross-cultural analysis of U.S. and Flemish applications. *Text, 15,* 457–475.

Connor, U., & Kaplan, R. B. (Eds.) (1997). *Writing across languages: Analysis of L2 text.* Reading, MA: Addison-Wesley.

Connor, U., & Kramer, M. G. (1995). Writing from sources: Case studies of graduate students in business management. In D. Belcher & G. Braine (Eds.), *Academic writing in a second language: Essays on research and pedagogy* (pp. 155–182). Norwood, NJ: Ablex.

Connor, U., & Lauer, J. (1988). Cross-cultural variation in persuasive student writing. In A. C. Purves (Ed.), *Writing across language and cultures: Issues in contrastive rhetoric* (pp. 138–159). Newbury Park, CA: Sage.

Connor, U., & Mauranen, A. (1999). Linguistic analysis of grant proposals: European Union research grants. *English for Specific Purposes, 18,* 47–62.

Connor, U., & McCagg, P. (1983). Cross-cultural differences and perceived quality in written paraphrases of English expository prose. *Applied Linguistics, 4,* 259–268.

Dyer, B., & Friederich, L. (2002). The personal narrative as cultural artifact: Teaching autobiography in Japan. *Written Communication, 19,* 265–296.

Eggington, W. G. (1987). Written academic discourse in Korean: Implications for effective communication. In U. Connor & R. B. Kaplan (Eds.),

Writing across languages: Analysis of L2 text (pp. 153–168). Reading, MA: Addison-Wesley.

Enkvist, N. E. (1987). Text linguistics for the applier: An orientation. In U. Connor & R. B. Kaplan (Eds.), *Writing across languages: Analysis of L2 text* (pp. 23–43). Reading, MA: Addison-Wesley.

Ferris, D., & Hedgcock, J. (1998). *Teaching ESL composition: Purpose, process, and practice.* Mahwah, NJ: Lawrence Erlbaum.

Folman, S., & Sarig, G. (1990). Intercultural rhetorical differences in meaning construction. *Communication and Cognition, 23*(1), 45–92.

Grabe, W. (1987). Contrastive rhetoric and text-type research. In U. Connor & R. B. Kaplan (Eds.), *Writing across languages: Analysis of L2 text* (pp. 115–137). Reading, MA: Addison-Wesley.

Grabe, W., & Kaplan, R. B. (1989). Writing in a second language: Contrastive rhetoric. In D. M. Johnson & D. H. Roen (Eds.), *Richness in writing: Empowering ESL students* (pp. 263–283). New York: Longman.

Grabe, W., & Kaplan, R. B. (1996). *Theory and practice of writing.* New York: Longman.

Hinds, J. (1983). Contrastive rhetoric: Japanese and English. *Text, 3,* 183–195.

Hinds, J. (1987). Reader versus writer responsibility: A new typology. In U. Connor & R. B. Kaplan (Eds.), *Writing across languages: Analysis of L2 text* (pp. 141–152). Reading, MA: Addison-Wesley.

Hinds, J. (1990). Inductive, deductive, quasi-inductive: Expository writing in Japanese, Korean, Chinese, and Thai. In U. Connor & A. M. Johns (Eds.), *Coherence in writing: Research and pedagogical perspectives* (pp. 87–110). Alexandria, VA: Teachers of English to Speakers of Other Languages.

Hirose, K., & Sasaki, M. (1994). Explanatory variables for Japanese students' expository prose: An exploratory study. *Journal of Second Language Writing, 3,* 203–230.

Hunt, E., & Agnoli, F. (1991). The Whorfian hypothesis: A cognitive psychology perspective. *Psychological Review, 98,* 377–389.

Jenkins, S., & Hinds, J. (1987). Business letter writing: English, French, and Japanese. *TESOL Quarterly, 21,* 327–354.

Johns, A. M. (1991). Interpreting an English competency exam: The frustrations of an ESL science student. *Written Communication, 8,* 379–401.

Johnstone, B. (1986). Arguments with Khomeni: Rhetorical situation and persuasive style in cross-cultural perspective. *Text, 6,* 171–187.

Kachru, Y. (1988). Writers in Hindi and English. In A. C. Purves (Ed.), *Writing across languages and cultures: Issues in contrastive rhetoric* (pp. 109–137). Newbury Park, CA: Sage.

Kachru, Y. (1995). Contrastive rhetoric in world Englishes. *English Today, 41*(1), 21–31.

Kamimura, T., & Oi, K. (1997). Contrastive rhetoric in letter writing: The interaction of linguistic proficiency and cultural awareness. *JALT Journal, 19,* 58–76.

Kaplan, R. B. (1966). Cultural thought patterns in inter-cultural education. *Language Learning, 16,* 1–20.

Kaplan, R. B. (1967). Contrastive rhetoric and the teaching of composition. *TESOL Quarterly, 1*(4), 10–16.

Kaplan, R. B. (1972). *The anatomy of rhetoric: Prolegomena to a functional theory of rhetoric.* Philadelphia: Center for Curriculum Development.

Kaplan, R. B. (1980). Cultural thought patterns in inter-cultural education. In K. Croft (Ed.), *Readings on English as a second language for teachers and teacher trainees* (2nd ed., pp. 399–418). Cambridge, MA: Winthrop.

Kaplan, R. B. (1983). Contrastive rhetoric: Some implications for the writing process. In A. Freedman, I. Pringle, & J. Yalden (Eds.), *Learning to write: First language/second language* (pp. 139–161). New York: Longman.

Kaplan, R. B. (1987). Cultural thought patterns revisited. In U. Connor & R. B. Kaplan (Eds.), *Writing across languages: Analysis of L2 text* (pp. 9–21). Reading, MA: Addison-Wesley.

Kaplan, R. B. (1988). Contrastive rhetoric and second language learning: Notes toward a theory of contrastive rhetoric. In A. C. Purves (Ed.), *Writing across language and cultures: Issues in contrastive rhetoric* (pp. 275–304). Newbury Park, CA: Sage.

Kobayashi, H. (1984). Rhetorical patterns in English and Japanese. *TESOL Quarterly, 18,* 737–738.

Kobayashi, H., & Rinnert, C. (1996). Factors affecting composition evaluation in an EFL context: Cultural rhetorical pattern and readers' background. *Language Learning, 46,* 397–437.

Kowal, K. H. (1998). *Rhetorical implications of linguistic relativity: Theory and application to Chinese and Taiwanese interlanguages.* New York: Peter Lang.

Kubota, R. (1997). A reevaluation of the uniqueness of Japanese written discourse. *Written Communication, 14,* 460–480.

Kubota, R. (1998). An investigation of L1–L2 transfer in writing among Japanese university students: Implications for contrastive rhetoric. *Journal of Second Language Writing, 7,* 69–100.

Leki, I. (1991). Twenty-five years of contrastive rhetoric: Text analysis and writing pedagogies. *TESOL Quarterly, 25,* 123–143.

Leki, I. (1997). Cross-talk: ESL issues and contrastive rhetoric. In C. Severino, J. C. Guerra, & J. E. Butler (Eds.), *Writing in multicultural settings* (pp. 234–244). New York: Modern Language Association.

Leki, I., & Carson, J. G. (1994). Students' perceptions of EAP writing instruction and writing needs across the disciplines. *TESOL Quarterly, 29,* 81–101.

Leki, I., and Carson, J. G. (1997). "Completely different worlds": EAP and the writing experiences of ESL students in university courses. *TESOL Quarterly, 31,* 39–69.

Li, X. (1996). *"Good writing" in cross-cultural context.* Albany: State University of New York Press.

Liebman, J. D. (1988). Contrastive rhetoric: Students as ethnographers. *Journal of Basic Writing, 7,* 6–27.

Liebman, J. D. (1992). Toward a new contrastive rhetoric: Differences between Arabic and Japanese rhetorical instruction. *Journal of Second Language Writing, 1,* 141–166.

Liebman-Kleine, J. (1987). Teaching and researching invention: Using ethnography in ESL writing classes. *ESL Journal, 41*(2), 104–111.

Maier, P. (1992). Politeness strategies in business letters by native and non-native English speakers. *English for Specific Purposes, 11,* 189–205.

Matalene, C. (1985). Contrastive rhetoric: An American writing teacher in China. *College English, 47,* 789–808.

Matsuda, P. K. (1995). *Contrastive rhetorics: Toward a pedagogical theory of second language writing.* Unpublished master's thesis, Miami University, Oxford, Ohio.

Matsuda, P. K. (1997). Contrastive rhetoric in context: A dynamic model of L2 writing. *Journal of Second Language Writing, 6,* 45–60.

Matsuda, P. K. (2001). On the origin of contrastive rhetoric: A response to "The origin of contrastive rhetoric revisited" by H. G. Ying (2000). *International Journal of Applied Linguistics, 11,* 257–260.

Matsuda, P. K. (2003). Coming to voice: Publishing as a graduate student. In C. P. Casanave & S. Vandrick (Eds.), *Writing for scholarly publication: Behind the scenes in language education* (pp. 39–51). Mahwah, NJ: Lawrence Erlbaum.

Mauranen, A. (1993). *Cultural differences in academic rhetoric.* Frankfurt: Peter Lang.

McCagg, P. (1996). If you can lead a horse to water, you don't have to make it drink: Some comments on reader and writer responsibilities. *Multilingua, 15,* 239–256.

Mohan, B., & Lo, W. A.-Y. (1985). Academic writing and Chinese students: Transfer and developmental factors. *TESOL Quarterly, 19,* 515–534.

Mok, W. E. (1993). Contrastive rhetoric and the Japanese writer of EFL. *JALT Journal, 15,* 151–161.

Nanri, K. (2001). Logical structures of Japanese texts. *Text, 21,* 373–409.

Oi, K., & Sato, T. (1990). Cross cultural rhetorical differences in letter writing: Refusal letter and application letter. *JACET Bulletin, 21,* 117–136.

Ostler, S. E. (1987). English in parallels: A comparison of English and Arabic prose. In U. Connor & R. B. Kaplan (Eds.), *Writing across languages: Analysis of L2 text* (pp. 169–185). Reading, MA: Addison-Wesley.

Ostler, S. E. (2002). Contrastive rhetoric: An expanding paradigm. In J. Flowerdew (Ed.), *Academic discourse* (pp. 167–181). Harlow, England: Longman/Pearson Education.

Panetta, C. G. (1997). Contrastive rhetoric in technical-writing pedagogy at urban institutions. *College ESL, 7*(2), 70–80.

Panetta, C. G. (Ed.). (2001). *Contrastive rhetoric revisited and redefined.* Mahwah, NJ: Lawrence Erlbaum.

Pére-Woodley, M. P. (1990). Contrasting discourses: Contrastive analysis and a discourse approach to writing. *Language Teaching, 23*(3), 143–151.

Pinker, S. (1994). *The language instinct: How the mind creates language.* New York: William Morrow.

Purves, A. C. (Ed.). (1988). *Writing across languages and cultures: Issues in contrastive rhetoric.* Newbury Park, CA: Sage.

Purves, A. C., & Purves, W. C. (1986). Viewpoints: Cultures, text models, and the activity of writing. *Research in the Teaching of English, 20,* 174–197.

Régent, O. (1985). A comparative approach to the learning of specialized written discourse. In P. Riley (Ed.), *Discourse and learning* (pp. 105–120). London: Longman.

Reid, J. M. (1993). *Teaching ESL writing.* Englewood Cliffs, NJ: Prentice-Hall.

Rinnert, C., & Kobayashi, H. (2001). Differing perceptions of EFL writing among readers in Japan. *Modern Language Journal, 85,* 189–209.

Sapir, E. (1949). *Language: An introduction to the study of speech.* New York: Harcourt Brace Jovanovich. (Original work published 1921)

Schneider, M. & Fujishima, N. K. (1995). When practice doesn't make perfect. The case of an ESL graduate student. In D. Belcher & G. Braine (Eds.), *Academic writing in a second language: Essays on research and pedagogy* (pp. 3–22). Norwood, NJ: Ablex.

Scollon, R. (2000). Generic variability in news stories in Chinese and English: A contrastive discourse study of five days' newspapers. *Journal of Pragmatics, 32,* 761–791.

Söter, A. O. (1988). The second language learner and cultural transfer in narration. In A. C. Purves (Ed.), *Writing across language and cultures: Issues in contrastive rhetoric* (pp. 177–205). Newbury Park, CA: Sage.

Swales, J. M. (1990a). *Genre analysis: English in academic and research settings.* New York: Cambridge University Press.

Swales, J. M. (1990b). Nonnative speaker graduate engineering students and their introductions: Global coherence and local management. In U. Connor & A. M. Johns (Eds.), *Coherence in writing: Research and pedagogical perspectives* (pp. 189–207). Alexandria, VA: Teachers of English to Speakers of Other Languages.

Swales, J. M., & Feak, C. B. (1994). *Academic writing for graduate students: Essential tasks and skills.* Ann Arbor: University of Michigan Press.

Swales, J. M., & Feak, C. B. (2000). *English in today's research world: A guide for writers.* Ann Arbor: University of Michigan Press.

Swales, J. M., & Najjar, H. (1987). The writing of research article introductions. *Written Communication, 4,* 175–191.

Takano, Y. (1989). Methodological problems in cross-cultural studies of linguistic relativity. *Cognition, 31,* 141–162.

Taylor, G., & Tingguang, C. (1991). Linguistic, cultural, and subcultural issues in contrastive discourse analysis: Anglo-American and Chinese scientific texts. *Applied Linguistics, 12,* 319–336.

Whorf, B. L. (1956). *Language, thought, and reality: Selected writings of Benjamin Lee Whorf* (J. B. Carroll, Ed.). Cambridge: MIT Press.

Wierzbicka, A. (1985). A semantic metalanguage for a crosscultural comparison of speech acts and speech genres. *Language in Society, 14,* 491–513.

Ying, H. G. (2000). The origin of contrastive rhetoric revisited. *International Journal of Applied Linguistics, 10,* 259–268.

Chapter 3
Paths to Improvement

"Written commentary on student papers is, of course, intended to produce improvement, but what constitutes improvement is not so clear. Much of the research on intermediate draft interventions only looks at improvements in students' subsequent drafts of the same piece of writing. In other words, there is little information on long-term improvement in writing." (Leki, 1990)

"Teachers and researchers hold a widespread, deeply entrenched belief that grammatical correction should, even must, be part of writing courses. But on what do they base this belief?" (Truscott, 1996)

"Good Writing: I Know It When I See It" (Title of article by Leki, 1995)

"[F]or the student, genres serve as keys to understanding how to participate in the actions of a community." (Miller, 1984)

"[W]riters often fit their words better to outside readers when they put those readers out of mind for a while and write privately to try to make sure their words fit themselves and their own experience of things." (Elbow, 1999)

"Sentimental realism . . . is a corrupt, if extraordinarily tempting genre." (Bartholomae, 1995)

"One of the language educator's responsibilities in college language classes is . . . to provide students with meaningful opportunities for some kind of intellectual engagement with ideas and issues along with their language practice." (Casanave, 1995)

LEADING QUESTIONS

- In L2 writing classes, what do we mean by "improvement"? How can teachers best help students improve?
- In what ways is practice in fluency and accuracy linked to improvement? Are these practices really incompatible?
- What are the central arguments in the process-product debate?
- Of the many kinds of responses to student writing, is there evidence that error correction leads to improvement?

Introduction to the Issues

Perhaps the most consuming of all dilemmas for L2 writing teachers is how to best help their students improve their writing. The dilemma involves not only the need for teachers to have a sense of what they mean by improvement but also an idea of what the diverse and sometimes competing and controversial opinions are about the approaches and practices that best lead to improvement. To help teachers make decisions about how to help students improve their writing, I present in this chapter several issues related to improvement that have been debated in the L1 and L2 writing literature. The first two issues are related: **the tensions between the goals of fluency and of accuracy in writing,** and **the process-product debate,** which lingers on in evolved and newly labeled forms. The third issue encompasses a more volatile debate on the role of response—**error correction in particular**—in helping students improve their writing (Ferris, 2002). Many L2 writing teachers cannot imagine *not* correcting at least some of students' errors, and many L2 students apparently feel the same way. What will not be considered controversial is the widely accepted belief that writing of all kinds, by all kinds of writers, improves with practice. Thus, regardless of what beliefs writing teachers hold about the controversial paths to improvement in their students' writing, practice, and more practice, is considered essential. As I recommend for issues in other chapters in this book, I urge readers who are unfamiliar with some of the influential literature in the various debates about improvement to read some of the original arguments and opinions, discuss the issues with colleagues, and consider all of the arguments in the context of their local teaching and research activities. Before introducing these three issues in more detail, I discuss briefly the difficulties we face in trying to figure out what we mean by improvement.

Broadly, improvement can be defined as positive change over time. However, a fundamental dilemma, one that influences how writing teachers approach specific paths to improvement, concerns how researchers and teachers identify specific characteristics of improvement in writing (Currie, 1994). To do this, we need to have some idea of what we consider "good writing" to be. It turns out to be quite difficult to characterize good writing in a clear and unambiguous way that would allow teachers to apply the characterizations to writing pedagogy. As Leki (1995) and others have noted, instructors in universities often hold tacit views of what good writing in their fields is. In other words, they can recognize it when they see it, but they have trouble explaining their criteria. Li (1996) is one of the few writing scholars to conduct an in-depth cross-cultural study to try to get at the heart of what "good writing" consists of in two cultures. She asked two writing teachers from the United States and two from her home country of China to respond to sets of student essays in English and Chinese, then discuss why they responded as they did. She found that they responded quite individually, but she noted as well that readers from both cultures believed that objective standards for good writing exist. Li's own experience as a writer in two cultures, however, convinced her that deciding what "good writing" consists of "is a messy and complex issue, anything but pure and simple" (Li, 1996, p. xiii).

In addition to asking readers to give reasons why they judge some writing as good and other writing as less successful, we can turn to assessment rubrics to see the criteria by which student writing is actually judged (see chap. 4; the chapter in Ferris & Hedgcock, 1998, on assessment; Weigle, 2002). By setting up criteria for assessment, writing teachers and evaluators necessarily characterize what they believe good writing to consist of. Criteria may be described in analytic schemes that focus on how effectively writers address a topic, provide a coherent and well-organized discussion, and use vocabulary and grammar to achieve their purposes. Holistic rubrics describe similar criteria but generally without breaking the features into discrete categories. Other criteria include maturity and flair (Casanave, 1994) and style and grace (Williams, 1997). It soon becomes obvious that criteria for good writing, particularly those that relate to thinking skills, such as coherence, flow, logic, clarity, and maturity, cannot themselves be easily characterized in ways that would satisfy the evaluator or researcher who wishes to count and quantify unambiguously what good writing is. It is perhaps for this reason, particularly in L2 writing, that teachers seem to focus so persistently on features of writing that can be seen and counted and easily corrected: grammar, vocabulary, and mechanics.

Finally, teachers and researchers of L2 writing need to try to distinguish between two very different conceptions of improvement in writing. One has to do with the quality of writing, however that is measured or characterized. This challenge faces L1 writing teachers and researchers as well. The second has to do with the development of students' second language proficiency, an issue facing those in L2 writing (Carson, 2001; Polio, 2001). These two may or may not be related. It is possible, in other words, for students to improve individual pieces of writing, with feedback and revision, without increasing their L2 proficiency at all, if by L2 proficiency we mean systematic changes in students' interlanguage (Carson, 2001; Yates & Kenkel, 2002). This dilemma has not been solved in L2 writing research. However, L2 writing teachers who are concerned mainly with helping students improve the quality of their writing will make certain kinds of decisions in their writing classrooms, and those concerned primarily with second language acquisition will make others.

It is not the purpose of this chapter to try to characterize good writing but to alert L2 writing teachers to the need to consider carefully what their own criteria for good writing are as they design activities to help students improve their writing. They will no doubt discover multiple criteria at many layers of attention, and they may find that they do not in fact need a stable and unambiguous characterization of good writing in order to help students along the path to improvement. They can attend to different criteria selectively, according to *who* the students are, *why* they are writing, *what* they are writing, and *whom* they are writing for. Indeed, if criteria for good writing change according to who readers are, we may be doing students a favor by convincing them that there are no universal standards for good writing and that their job is to learn as much as they can about what their readers (and realistically this usually means individual teachers) expect (see chap. 5, "Interaction"). The point is that teachers need to reflect on their criteria in conjunction with their goals and contexts for teaching and to realize they cannot, and need not, do everything at once. Now let me turn to the main issues in this chapter.

I first introduce the tensions between the two different, but equally desired, goals for L2 writers: that of developing fluent writing (with attendant loss of fear of taking risks and making mistakes) and that of developing writing that is grammatically accurate and formally acceptable. Some of the arguments for and against attention to fluency and accuracy are revisited in the process-product debate, the second issue I discuss. I then review the debate concerning error correction and response.

It is probably safe to say that every L2 writing teacher hopes that all students develop both fluency and accuracy in their writing, even though neither one can be linked clearly to improvement in writing quality (Polio, 2001). *Fluency* can be seen as writers' ability to produce a lot of language (or to read) without excessive hesitations, blocks, and interruptions. Fluent writers write without fear of making mistakes, knowing that they can go back to their writing at any time to make changes and corrections. Although very little research has focused on fluency (Polio, 2001), it is usually measured by the total number of words a writer can produce within a specified time limit (Wolfe-Quintero, Inagaki, & Kim, 1998). *Accuracy,* on the other hand, usually refers to a writer's ability to produce language that is free of language errors at the word and sentence level. In this meaning it does not refer to a writer's accurate reporting of content. Accuracy in research is usually measured by error counts, such as the number of error-free T-units (a "minimal terminable unit" consisting of an independent clause and any attached dependent clauses or phrases, as defined by Hunt [1977]) or analytic scales (Polio, 2001). The problem for students and their writing teachers is that fluency and accuracy are inversely related: As attention to one goes up, attention to the other goes down. This means that students may see more errors in writing that they do as part of fluency exercises than in writing that is done more slowly and deliberately, where they can either attend more systematically to errors or consciously avoid taking risks that might produce them. Both researchers and teachers continue to ponder the relationship between these two aspects of writing, on the one hand, and improvement in writing, on the other.

As for the process-product debate, the discussions that began in the 1970s continue to be relevant, even though the either-or dichotomy is considered invalid. Expanded discussions include attention to genre (a kind of socially situated product orientation) and to more social and political aspects of writing (see also chap. 6, "Politics and Ideology").

There probably has not been a time in which L1 and L2 writing educators have totally focused attention on the finished products of students' writing at the expense of attention to how they got there (see the historical review by Matsuda [2003]). In a nutshell, when they focus on writing as a product, researchers and teachers look at the textual characteristics of writing samples, counting various features, analyzing rhetorical structures, and teaching and evaluating grammatical, linguistic, and rhetorical forms that suit different genres. Their concerns do not lie with how writers got to the final stage of writing nor with how to help writers recognize the strategies they use before and during the act of writing but with the form and evaluation of the resulting product. Improvement is signaled by changes in these features, toward language that is more "native-like." In contrast, when they focus on writing as a process, researchers and teachers define the act of writing as a nonlinear, recursive activity of meaning-making, discovery, and problem solving that may begin well before writers begin drafting. If students' writing processes become more similar to those used by experts, the argument goes, we can expect the quality of the writing to improve. Experts know that writing is social, strategic, and purposive, that it can be used to both generate and clarify ideas, and that it may require multiple revisions of ideas and content rather than just correction at the levels of word, sentence, and paragraph. In a process-oriented classroom, students work together, and the teacher is more a collaborator than an evaluator. It is not clear how either of these approaches to writing instruction is linked to improvement over time in students' writing.

The third issue concerns response. In this chapter, I concentrate on the unresolved debate about the value of error correction, although I touch on several other issues as well.

Writing teachers are genetically endowed with a paper-marking reflex that makes it difficult for them to read their students' papers without (red) pen in hand. Whether the responses consist of error corrections or comments on content, they see marking papers as such an inherent part of their job that they easily slip into mindless routines of responding and do not stop to ask themselves what purposes their responding is designed to serve or whether those purposes are being fulfilled.

Responses to writing include two basic kinds: (1) commentary on content and ideas and (2) responses designed to address the formalities of global and local writing problems. There are a number of reasons why teachers might respond to students' writing in these ways, such as motivating and encouraging students (as people, as writers), helping students deal with content, or providing them information or clues about specific linguistic or rhetorical features of their writing (Duppenthaler, 2002a, 2002b). In all cases, writing teachers hope that their students' writing will improve. Research on the effects of different kinds of response on students' improvement continues to be conducted. However, it is still notoriously inconclusive and rife with methodological problems (Goldstein, 2001). I do not, therefore, have generic answers to questions about the effectiveness of responding. I recommend that teachers reflect carefully on what they mean by improvement and link their beliefs about improvement to their responding practices. Underlying the responses that teachers make to writing are beliefs, tacit or overt, about what improvement in writing means and what students need to do to improve.

Discussions in the Literature

Fluency and Accuracy

A number of arguments have been made that favor a fluency-first approach to improvement in writing and reading (e.g., MacGowan-Gilhooly, 1991; some of the work of Peter Elbow; and L1 and L2 writing scholars interested in journal writing). Some scholars, on the other hand, and many students, worry that too much attention to fluency at the expense of accuracy will not help students efficiently develop writing that is acceptable to readers such as teachers in school settings or evaluators of essay tests.

In her influential article urging a fluency-first approach to ESL writing and reading, MacGowan-Gilhooly (1991) describes a common problem faced by ESL students and educators in English-medium college settings, that of students' poor success rates at meeting college writing standards. At her public college in New York, in spite of many years of grammar instruction, many ESL students could not pass the college's required writing test. To address this problem, a group of ESL faculty devised a whole-language approach to literacy instruction (Freeman & Freeman, 1989), in which language and ideas emerge from the learners rather than from textbooks. Importantly, language is not broken up into uncontextualized segments of sounds, words, and sentences but kept whole and contextualized.

Following Mayher, Lester, and Pradl (1983, as cited in MacGowan-Gilhooly, 1991), the teachers devised a three-course sequence in which the goals were fluency first, then clarity, then correctness. Of particular interest to L2 teachers of writing was the experience of the students in the lowest of the ESL courses. These students, described as having a basic knowledge of English but weak reading and writing skills, were given no grammar instruction but instead were required to do extraordinary amounts of reading and writing. To be specific, in one semester the students read about 70 pages a week of popular fiction, kept a journal in which they copied and responded to passages they liked, discussed responses in small groups, and completed a 10,000-word writing project of their own choosing, such as personal memoirs or fictional stories. None of the writing was corrected. The students in this section and in the second course in the sequence doubled their reading scores and raised their writing test scores by 20 percentage points. The teachers reported that students increased their fluency in written English very fast, often doubling the amount they wrote by the fourth week of the term. They also reported that the students seemed to take more risks in trying out new vocabulary; to write clearer, more interesting pieces; and to read with greater comprehension and enjoyment. Although they did not have quantitative evidence, the teachers also reported that students' control of language, including grammar, improved. The students themselves saw great improvements, surprising themselves at the quantity of reading and writing they did and at the improvement in their speaking abilities as well. As has been found in other surveys of student opinion, however, these students still reported that they wanted more grammar instruction in spite of the extraordinary growth they saw in their L2 language skills.

In another North American setting, the work of L1 writing educator Peter Elbow has influenced the thinking of L1 and L2 writing teachers alike. Elbow himself has been at the center of debates about the value of personal and expressive writing as opposed to "academic" writing (see Bartholomae, 1995; Bishop, 1995; Elbow, 1994, 1995, 1999). But one of his most influential books, *Writing Without Teachers* (Elbow, 1973), advocated "freewriting" in which the purpose is to write nonstop for at least 10 minutes, without concern for correctness, coherence, or conventions of any kind. Many years later, Elbow (1993) continued to argue the benefits of this kind of unevaluated fluency exercise in helping students build confidence, self-knowledge, and liking of their own writing.

The final part of my discussion of fluency concerns the literature on journal writing. In the L2 setting, both in English-medium countries and in settings where English is a foreign language, regular journal writing has been touted as benefiting students in a variety of ways, including in their development of fluency. The argument is both simple and powerful: In learning an L2, students are bound to make mistakes. Mistakes are normal, inevitable, and indeed desirable when we consider that they help students experiment and test their own interlanguage hypotheses about their evolving L2. Fear of making mistakes will hinder students' progress—they are less likely to experiment and more likely to be overly concerned with small language matters that prevent them from seeing the forest for the trees. Although journal-writing practices have been characterized in a number of ways, a common feature is that journals are usually uncorrected and unrevised. Students use them to build fluency of language, fluency of thinking, and fluency and confidence in exploration of ideas and content (Casanave, 1994, 1995; Duppenthaler, 2002a, 2002b; Fulwiler, 1987; Lucas, 1992; Mlynarczyk, 1998; Peyton & Staton, 1993).

Research results of studies on journal writing are somewhat mixed but generally positive. Some problems were captured by Lucas (1992) in her study of the journal-writing experiences of eight female adult students in a class that was expressly devoted to building fluency. In this class, journals by both students and the teacher consisted of descriptions of and responses to personal events. Lucas found that the eight students all responded quite differently, including one who dropped the class and two who developed their own, less personal agendas in their journals. The other problematic issue for students was one of audience—they were unclear who they were writing their journals for.

Dialogue journals, a particular kind of journal in which teacher and students interact regularly through their journal writing, came to the attention of L2 writing educators with the work of Jana Staton and Joy Kreeft Peyton, who worked with one sixth-grade teacher following her daily written interactions with her students (Staton, Shuy, Peyton, & Reed, 1988). This study and other dialogue journal studies (e.g., Peyton, 1990b; Peyton & Staton, 1993) offer evidence that dialogue journals "provide a means for individualizing instruction in classrooms in which students represent various cultural and language backgrounds and various levels of English proficiency, and for communicating with students at their level of proficiency" (Peyton, 1990a, p. 67).

Journals are often stereotyped as being only intensely personal, but journals of other kinds help students build fluency of language and thought as well. My own studies of journal writing with undergraduate students at a Japanese university showed that students improved their fluency greatly, as suggested by the self-reports of how much less time they spent writing the equivalent number of words at the end of the semester than at the beginning. Evidence from their journals also indicates that many students deepened their thinking, not only about personal topics, but about issues that they were responding to from films and discussions. Students themselves recognized these changes (Casanave, 1993b, 1995). In Casanave 1994 I further reported that in spite of no systematic grammar instruction or correction, students' proficiency with English language developed in a number of different ways: In addition to writing more fluently, some students wrote more accurately over time (as measured by error-free

T-units); some wrote on more mature topics; and some wrote with more detail, depth, and expressiveness. I consider all of these changes to be signs of improvement. (For other evidence that language proficiency improves via journal writing, see Duppenthaler, 2002b; Peyton, 1990a; Weissberg, 1998.)

Although all writing teachers hope that their students acquire both fluency and accuracy in their writing, not all are so sanguine about the benefits of fluency practices in the L2 writing classroom. Taken to an extreme, teachers who focus on fluency can do students a disservice by neglecting attention to the language features that students need to master in order to succeed in content classes and to meet required writing standards. Infelicities in the accuracy of students' written language can distract content teachers and evaluators such that students' knowledge and abilities may be masked by the surface appearance of their writing. It is also the case that a focus on fluency above accuracy may not meet with students' expectations about what they are supposed to be learning in their L2 writing class and what their teachers' role should be. Some students, such as one of the participants in Lucas's (1992) study, resist writing on the intensely personal topics that some teachers expect in journal writing. (Note, however, that many journal-writing activities do not deal with personal topics, but academic ones: see, e.g., Hamada & Izawa, 1998; Mlynarczyk, 1991; Vanett & Jurich, 1990.) Some students may also understandably resist a method of teaching writing that eschews all correction of language errors, as was the case for Dang, the lone "contrarian" journal writer in a study by Holmes and Moulton (1995). Although both Dang and his teachers saw improvements in his writing, he still believed that he needed to have his language errors marked in order to improve. Finally, not all writing teachers are able to implement fluency-first approaches if their time with a particular group of students is limited or if there is pressure to prepare students for an imminent writing assessment where they will be evaluated at least in part on the accuracy of their writing (Horowitz, 1986b). Arguments in favor of paying attention to accuracy will be further explored in the next section.

The conflict between fluency and accuracy is less a debate than it is a dilemma. L2 writing teachers tend to agree that both are important, but we have not yet designed and rationalized pedagogies that effectively attend to both within the limited time that most students have in their writing classes. L2 writing teachers are therefore faced with daily decisions about how to divide their class time between these two competing goals.

Product, Process, Genre, and the Social Turn

Product and Process

In this section, aspects of the fluency-accuracy debate overlap in the discussion over which aspects of writing merit more attention in the classroom by writing teachers—writers' processes or the products by which writers are ultimately evaluated. All writing teachers no doubt hope to find balanced ways to help students improve the effectiveness of their writing processes on their way to producing a satisfactory written product. However, by the 1970s, resistance began to arise to what Young (1978) called the "current-traditional paradigm" in L1 writing. According to Young, this traditional product-focused approach was tacit rather than set forth in a clear theoretical or pedagogical set of precepts. It included

> emphasis on the composed product rather than the composing process; the analysis of discourse into words, sentences, and paragraphs; the classification of discourse into description, narration, exposition, and argument; the strong concern with usage (syntax, spelling, punctuation) and with style (economy, clarity, emphasis); the preoccupation with the informal essay and the research paper; and so on. (p. 31)

With little research on students' composing processes at that time, in particular at the prewriting stage or on the thinking skills needed for writing, the L1 writing field was ripe for change. Janet Emig's (1971) groundbreaking study of the composing processes of twelfth graders helped the field come to see composition as a process and to shift attention away from "frivolous basics" such as spelling and punctuation, which Emig claimed represent "merely the conventions, the amenities for recording the outcome of the process" (Emig, 1978, p. 59). What was needed in teaching was a way to help students understand their own composing processes and to use invention strategies (Young, 1978), and what was needed in research was a way to get inside the heads of writers to learn what was going on as they composed (Flower & Hayes, 1981). Whether this shift really constituted a Kuhnian revolution in composition (Hairston, 1982; Young, 1978) is debatable (Faigley, 1986, 1992; Matsuda, 2003), given the historical diversity of the field of composition studies and a lack of evidence that the persuasive ideas of process pedagogies were ever fully turned into practice (Applebee, 1986; Susser, 1994). Part of the history of the debate, then, is a debate about perceptions and even misunderstandings rather than about realities of what writing educators actually did and said. Nevertheless, there was at the very least a perception among L1 and L2 writing educators that by the early 1980s things had indeed changed.

At that time, many people believed that by understanding more about writing processes, L2 writing teachers can potentially help students develop effective invention, drafting and revising strategies, awareness and control, expressivity, and fluency—all of which can be considered aspects of improvement. At least two versions of process writing influenced both L1 and L2 writing educators. One was the view of writing as a cognitive problem-solving process, inspired by the research of L1 writing scholars Flower and Hayes (1981). This line of research aimed to get inside the heads of experienced and inexperienced writers as they composed in order to understand the decisions that they made through the several iterations of a piece of writing. Researchers used a technique called "think-aloud composing," in which writers were trained to talk into a tape recorder as they wrote, voicing their problems, decisions, and strategic choices. Expert writers, this strand of research concluded, compose quite differently from novices in that they establish plans before writing, attend to large issues of meaning first, revise and rethink their content, and postpone attention to mechanics.

Findings from this work found their way into L2 writing via review articles such as those by Zamel (1976, 1982). Case study research, such as that by Zamel (1983a), in which writers talked and wrote about their writing processes, similarly concluded that experienced L2 writers use their writing to discover and explore ideas and that their writing processes are not interrupted by language-level concerns. Process pedagogies that developed from this research were intended to help novice writers understand the roles of invention, planning, discovery, and revising and the inevitable place of errors and imperfections of language and thinking during the overall process of composing (Raimes, 1985, 1991; Spack, 1984; Zamel, 1982, 1987). Teaching writing as discrete skills or as a linear step-by-step process was severely criticized. An unproven assumption underlying this work was that novice writers, L1 or L2, would improve by learning how to write more like the experts (Casanave, 1988; see Susser, 1994, for a more detailed discussion).

Another view of process writing links it with expressivist movements in which the act of writing liberates student writers from the formal constraints of academic assignments and evaluations and helps them explore issues of personal importance. Perhaps the most influential liberator of all has been L1 writing educator Peter Elbow, who, as I mentioned earlier, has been promoting the benefits of unevaluated personal writing for many years. Writers need to know themselves, Elbow argues, and writing can help them do that, but not the kind of tightly constrained, rule-bound writing that characterizes typical academic assignments. Student writers also need to satisfy themselves as readers of their own writing—to like their own writing and to have teachers like their writing and therefore respond more as interested readers than as evaluators (Elbow, 1993). Such a view of writing need not be harmful, Elbow says to his critics; indeed, "[s]elf-exploration usually increases people's ability to identify with others" (Elbow, 1999, p. 156).

Writing pedagogies that have evolved from expressivist traditions use freewriting, brainstorming, personal journal writing, and personal essay writing. Much of the writing may not be revised at all. Topics emerge from students' own lives rather than from academic fields or from topics of supposedly general interest assigned by writing teachers. Every student, in theory, thus has something important and meaningful to say and unconstrained and creative ways to say it—central requirements of process pedagogies. The exploration of self through narrative and reflection that is thought to occur within expressivist writing contributes both to self-knowledge and to in-depth thinking, qualities that can benefit students in their more formal academic writing.

However, in the L2 writing literature, vocal critics to process writing surfaced in the mid-1980s. Some critics understood process gurus such as Zamel and Raimes to be saying that we do not need to concern ourselves with written products and that personal narratives will do (Barnes, 1983; Horowitz, 1986a, 1986b) and that writing as a discovery process refers to creative, rather than academic, writing (Reid, 1984a). Horowitz (1986b), for example, claimed that the bandwagon enthusiasm for process approaches neglected the kinds of writing that students needed to do to survive in academic settings, such as essay examinations. Criticizing Raimes for claiming that essay exams cannot be considered "real writing," Horowitz (1986b) argued that in a school setting nothing was quite so real for students as an essay exam. For Horowitz, then, improvement might be measured by passing rates on such exams. A longtime process advocate, Raimes (1991, pp. 414–415) conceded that "[t]he issue of what university writing is and what kind of writing ESL students should be doing is a thorny one, and the use of the term *real* relates to this issue in practice as well as in theory."

Still, the belief of critics persisted that process approaches demanded personal and expressive writing to the exclusion of explicit instruction in structured academic writing and that such writing could not help students improve in the ways they need to in school settings. In the L2 writing scene, Leki and Carson (1994, 1997) surveyed and interviewed ESL students who had moved into academic classes, and they learned that at least some ESL writing classes provided students with too much personal and narrative writing and not enough challenging, text-responsible academic writing of the kind that they encountered when they left their L2 writing classes. In L1 writing in the mid-1990s, Bartholomae (1995) was still criticizing Elbow for not being more concerned about the formal writing that students need to do in schools and for not acknowledging the roles of teachers in giving students explicit guidance. There is no writing that is "writing without teachers," Bartholomae asserted, just as "there is no writing done in the academy that is not academic writing" (p. 63). But he also equated personal writing with "sentimental realism" and asked whether all students should be "required to participate in a first person narrative or expressive genre whose goal it is to reproduce the ideology of sentimental realism" (p. 69)—full of livid details, but not conducive to the critical thinking needed in the academy. For her part in this debate, Bishop (1995) claimed she did not recognize Bartholomae's caricature of expressive writing in her own composition classes or her own expressive writing. Both she and her students used personal writing to deepen and critically reflect on their thinking. In his own defense, Elbow (1995) argued that he wants to help his students become writers as well as academics, goals that he believes conflict.

Scholars who responded to these critiques tended to point out that paying attention to students' writing processes and exploration of self, on the one hand, and easing students into academic writing, on the other, are not mutually exclusive (Hamada & Izawa, 1998; Hamp-Lyons, 1986; Leibman-Kleine, 1986; Spack & Sadow, 1983; Vanett & Jurich, 1990). For example, Zamel (1983a, 1984) disagreed with the view that process writing of the personal expressive type dominated writing instruction, pointing out that her own students wrote academic essays. She further pointed out that because of their attention to revision, process pedagogies inevitably are intended to improve the products of students' writing (Zamel, 1983a). In other words, accuracy is not necessarily neglected. Furthermore, journal writing, often portrayed as personal memoir and reflection, can link personal, process-oriented writing and academic writing, particularly when journals consist of learning logs and responses to classes and readings (Carroll, 1994; Cole, Raffier, Rogan, & Schleicher, 1998; Mlynarczyk, 1991, 1998; Vanett and Jurich, 1990). In my own work on journal writing, I found that my Japanese students could use personal and reflective topics in their journals to develop both fluency and depth of thinking, the latter characterized as detailed and thoughtful treatment of subject matter. Both fluency and depth of treatment can contribute to improved academic writing, which ultimately always requires accuracy (Casanave, 1994, 1995). With Bishop (1995), we can thus counter the assumption that personal writing is not challenging, critical, or text-based.

The critiques and responses I have discussed so far deal mainly with the typical subject matter (the self) and reflective nature of process writing approaches. Another kind of critique is aimed at the assumptions in process approaches of how writing actually gets done (Casanave, 1988). Expert writers are thought to discover meaning through (rather than before) writing, to revise multiple times, to postpone attention to mechanics, to be personally engaged with their writing, and so on. However, there is little evidence to support such a uniform view of expert writers, particularly if we do not consider purpose, genre, and individual styles and strategies of writing. Reid (1984b), an expert writer by anyone's account, labels herself a "radical outliner," unlike her husband, a "radical brainstormer." The outliner may not use writing as discovery, in other words, but may employ discovery heuristics before beginning to draft. Such writers may also revise less than the "brainstormers," given that meticulous planning takes place in the first stages of writing rather than recursively, as predicted by process writing research. Moreover, some expert writers do not postpone attention to mechanics until all drafting gets done (I am one of them) but either weave attention to mechanics into every stage of writing or (rarer?) attempt to perfect each sentence before moving on to the next, as Annie Dillard (1989) described in her writing autobiography. Likewise, being personally involved with one's topics sounds wonderful. However, it is probable that most of the required writing we do throughout all our years of schooling does not engage us personally in the ways that process advocates would wish and is evaluated only in its finished form as a product. Such realities do not necessarily damage the quality of our writing. It is therefore important in this debate, indeed in any debate, to lay out and examine the assumptions that underlie the various positions. The assumptions may not be based on accurate depictions of writers and their writing processes.

Nevertheless, the writing process movement has had a great impact on how writing scholars and teachers think about writing. We recognize that writing is often a lengthy messy process and that voice and identity are represented in our writing whether we intend them to be or not (Ivanič, 1998; see also the different points of view on this in the 2001 special issue of the *Journal of Second Language Writing* [*10*(1)], on voice). We also recognize that effective writing instruction involves writing teachers in helping students develop their writing from the earliest stages and continuing to the final product, whatever the interim processes and strategies and whatever the final product might be. The point is that the debates in the published literature—the "discursive history" (Matsuda, 2003)—tend to simplify and misrepresent the views of spokespeople on both sides of the debate, to neglect the diversity of ways that writing actually gets done and taught, and to underplay the many purposes and audiences for writing. As pointed out by Matsuda (2003) and Susser (1994), the process-product debate in its discursive form in some of the published literature seems quite straightforward, but a historical look at the reality of different approaches to writing indicates that there is now, and always has been, a multiplicity of theoretical and practical views of what students need to do to improve their writing.

Genre: A Socially Situated Product Perspective?

Attention to written product in discussions of how students' writing improves has not disappeared. In recent years, another wave of resistance to the personal and expressivist writing thought to characterize process pedagogies has surfaced in the form of genre approaches to writing. Genre research and pedagogy indeed focuses on the features of written products, but with a social context thrown in, in that genres are produced for social purposes of communication within groups that share purposes, understandings, and ways of using language (Hyland, 2002; Johns, 2002a; Miller, 1984; Swales, 1990). Two basic types of research are conducted in genre studies: those with a textual or linguistic focus and those with a contextual or socially situated focus (Flowerdew, 2002; Johns, 2002b). Genre research with a textual focus tries to identify the salient features of different genres (necessary if we are to know what to teach) either for the purpose of characterizing the formal features of different genres (Connor, 2000; Swales, 1990) or for inferring the social and interactive nature of academic and professional writing (Hyland, 1996, 1997, 1998, 1999, 2000). In Hyland's work, corpus studies use computer search software to locate language features in large authentic data samples from different disciplines. Additionally, textual analyses of professional writing at the rhetorical level help scholars and writing teachers identify larger structural and cohesive patterns in different genres (Connor, 1996, 2000; Posteguillo, 1999; Swales, 1990). If salient formal features of genres can indeed be identified, this information can then be used to argue for a pedagogy that values explicitness over exploration and discovery (Cope & Kalantzis, 1993; Williams & Colomb, 1993). In contrast, genre research with a contextual or situational focus tends to be more descriptive of people and situations—more ethnographic—and less focused on specific linguistic items (Casanave, 2002b; Freedman, Adam, & Smart, 1994; Freedman & Medway, 1994). In this view, novice writers improve their ability to control genres by actually participating in the writing and writing-related activities of different communities of writers (cf. Lave & Wenger, 1991).

As for teaching that follows from these orientations, genre enthusiasts from Australia, for instance, advocate that we explicitly teach the formal features, including the grammar, of different genres to minority students—indeed that we are ethically obligated to do so as a way to remedy discriminatory practices in society (Cope & Kalantzis, 1993; Flowerdew, 2002; Martin, 1997). Followers of contrastive rhetoric (see chap. 2) presume as well that we can identify the formal features, such as patterns of rhetorical organization, of different genres across cultures and that our knowledge can be used to help students write in culturally and rhetorically appropriate ways (Connor, 1996, 1997; Kaplan, 1987). Explicit comparisons and explicit instruction, in the view of some scholars, grow naturally out of genre approaches to writing.

However, others argue that there is enough diversity within and across genres to make it problematic to try to apply the findings of genre studies explicitly to instructional situations. Hyland (2000) found many differences across disciplines in his studies of the socially motivated language forms and functions in research articles and other academic genres, such that it would be impossible to apply his findings to an undifferentiated genre called academic writing. He therefore argues that explicit rules and conventions should not be taught as formalities to students but that students themselves should explore the textual forms and functions within the genres of their own fields. Others assert that writing is learned in situ, not through explicit instruction. School writing, for example, is learned through immersion in school writing practices, and workplace or professional writing is learned through immersion in workplace practices (Freedman, Adam, & Smart, 1994). The L2 bilingual faculty that I studied in Japan indeed learned to write in situ, without having taken a single ESL or EAP class (Casanave, 1998). Instead, they improved over time with practice, using models from their readings and feedback from mentors.

Still, in the case of L2 writers trying to improve their writing through increased attention to and practice with particular genres, we are faced with the confounding factor of basic language proficiency. Silva (1993) argues that L2 writers have special needs related to language proficiency. Should L2 writers learn basic grammar and academic vocabulary first and then attend to features of different genres, presuming we can identify those features in a relatively unambiguous way? As some have argued, do L2 writers benefit from explicit instruction in rules and conventions of genres and in how to model their writing on different genres? Or do they improve equally well from sink-or-swim immersion as is often the case outside the writing class and in education systems where writing is not taught as a subject? These questions merit ongoing attention within the contexts of L2 writing instructors' own classes.

Adding a Social Orientation

Finally, I conclude this discussion of the process-product debate with a brief reference to what has been referred to as a post-process movement (Atkinson, 2003; Casanave, 2003; Matsuda, 2003; Kent, 1999; Trimbur, 1994). In this movement, the interest of L2 writing scholars who favor this perspective has turned to the socially and politically situated contexts of writing and how these contexts influence both how writing gets done and the end products of writing. If this is true, a vast new arena of decision making faces L2 writing teachers, requiring that they see writing as involving far more than texts, cognitive or expressive writing strategies, and formalities of language. They will need to consider how the social and political dimensions of writing influence their attempts to help students improve their writing.

As is the case in the process-product debate, spokespeople in the post-process camp tend to pit themselves against something they are not and then fill in gaps, correct mistaken past views, or expand our conception of writing. Beginning in the L1 composition field, Trimbur (1994) brings the term *post-*

process into our vocabulary in his review of three books on L1 composition from the 1990s. He refers to the "social turn" of the 1980s, in which a "post-process, post-cognitivist theory and pedagogy . . . represent literacy as an ideological arena and composing as a cultural activity by which writers position and reposition themselves in relation to their own and others' subjectivities, discourses, practices, and institutions" (p. 109).

Although the prefix *post-* may link the movement to then popular views on postmodernism, it also implies a movement that came after (and replaced) process approaches. Matsuda (2003) rightly points out that the label *post-process* is a misnomer because it does not reject process pedagogies or theories. Rather, it rejects "the dominance of process at the expense of other aspects of writing and writing instruction" (pp. 78–79). However, as is the case in all the debates and controversies in writing and composition, such movements get discursively constructed and labeled and, in the process, simplified and used to tell stories ("metadisciplinary narratives") of the field (Casanave, 2002a; Matsuda, 2003). As Matsuda (2003) explains, in order for a notion like "the post-process movement" to make sense, it needs to be seen in relation to a caricature of something else, in this case, the process movement, just as the process proponents created caricatures of what they saw as an overemphasis on written products in current-traditional writing pedagogy. In my own commentary on my belief that L2 writing researchers and teachers need to consider social and political factors that influence writing, I concur with Matsuda (2003) that the term *post-process* is a misnomer because as a label it not only does not capture the idea of an expanded sociopolitical orientation but also has little meaning in countries like Japan that never experienced a process revolution in the first place (Casanave, 2003, p. 98).

Debates, controversies, and dilemmas arise in part because these simplified caricatures of complex ideas and activities are pitted against one another in our discussions of pedagogy and theory. L2 writing teachers, then, need to be aware that even though such simplification captures some of the changing perceptions of how we conceptualize and teach writing, it obscures the complexities both of historical changes and of what really goes on in each teacher's writing class. I thus urge L2 writing teachers to stay abreast of these ongoing discussions and to stay off the bandwagon.

How does a socially oriented approach to writing instruction relate to improvement in students' writing? Any movement in writing research and pedagogy that views writing as a complex social and political practice necessarily links improvement in students' writing to how students understand, and are able to locate themselves within, the social and political contexts of their writing. With such understanding presumably comes greater control of writers' own decisions about how to interact with and respond to the instruction they receive. With greater control comes greater agency and an ability to participate in, and possibly resist, the literacy practices of their academic and workplace communities (see chap. 6, "Politics and Ideology").

To conclude this section, L2 writing teachers who consider the debates on process and product, genre, and post-process in light of their own writing classes face a number of decisions about how they will help students improve their writing. All of these movements potentially influence L2 writing pedagogies in the classrooms of individual writing teachers. Each teacher or writing-program group decides which teaching materials to use or design, how much importance to place on drafts or finished texts, whether and when to help students develop both fluency and accuracy, and whether to contextualize writing pedagogies within broader social, political, and ideological contexts.

Response (The Error Correction Debate)

In this section I review some of the issues that have been associated with teacher response to student writing, highlighting the question of whether responses of various kinds can be linked to improvement in students' writing. Central to this argument is the debate over the value of error correction.

It is difficult to define and therefore study writing problems and writing quality at the levels of content and rhetoric. Therefore, much research on responding to writing concerns either students' attitudes toward different kinds of teacher response or the style and effects of language-level error treatment on students' attitudes, receptivity, and motivation (Cohen & Cavalcanti, 1990; Duppenthaler, 2002a; Ferris, 1995; Goldstein, 2001; Hedgcock & Lefkowitz, 1994, 1996; Holmes & Moulton, 1995; Radecki & Swales, 1988; Saito, 1994). Not surprisingly, most students report that they want and appreciate teachers' commentary, but in particular they claim to want help with grammar and vocabulary and may feel that a teacher who does not correct these language errors is not doing her job (Holmes & Moulton, 1995). Students tend to believe (as do many teachers) that corrections help regardless of whether they see actual improvement in their writing over time and regardless of whether they actually incorporate the corrections into revisions. But as many experienced writing teachers confess, there is little evidence that responding practices lead students to improve their writing on new tasks. The primary controversy in the L2 writing literature on response thus revolves around the question of error treatment: Does it help students improve their writing or not?

It may surprise teachers who are new to the field of writing that little evidence exists in either L1 and L2 writing research that teacher or peer feedback on students' writing has the positive effects that are intended (Leki, 1992; Robb, Ross, & Shortreed, 1986; Truscott, 1996). Based on her review of some of this literature, Leki (1992) explains this failure from several angles. She notes the following: Students have no reason to pay attention to feedback on final drafts; they may not be developmentally (cognitively, linguistically) ready for the kinds of responses they receive from teachers; they may not understand teachers' comments clearly enough to be able to take action on them; they may reject comments on content as a way to maintain ownership of their texts; they may know more about the content and form of certain professional genres than their teachers and so reject comments because they see their teachers primarily as English experts; and students who accept teachers' feedback too readily do not learn to take responsibility for their own writing and so do not improve over time (Leki, 1992, pp. 122–123).

As I indicated earlier, there is a specific debate about the value of treating grammatical errors in students' writing. This issue has been articulated most prominently in the published literature by Truscott (1996, 1999) on the anti-treatment side and by Ferris (1999a, 2002; Ferris & Helt, 2000; Ferris & Roberts, 2001) on the pro-treatment side. In this debate, "improvement" refers to increased grammatical accuracy in students' writing. Truscott (1996) does not condemn all responses to student writing, just grammar correction, which is what many teachers spend most of their time on. He makes the strong, unhedged assertion that, according to his review of the literature, teachers' correction of grammatical errors does students no good and may actually harm them by discouraging them from further efforts and by robbing them and their teachers of time that could be spent on more productive activities.

Truscott makes three major points about error correction. He first provides evidence to show that grammar correction does not work to improve the grammatical accuracy of students' writing, either in L1 or in L2. He further argues that even in the case of studies that claim to find positive effects of grammar correction, such as Fathman and Whalley (1990), there is no evidence that "grammar correction in writing classes make[s] students better writers in any sense" beyond revisions on the same piece of writing (Truscott, 1996, p. 338). Truscott argues secondly that these findings can be explained by recognizing that L2 learners' grammatical accuracy improves mainly through a process of interlanguage development rather than through one of noticing and conscious self-correction. Truscott's third point is that grammar correction can actually harm students: "Even students who believe that correction is a necessary part of learning do not enjoy the sight of red ink all over their writing and probably find the experience extremely discouraging" (p. 354). Truscott's position is that there is no reason to correct grammatical errors in students' writing until evidence conclusively demonstrates the effectiveness of correction (Truscott, 1996, 1999). He concludes that until that time, "grammar correction should be abandoned" (Truscott, 1996, p. 360).

In making these arguments, Truscott does not reject the importance of grammatical accuracy in writing or the value of other kinds of feedback, such as to the "content, organization, and clarity of a composition"; the issue, he asserts "is whether or not grammar correction can contribute to [the] development [of grammatical accuracy]" (Truscott, 1996, p. 329).

For her part, Ferris (1999a, 2002; Ferris & Helt, 2000) acknowledges with Truscott and others (e.g., Leki, 1992; Polio, Fleck, & Leder, 1998) that current research has not yet demonstrated unambiguously that error correction benefits students' writing. She nevertheless asserts that error treatment is "necessary for L2 writers" (Ferris, 2002, chap. 1) for a number of compelling reasons. First, she notes that some studies have shown that error correction helps students improve in the short term, for example on drafts of the same essay or on targeted errors (e.g., Fathman & Whalley, 1990). She argues that even if there is no evidence of long-term improvement, "long-term development is unlikely without observable short-term improvement" (Ferris, 2002, p. 8). Second, Ferris claims correctly that students like feedback and that they believe it helps them (e.g., Cohen & Cavalcanti, 1990; Ferris, 1995). Truscott (1996) does not see this as a reason for providing students with feedback that he believes is useless, but Ferris (1999a, 2002) argues that students who do not get what they believe they need may lose motivation. Finally, Ferris argues that because accuracy in writing is important in the real world, students need to learn how to edit their own work. Teachers, she says, have a responsibility for helping students learn to do this (Ferris, 2002, p. 9).

Let me now review just two studies that attempted to define improvement and to compare the effects of different kinds of responses on student writing. First, in one of the few carefully designed quantitative studies of L2 writing improvement at the high school level, Duppenthaler (2002a, 2002b) investigated the effects of regular year-long journal writing under three feedback conditions on improvements in the writing and motivation of 99 high school girls in Japan. Duppenthaler (2002b) defined improvement as a significant increase in quantity of writing over a year, a significant increase in accuracy as measured by error-free clauses, and a significant increase in quality (defined as the number of clauses per entry), readability (according to a standard readability index), and vocabulary (as measured by several vocabulary indices). Duppenthaler divided the students into three groups and provided each group with different kinds of feedback. One group received meaning-focused feedback in the form of Duppenthaler's comments on specific aspects of the content of the students' journals. A second group received only encouraging responses (e.g., "Good, keep writing") but no specific remarks about content and no correction. The third group had all of their errors corrected but received no encouraging remarks or comments on content. Duppenthaler found that only the meaning-focused group showed improvements of various kinds in subsequent journals but that none of the feedback groups demonstrated significant improvements on a separate measure of in-class writing. In other words, improvement did not seem to transfer to other kinds of writing, even for the group whose errors were corrected, the latter a finding that supports Truscott's claims.

In an article written from his 2002 dissertation, Duppenthaler (2002a) reported only the results of questionnaire items designed to measure the attitudes and motivation of the three groups of students. He found that the group that received meaning-focused comments most enjoyed journal writing but that the other two groups enjoyed it as well. The only significant difference among the groups was that the group that received only encouraging remarks, without either meaningful comments or error corrections, did not look forward to getting their journals back each week as much as did the other two groups. Duppenthaler's (2002a, 2002b) study lends credence to the belief by some researchers and teachers that improvement in writing happens over time with regular writing practice regardless of feedback type and that specific commentary on content helps students develop positive attitudes toward L2 writing.

The other study on response type looks at several patterns of teacher response over multiple drafts of one composition written by 50 Japanese university students (Ashwell, 2000). Ashwell wanted to know if a process-oriented response style that focused on content first and form later would lead to greater improvement in subsequent drafts than a response style that targeted formal errors from the beginning. In this study, Ashwell defined improvement as increases in formal accuracy (grammar, lexicon, mechanics) and in content, as measured by an adaptation of several existing analytic scales. The content categories consisted of communicative quality, organization, paragraphing, cohesion, and relevance and adequacy (Ashwell, 2000, p. 236). Three native English speakers scored all three drafts of students' essays. The 50 students were divided into four groups: content feedback before form, form feedback before content, simultaneous content and form feedback, and no feedback at all. Results showed that the three groups that received feedback, regardless of kind, improved their formal accuracy and their content scores. However, the group that received no feedback also improved their content scores, whereas their scores on formal accuracy dropped. Content can apparently improve "simply by rewriting" (p. 243), a conclusion also reached by Fathman and Whalley (1990) and by Robb, Ross, and Shortreed (1986). What we do not learn from Ashwell (2000) is whether feedback on form, which seems to help from draft to draft, transfers to new pieces of writing. Duppenthaler (2002b) found that it did not. It can be argued that it is natural to expect that teacher feedback on form be incorporated into subsequent drafts of the same composition and that this kind of revising tells us nothing about what students have actually learned that might apply to new pieces of writing. (For more on response and error correction, see Ferris, 2002.)

To conclude, both teachers and researchers need to carefully consider what they mean by improvement and whether it is possible or desirable to measure improvement quantitatively or to treat it more qualitatively and descriptively. Moreover, as Goldstein (2001) and Hedgcock and Lefkowitz (1996) have pointed out, much more research needs to be done in order to learn what the effect of teacher response is on students' writing, particularly on new pieces of writing and on writing improvement over time. If writing improves mainly through practice and natural development rather than through intervention (Polio, 2001), via a kind of written interlanguage (Yates & Kenkel, 2002), L2 writing teachers are left to ponder what the purposes of their responses are and perhaps to rethink how they and their students spend their time in the L2 writing class.

Classroom Perspectives

It is difficult to provide useful examples of how classroom writing teachers help their students improve their writing, because each teacher, group of students, class goals, and practical constraints differ so greatly. I here provide one brief example from my own experiences teaching in Japan, simply as a demonstration of the kinds of decisions I faced in helping my students improve their English and their writing in particular (see also Casanave, 1994).

For several years, I taught what might be called intermediate-level undergraduate students at a Japanese university (TOEFL about 400–450). The students were required to take three semesters of intensive foreign language classes, defined as four 90-minute classes a week. I taught several classes of about 35 students two times a week for at least two consecutive semesters. A number of us at that time taught content/project-based courses, centered around some general theme such as human relationships, education, or culture, allowing us great flexibility with specific lessons and projects. We did not use textbooks. Students watched films, did short readings, discussed issues, and did some kind of semester-long project that would involve them in a variety of English skills.

I had to decide what I meant by "improvement" for a group of students who had never before been taught in English as the language of instruction and who for the most part had written no extended discourse in English. Many students were also reticent to speak out or write much, for fear of making mistakes. Because they had studied grammar and translation for up to six years and taken many tests in English where there was always a right answer, I decided to define improvement as the development of fluency and expression of their own ideas, increased willingness to take risks without fear of making mistakes, and the ability to write and revise one or more pieces of writing for a class "book" of their own work. I therefore asked the students to write personal journals (double-spaced and typed) once a week on topics of their choice and to form small groups of five or six students that would work on a "book" project. These groups discussed their ideas together during the semester, primarily in Japanese.

I responded each week to the ideas in the journals, without making more than a few language corrections (a bit on grammar and vocabulary if problems seemed to interfere with meaning), but I did not ask students to revise their journals. Rather, they collected them week by week, until by the end of the semester they had a collection of 30 or more pages of journal entries, much to their amazement. As for the separate "book" project, each group of students designed its own "book" (title, cover, contents). I set a schedule, helped them revise their short essays or poems and write bio-statements, and copied the final products for group members.

Did these students improve their writing? According to the criteria I established at the beginning of the semester, they did, although as a practicing classroom teacher I had no irrefutable proof. By the end of the term, most of the students reported that they wrote more in their journals in less time than at the beginning; they showed no signs of being afraid of making mistakes (e.g., no more apologies for bad grammar or lack of vocabulary and plenty of evidence that they did not proofread their journals!); and they expressed pride in and enthusiasm about their final products. These aspects of their improvement carried over into the second semester, which I also had with them. In short, many students had gone from fearing or disliking English to showing confidence in and engagement with their written tasks. In a separate study of journal writing, I also showed specific changes in the writing of some students in several intermediate classes, such as greater detail, depth, and maturity in their journal writing. Additionally, I documented improvements in grammatical accuracy in some cases and drops in accuracy in others, the latter of which I took to be a possible sign of more risk taking (Casanave, 1994). However, I believe that if my only definition of improvement had been tied to specific linguistic and rhetorical changes that I could have specified beforehand and then taught, I might have been disappointed. My written corrections to some of the errors in students' journals seemed to have little effect on later journals, whereas the regular weekly practice did. It may have been that students improved the language of their journals through means other than my teaching and explicit feedback. For example, they could have used my feedback as a model of syntax and vocabulary, and readings and class discussion as a source of input waiting to be absorbed when they were developmentally ready. Such questions about improvement, and many others, remain to be investigated.

Ongoing Questions

It is frustrating for L2 writing teachers to have so few answers to important questions such as how to characterize and facilitate improvement in their students' writing. Of all the dilemmas in L2 writing pedagogy, perhaps this is the largest, most important, and most problematic. We recognize the essential role that a great deal of practice in both reading and writing plays in helping students improve, and probably most teachers and researchers agree that real improvement refers to positive changes in new writing tasks. However, we seem stuck for now with local characterizations and solutions that fit the needs, purposes, and beliefs of particular teachers and students. This is fine, as long as teachers are reflective about the sometimes tenuous connections between their labor-intensive work and real improvement in their students' writing.

In my own teaching with intermediate-level students in Japan, as I mentioned, I perceived that students lacked fluency and depth above all else in their writing, so I worked hard to help them improve in this area. However, their own questions and mine about how to improve the long-term accuracy of their writing remained. With small groups of upper-division and graduate students, I helped students edit papers much the way a professional editor would, without worrying much about whether students learned specific things about their writing for the next time. Naturally their revisions improved, but I don't really know what students acquired in the way of long-term improvement.

Can we assume that our instruction and feedback help, even in the short time that most of us have with our students? What is our evidence, and to what extent do we or others need to see "proof"? Or, lacking evidence, are we assuming and hoping that various kinds of instruction (in fluency, accuracy, writing processes, genre structure and purpose, response, etc.) help our students, if not now, then in the long run? Where does the burden of proof lie, with doubters or believers? And, a point on which Truscott (1996) and Ferris (1999a, 2002) disagree, do we provide students with what they think they need (e.g., error correction) even if we have little evidence from research or from our own teaching that it helps? What is the role of a positive and motivated attitude—of committed engagement in a writing task—in helping students improve? L2 writing teachers can begin to sort out some of the answers to these questions for themselves by reflecting on, looking at, and attending to their own decisions, and the consequences of their decisions, about how to help their students down the path to improvement.

Beliefs and Practices

Beliefs

1. In the context of your own teaching and/or learning of L2 writing, how do you characterize "improvement" in writing? Try to define what you believe each of the following improvements consists of, adding your own. Then rank order them from most important (1) to least important at two different points in a class term, early and late.

AREA	IMPORTANCE (early)	IMPORTANCE (late)
Increase in fluency	——	——
Increase in grammatical accuracy	——	——
Clearer expression of personal involvement and voice	——	——
More detail and depth of content	——	——
More effective use of "expert" writing processes	——	——
More confidence and motivation	——	——
Increased knowledge of genre conventions of writing	——	——
Better ability to revise in response to teacher's feedback	——	——

Increased ability to   —   —
self-edit

Other_____   —   —

_____

Other_____   —   —

_____

Other_____   —   —

_____

2. Look at the following list of beliefs. Explain why you agree or disagree with them.
   a. Adult (or child) L2 writing students benefit greatly from explicit instruction and feedback from a teacher.
   b. Adult (or child) L2 writing students improve primarily through a process of natural development that occurs as a result of practice.
   c. Teachers should provide L2 writing students with the kinds of feedback they want even if there is little evidence that it leads to improved writing.
   d. A fluency-first approach makes a lot of sense with beginning writers.
   e. L2 writing students can and should be taught particular writing processes and strategies.
   f. Personal and expressive writing, focusing on fluency and depth of expression, benefits students, even in academic contexts.
   g. In school settings, L2 writing students should be taught the formal structures and conventions for the kinds of writing they will probably need, including explicit instruction in genre; time should not be wasted on other kinds of writing.
   h. Students' writing and images of themselves as writers will improve if students become aware of the complex social nature of writing.
   i. Even if it does not reflect the complex realities of writing, L2 students improve most from a pattern-governed, "keep-it-simple" approach.

Practices

1. Describe some fluency exercises you have done/could do with particular L2 writing students (specify who). Then design some new fluency exercises.
2. In your own teaching or belief system, how concerned are you with the grammatical accuracy of L2 students' writing? In what kinds of writing situations are you most and least concerned with accuracy? What examples do you have from your own L2 writing experiences?
3. Describe how you demonstrate to students your concern (or lack thereof) for fluency. Describe how you demonstrate to students your concern (or lack thereof) for accuracy.
4. What aspects of process approaches, if any, have you used or do you plan to use with your L2 writing students? Why?
5. What kinds of finished products have you asked or do you plan to ask students to complete? Why? What steps do you take to help your students finish a piece of writing?
6. Examine several samples of your written responses to some L2 students' writing. What do you notice about the patterns, emphases, gaps, inconsistencies, and in general the choices that you make in your responses? What kinds of improvements do you hope will result from your responses?
7. Putting yourself in your students' shoes, what effects do you believe your responses have on students' attitudes toward writing? On their improvement? What have been the effects on you of different kinds of responses to L2 writing that you yourself have done?
8. If you or your colleagues have used or designed any writing assessment rubrics, what do those rubrics tell you about your conceptualizations of improvement in writing?

References and Relevant Readings

Anderson, J. (1993). Journal writing: The promise and the reality. *Journal of Reading, 36,* 304–309.

Anson, C. M. (Ed.). (1989). *Writing and response: Theory, practice, and research.* Urbana, IL: National Council of Teachers of English.

Applebee, A. (1986). Problems in process approaches: Toward a reconcep-
tualization of process instruction. In A. R. Petrosky & D. Bartholomae
(Eds.), *The teaching of writing: Eighty-fifth yearbook of the National Society for the Study of Education, part II* (pp. 95–113). Chicago: National
Society for the Study of Education.

Ashwell, T. (2000). Patterns of teacher response to student writing in a
multiple-draft composition classroom: Is content feedback followed by
form feedback the best method? *Journal of Second Language Writing, 9,*
227–257.

Atkinson, D. (2003). L2 writing in the post-process era: Introduction. *Journal of Second Language Writing, 12,* 3–15.

Bamsforth, R. (1993). Process versus genre: Anatomy of a false dichotomy.
Prospect, 8(2), 89–99.

Barkhuizen, G. P. (1995). Dialogue journals in teacher education revisited.
College ESL, 5(1), 22–35.

Barnes, G. A. (1983). Comments on Vivian Zamel, "Writing: The process of
discovering meaning." *TESOL Quarterly, 17,* 137–138.

Bartholomae, D. (1995). Writing with teachers: A conversation with Peter
Elbow. *College Composition and Communication, 46,* 62–71.

Berger, V. (1990). The effects of peer and self-feedback. *CATESOL Journal,
3,* 21–35.

Bishop, W. (1995). Responses to Bartholomae and Elbow: If Winston Weath-
ers would just write me on e-mail. *College Composition and Communication, 46,* 97–103.

Blanton, L. L. (1995). Elephants and paradigms: Conversations about teaching L2 writing. *College ESL, 5*(1), 1–21.

Brice, C. (1995). *ESL writers' reactions to teacher commentary: A case study.*
(ERIC Document Reproduction Service No. ED394312)

Britton, J. (1978). The composing processes and the functions of writing. In
C. R. Cooper & L. Odell (Eds.), *Research on composing: Points of departure* (pp. 13–28). Urbana, IL: National Council of Teachers of English.

Brumfit, C. (1984). Communicative methodology in language teaching:
The roles of fluency and accuracy. Cambridge: Cambridge University
Press.

Burns, A. (1990). Genre-based approaches to writing. *Prospect, 5*(3), 62–71.

Carroll, M. (1994). Journal writing as a learning and research tool in the
adult classroom. *TESOL Journal, 4*(1), 19–22.

Carson, J. (2001). Second language acquisition and second language writing. In T. Silva & P. K. Matsuda (Eds.), *On second language writing* (pp. 191–199). Mahwah, NJ: Lawrence Erlbaum.

Casanave, C. P. (1988). The process approach to writing instruction: An examination of issues. *CATESOL Journal, 1,* 29–39.

Casanave, C. P. (Ed.). (1993a). *Journal writing: Pedagogical perspectives.* Keio University SFC Monograph No. 3. (ERIC Document Reproduction Service No. ED423682)

Casanave, C. P. (1993b). Student voices: The insiders speak out on journal writing. In C. P. Casanave (Ed.), *Journal writing: Pedagogical perspectives* (pp. 95–115). Keio University SFC Monograph No. 3. (ERIC Document Reproduction Service No. ED423682)

Casanave, C. P. (1994). Language development in students' journals. *Journal of Second Language Writing, 3,* 179–201.

Casanave, C. P. (1995). Journal writing in college English classes in Japan: Shifting the focus from language to education. *JALT Journal, 17,* 95–111.

Casanave, C. P. (2002a, October). *Uses of narrative in L2 writing research.* Paper presented at the Second Purdue Symposium on Second Language Writing, Purdue University, West Lafayette, Indiana.

Casanave, C. P. (2002b). *Writing games: Multicultural case studies of academic literacy practices in higher education.* Mahwah, NJ: Lawrence Erlbaum.

Casanave, C. P. (2003). Looking ahead to more sociopolitically-oriented case study research in L2 writing scholarship (But should it be called "postprocess"?). *Journal of Second Language Writing, 12,* 85–102.

Chandler, J. (2000, March). *The efficacy of error correction for improvement in the accuracy of L2 student writing.* Paper presented at the American Association of Applied Linguistics Conference, Vancouver, British Columbia.

Chapin, R., & Terdal, M. (1990). *Responding to our response: Student strategies for responding to teacher written comments.* (ERIC Document Reproduction Service No. ED328098)

Ching, L. P., & Ai, N. C. (1991). How journal writing improved our English classes. *English Teaching Forum, 29*(3), 43–44.

Cohen, A., & Cavalcanti, M. (1990). Feedback on written compositions: Teacher and student verbal reports. In B. Kroll (Ed.), *Second language writing: Research insights for the classroom* (pp. 155–177). Cambridge: Cambridge University Press.

Cole, R., Raffier, L. M., Rogan, P., & Schleicher, L. (1998). Interactive group journals: Learning as a dialogue among learners. *TESOL Quarterly, 32*, 556–568.

Connor, U. (1996). *Contrastive rhetoric: Cross-cultural aspects of second-language writing.* Cambridge: Cambridge University Press.

Connor, U. (1997). Contrastive rhetoric: Implications for teachers of writing in multicultural classrooms. In C. Severino, J. C. Guerra, & J. E. Butler (Eds.), *Writing in multicultural settings* (pp. 198–208). New York: Modern Language Association.

Connor, U. (2000). Variation in rhetorical moves in grant proposals of U.S. humanists and scientists. *Text, 20*, 1–28.

Cope, B., & Kalantzis, M. (Eds.). (1993). *The powers of literacy: A genre approach to teaching writing.* London: Falmer Press.

Currie, P. (1994). What counts as good writing? Enculturation and writing assessment. In A. Freedman & P. Medway (Eds.), *Teaching and learning genre* (pp. 63–79). Portsmouth, NH: Boynton/Cook.

Delpit, L. D. (1986). Skills and other dilemmas of a progressive Black educator. *Harvard Educational Review, 56*, 379–385.

Delpit, L. D. (1988). The silenced dialogue: Power and pedagogy in educating other people's children. *Harvard Educational Review, 58*, 280–298.

Dillard, A. (1989). *The writing life.* New York: Harper and Row.

Duppenthaler, P. M. (2002a). The effect of three types of written feedback on student motivation. *JALT Journal, 24*, 130–154.

Duppenthaler, P. M. (2002b). *Feedback and Japanese high school English language journal writing.* Unpublished doctoral dissertation, Temple University, Philadelphia, PA.

Edelsky, C. (1990). Whose agenda is this anyway? A response to McKenna, Robinson, and Miller. *Educational Researcher, 19*(8), 7–10.

Edelsky, C. (1997). Working on the margins. In C. P. Casanave & S. R. Schecter (Eds.), *On becoming a language educator: Personal essays on professional development* (pp. 3–17). Mahwah, NJ: Lawrence Erlbaum.

Elbow, P. (1973). *Writing without teachers.* New York: Oxford University Press.

Elbow, P. (1993). Ranking, evaluating, and liking: Sorting out three forms of judgment. *College English, 55*, 187–206.

Elbow, P. (1994). Closing my eyes as I speak: An argument for ignoring audience. In G. Tate, E. P. J. Corbett, & N. Myers (Eds.), *The writing teacher's sourcebook* (3rd ed., pp. 258–276). New York: Oxford University Press.

Elbow, P. (1995). Being a writer vs. being an academic: A conflict in goals. *College Composition and Communication, 46,* 72–83.

Elbow, P. (1999). In defense of private writing: Consequences for theory and research. *Written Communication, 16,* 139–170.

Emig, J. (1971). *The composing processes of twelfth graders* (NCTE Research Report No. 13). Urbana, IL: National Council of Teachers of English.

Emig, J. (1978). Hand, eye, brain: Some "basics" in the writing process. In C. R. Cooper & L. Odell (Eds.), *Research on composing: Points of departure* (pp. 59–71). Urbana, IL: National Council of Teachers of English.

Eskey, D. E. (1983). Meanwhile, back in the real world . . . : Accuracy and fluency in second language teaching. *TESOL Quarterly, 17,* 315–323.

Faigley, L. (1986). Competing theories of process: A critique and a proposal. *College English, 48,* 527–542.

Faigley, L. (1992). *Fragments of rationality: Postmodernism and the subject of composition.* Pittsburgh: University of Pittsburgh Press.

Fathman, A., & Whalley, E. (1990). Teacher response to student writing: Focus on form versus content. In B. Kroll (Ed.), *Second language writing: Research insights for the classroom* (pp. 178–190). Cambridge: Cambridge University Press.

Ferris, D. R. (1995). Student reactions to teacher response in multiple-draft composition classrooms. *TESOL Quarterly, 29,* 33–53.

Ferris, D. R. (1997). The influence of teacher commentary on student revision. *TESOL Quarterly, 31,* 315–339.

Ferris, D. R. (1999a). The case for grammar correction in L2 writing classes: A response to Truscott (1996). *Journal of Second Language Writing, 8,* 1–11.

Ferris, D. R. (1999b). One size does not fit all: Response and revision issues for immigrant student writers. In L. Harklau, K. M. Losey, & M. Siegal (Eds.), *Generation 1.5 meets college composition: Issues in the teaching of writing to U.S.-educated learners of ESL* (pp. 143–157). Mahwah, NJ: Lawrence Erlbaum.

Ferris, D. R. (2002). *Treatment of error in second language student writing.* Ann Arbor: University of Michigan Press.

Ferris, D., & Hedgcock, J. (1998). *Teaching ESL composition: Purpose, process, and practice.* Mahwah, NJ: Lawrence Erlbaum.

Ferris, D. R., & Helt, M. (2000, March). *Was Truscott right? New evidence on the effects of error correction in L2 writing classes.* Paper presented at the American Association of Applied Linguistics Conference, Vancouver, British Columbia.

Ferris, D. R., Pezone, S., Tade, C., & Tinti, S. (1997). Teacher commentary on student writing: Descriptions and implications. *Journal of Second Language Writing, 6,* 155–182.

Ferris, D. R., & Roberts, B. (2001). Error feedback in L2 writing classes: How explicit does it need to be? *Journal of Second Language Writing, 10,* 161–184.

Flower, L., & Hayes, J. R. (1981). A cognitive process theory of writing. *College Composition and Communication, 32,* 365–387.

Flowerdew, J. (2002). Genre in the classroom: A linguistic approach. In A. M. Johns (Ed.), *Genre in the classroom: Multiple perspectives* (pp. 91–102). Mahwah, NJ: Lawrence Erlbaum.

Freedman, A. (1993). Show and tell? The role of explicit teaching in the learning of new genres. *Research in the Teaching of English, 27,* 222–251.

Freedman, A., Adam, C., & Smart, G. (1994). Wearing suits to class: Simulating genres and simulations as genre. *Written Communication, 11,* 193–226.

Freedman, A., & Medway, P. (Eds.), (1994). *Learning and teaching genre.* Portsmouth, NH: Boynton/Cook.

Freedman, S. W. (1987). *Response to student writing.* Urbana, IL: National Council of Teachers of Writing.

Freeman, Y., & Freeman, D. E. (1989). Whole language approaches to writing with secondary students of English as a second language. In D. M. Johnson & D. H. Roen (Eds.), *Richness in writing: Empowering ESL students* (pp. 177–192). New York: Longman.

Fulwiler, T. (Ed.). (1987). *The journal book.* Portsmouth, NH: Boynton/Cook.

Goldstein, L. (2001). For Kyla: What does the research say about responding to ESL writers? In T. Silva & P. K. Matsuda (Eds.), *On second language writing* (pp. 73–89). Mahwah, NJ: Lawrence Erlbaum.

Gomez, R., Jr., Parker, R., Lara-Alecio, R., & Gomez, L. (1996). Process versus product with limited English proficient students. *Bilingual Research Journal, 20,* 209–233.

Green, C., & Green, J. M. (1993). Secret friend journals. *TESOL Journal, 2*(3), 20–23.

Gutstein, S. (1987). *Toward the assessment of communicative competence in writing: An analysis of the dialog journal writing of Japanese adult*

ESL students. Washington, DC: Georgetown University Dissertation Abstracts, No. AAG8804261.

Hairston, M. (1982). The winds of change: Thomas Kuhn and the revolution in the teaching of writing. *College Composition and Communication, 33,* 76–88.

Hamada, M., & Izawa, H. (1998). Students' journal work. *Journal of the University of Marketing and Distribution Sciences, 10*(2), 93–116.

Hammersly, H. (1991). *Fluency and accuracy.* Clevedon, England: Multilingual Matters.

Hamp-Lyons, L. (1986). No new lamps for old yet, please. *TESOL Quarterly, 20,* 790–796.

Harrison, M. R. (1993). The role of teacher response in high school journal writing. In C. P. Casanave (Ed.), *Journal writing: Pedagogical perspectives* (pp. 71–77). Keio University SFC Monograph No. 3. (ERIC Document Reproduction Service No. ED423682)

Hedgcock, J., & Lefkowitz, N. (1994). Feedback on feedback: Assessing learner receptivity in second language writing. *Journal of Second Language Writing, 3,* 141–163.

Hedgcock, J., & Lefkowitz, N. (1996). Some input on input: Two analyses of student response to expert feedback on L2 writing. *Modern Language Journal, 80,* 287–308.

Holmes, V. L., & Moulton, M. R. (1995). A contrarian view of dialogue journals: The case of a reluctant participant. *Journal of Second Language Writing, 4,* 223–251.

Horowitz, D. (1986a). The author responds to Liebman-Kleine. *TESOL Quarterly, 20,* 788–790.

Horowitz, D. (1986b). Process, not product: Less than meets the eye. *TESOL Quarterly, 20,* 141–144.

Hunt, K. W. (1977). Early blooming and late blooming syntactic structures. In C. R. Cooper & L. Odell (Eds.), *Evaluating writing: Describing, measuring, judging* (pp. 91–106). Urbana, IL: National Council of Teachers of English.

Hyland, K. (1996). Talking to the academy: Forms of hedging in science research articles. *Written Communication, 13,* 251–281.

Hyland, K. (1997). Scientific claims and community values: Articulating an academic culture. *Language and Communication, 16,* 19–32.

Hyland, K. (1998). Persuasion and context: The pragmatics of academic metadiscourse. *Journal of Pragmatics, 30,* 437–455.

Hyland, K. (1999). Academic attribution: Citation and the construction of disciplinary knowledge. *Applied Linguistics, 20,* 341–367.

Hyland, K. (2000). *Disciplinary discourses: Social interactions in academic writing.* London: Longman.

Hyland, K. (2002). Genre: Language, context, and literacy. *Annual Review of Applied Linguistics, 22,* 113–135.

Ivanič, R. (1998). *Writing and identity: The discoursal construction of identity in academic writing.* Philadelphia: John Benjamins.

Janopolous, M. (1992). University faculty tolerance of NS and NNS writing errors. *Journal of Second Language Writing, 1,* 109–122.

Johns, A. M. (Ed.). (2002a). *Genre in the classroom: Multiple perspectives.* Mahwah, NJ: Lawrence Erlbaum.

Johns, A. M. (2002b). Introduction: Genre in the classroom. In A. M. Johns (Ed.), *Genre in the classroom: Multiple perspectives* (pp. 3–13). Mahwah, NJ: Lawrence Erlbaum.

Kaplan, R. B. (1987). Cultural thought patterns revisited. In U. Connor & R. B. Kaplan (Eds.), *Writing across languages: Analysis of L2 text* (pp. 9–21). Reading, MA: Addison-Wesley.

Kent, T. (Ed.). (1999). *Post-process theory: Beyond the writing process paradigm.* Carbondale: Southern Illinois University Press.

Kepner, C. G. (1991). An experiment in the relationship of types of written feedback to the development of second-language writing skills. *Modern Language Journal, 75,* 305–313.

Krapels, A. (1990). An overview of second language writing process research. In B. Kroll (Ed.), *Second language writing: Research insights for the classroom* (pp. 37–56). Cambridge: Cambridge University Press.

Lalande, J. F., II. (1982). Reducing composition errors: An experiment. *Modern Language Journal, 66,* 140–149.

Lave, J., & Wenger, E. (1991). *Situated learning: Legitimate peripheral participation.* Cambridge: Cambridge University Press.

Lee, C. (1997). Giving effective written feedback to ESL global errors. In J. C. Richards (Ed.), *Teaching in action: Case studies from second language classrooms* (pp. 261–264). Alexandria, VA: Teachers of English to Speakers of Other Languages.

Leki, I. (1990). Coaching from the margins: Issues in written response. In B. Kroll (Ed.), *Second language writing: Research insights for the classroom* (pp. 57–68). Cambridge: Cambridge University Press.

Leki, I. (1991). The preferences of ESL students for error correction in college-level writing classes. *Foreign Language Annals, 24,* 203–218.

Leki, I. (1992). *Understanding ESL writers: A guide for teachers.* Portsmouth, NH: Boynton/Cook Heinemann.

Leki, I. (1995). Good writing: I know it when I see it. In D. Belcher & G. Braine (Eds.), *Academic writing in a second language: Essays on research and pedagogy* (pp. 23–46). Norwood, NJ: Ablex.

Leki, I., & Carson, J. G. (1994). Students' perceptions of EAP writing instruction and writing needs across the disciplines. *TESOL Quarterly, 29,* 81–101.

Leki, I., & Carson, J. (1997). "Completely different worlds": EAP and the writing experiences of ESL students in university courses. *TESOL Quarterly, 31,* 39–69.

Li, X. (1996). *"Good writing" in cross-cultural context.* Albany: State University of New York Press.

Liebman-Kleine, J. (1986). In defense of teaching process in ESL composition. *TESOL Quarterly, 20,* 783–788.

Lucas, T. (1992). Diversity among individuals: Eight students making sense of classroom journal writing. In D. E. Murray (Ed.), *Diversity as resource: Redefining cultural literacy* (pp. 202–232). Alexandria, VA: Teachers of English to Speakers of Other Languages.

MacGowan-Gilhooly, A. (1991). Fluency first: Reversing the traditional ESL sequence. *Journal of Basic Writing, 10,* 73–87.

Martin, J. R. (1997). Analyzing genre: Functional parameters. In F. Christie & J. R. Martin (Eds.), *Genre and institutions* (pp. 3–39). London: Continuum.

Matsuda, P. K. (2003). Process and post-process: A discursive history. *Journal of Second Language Writing, 12,* 65–83.

McCornick, A. J. (1993). Journal writing and the damaged language learner. In C. P. Casanave (Ed.), *Journal writing: Pedagogical perspectives* (pp. 6–17). Keio University SFC Monograph No. 3. (ERIC Document Reproduction Service No. ED423682)

McKay, S. (Ed.). (1984). *Composing in a second language.* Rowley, MA: Newbury House.

Miller, C. R. (1984). Genre as social action. *Quarterly Journal of Speech, 70,* 151–167.

Mlynarczyk, R. W. (1991). Is there a difference between personal and academic writing? *TESOL Journal, 1*(1), 17–20.

Mlynarczyk, R. W. (1998). *Conversations of the mind: The uses of journal writing for second-language learners.* Mahwah, NJ: Lawrence Erlbaum.

Moulton, M. R., & Holmes, V. L. (1994). Writing in a multicultural classroom: Using dialogue journals to ease transitions. *College ESL, 4*(2), 12–25.

Murray, D. M. (1984). Teach writing as a process not product. In R. L. Graves (Ed.), *Rhetoric and composition: A sourcebook for teachers and writers* (pp. 89–93). Upper Montclair, NJ: Boynton/Cook.

Nelson, G. L., & Carson, J. G. (1998). ESL students' perceptions of effectiveness in peer response groups. *Journal of Second Language Writing, 7*, 113–132.

Pennington, M., & Cheung, M. (1995). Factors shaping the introduction of process writing in Hong Kong secondary schools. *Language, Culture and Curriculum, 8*(1), 15–34.

Perl, S. (1980). Understanding composing. *College Composition and Communication, 31*, 363–369.

Peyton, J. K. (1990a). Dialogue journal writing and the acquisition of English grammatical morphology. In J. K. Peyton, (Ed.), *Students and teachers writing together: Perspectives on journal writing* (pp. 65–97). Alexandria, VA: Teachers of English to Speakers of Other Languages.

Peyton, J. K. (Ed.). (1990b). *Students and teachers writing together: Perspectives on journal writing.* Alexandria, VA: Teachers of English to Speakers of Other Languages.

Peyton, J. K., & Reed, L. (1990). *Dialogue journal writing with nonnative English speakers: A handbook for teachers.* Alexandria, VA: Teachers of English to Speakers of Other Languages.

Peyton, J. K., & Staton, J. (Eds.). (1993). *Dialog journals in the multi-lingual classroom: Building language fluency and writing skills through written interaction.* Norwood, NJ: Ablex.

Polio, C. (2001). Research methodology in second language writing research: The case of text-based studies. In T. Silva & P. K. Matsuda (Eds.), *On second language writing* (pp. 91–115). Mahwah, NJ: Lawrence Erlbaum.

Polio, C., Fleck, C., & Leder, N. (1998). "If only I had more time:" ESL learners' changes in linguistic accuracy on essay revisions. *Journal of Second Language Writing, 7*, 43–68.

Posteguillo, S. (1999). The schematic structure of computer science research articles. *English for Specific Purposes, 18*, 139–160.

Radecki, P. M., & Swales, J. M. (1988). ESL student reaction to written comments on their written work. *System, 16*, 355–365.

Raimes, A. (1985). What unskilled ESL students do as they write: A classroom study of composing. *TESOL Quarterly, 19*, 529–534.

Raimes, A. (1991). Out of the woods: Emerging traditions in the teaching of writing. *TESOL Quarterly, 25*, 407–430.

Raimes, A. (1992). *Exploring through writing: A process approach to ESL composition* (2nd ed.). Boston: Allyn and Bacon.

Reid, J. (1984a). Comments on Vivian Zamel's "The composing processes of advanced ESL students: Six case studies." *TESOL Quarterly, 18*, 149–153.

Reid, J. (1984b). The radical outliner and the radical brainstormer. *TESOL Quarterly, 18*, 529–533.

Reid, J. (1994). Responding to ESL students' texts: The myths of appropriation. *TESOL Quarterly, 28*, 273–292.

Reid, J. (1998). Responding to ESL student language problems: Error analysis and revision plans. In P. Byrd & J. Reid (Eds.), *Grammar in the composition classroom* (pp. 118–137). Boston: Heinle & Heinle.

Robb, T., Ross, S., & Shortreed, I. (1986). Salience of feedback on error and its effect on EFL writing quality. *TESOL Quarterly, 20*, 83–93.

Rose, M. (1980). Rigid rules, inflexible plans, and the stifling of language: A cognitivist analysis of writer's block. *College Composition and Communication, 31*, 389–401.

Saito, H. (1994). Teachers' practices and students' preferences for feedback on second language writing: A case study. *TESL Canada Journal, 11*(2), 46–70.

Sandler, K. W. (1987). Letting them write when they can't even talk? Writing as discovery in the foreign language classroom. In T. Fulwiler (Ed.), *The journal book* (pp. 312–320). Portsmouth, NH: Boynton/Cook.

Semke, H. D. (1984). The effects of the red pen. *Foreign Language Annals, 17*, 195–202.

Sheppard, K. (1992). Two feedback types: Do they make a difference? *RELC Journal, 23*, 103–110.

Silva, T. (1990). Second language composition instruction: Developments, issues, and directions in ESL. In B. Kroll (Ed.), *Second language writing: Research insights for the classroom* (pp. 11–23). Cambridge: Cambridge University Press.

Silva, T. (1993). Toward an understanding of the distinct nature of L2 writing: The ESL research and its implications. *TESOL Quarterly, 27*, 657–675.

Sommers, N. (1980). Revision strategies of student writers and experienced adult writers. *College Composition and Communication, 31,* 378–388.

Sommers, N. (1982). Responding to student writing. *College Composition and Communication, 33,* 148–156.

Spack, R. (1984). Invention strategies and the ESL composition student. *TESOL Quarterly, 18,* 649–670.

Spack, R., & Sadow, C. (1983). Student-teacher working journals in ESL freshman composition. *TESOL Quarterly, 17,* 575–593.

Staton, J. (1993). Dialog journals as a means of assisting written language acquisition. In J. K. Peyton & J. Staton (Eds.), *Dialog journals in the multilingual classroom: Building language fluency and writing skills through written interaction* (pp. 103–122). Norwood, NJ: Ablex.

Staton, J., Shuy, R., Peyton, J. K., & Reed, L. (1988). *Dialogue journal communication: Classroom, linguistic, social, and cognitive views.* Norwood, NJ: Ablex.

Straub, R. (1997). Students' reactions to teacher comments: An exploratory study. *Research in the Teaching of English, 31,* 91–119.

Susser, B. (1994). Process approaches in ESL/EFL writing. *Journal of Second Language Writing, 3,* 31–47.

Swales, J. M. (1990). *Genre analysis: English in academic and research settings.* New York: Cambridge University Press.

Talburt, S. (1995). Dialogue journals in adult ESL: Exploring and creating possibilities. *College ESL, 5*(2), 67–82.

Thornbury, S. (1991). Watching the whites of their eyes: The use of teaching-practice logs. *ELT Journal, 45,* 140–146.

Tobin, L. (1994). Introduction: How the writing process was born—and other conversion narratives. In L. Tobin & T. Newkirk (Eds.), *Taking stock: The writing process movement in the '90s* (pp. 1–14). Portsmouth, NH: Boynton/Cook Heinemann.

Trimbur, J. (1994). Taking the social turn: Teaching writing post-process. *College Composition and Communication, 45,* 108–118.

Truscott, J. (1996). The case against grammar correction in L2 writing classes. *Language Learning, 46,* 327–369.

Truscott, J. (1999). The case for "The case against grammar correction in L2 writing classes": A response to Ferris. *Journal of Second Language Writing, 8,* 111–122.

Ulanoff, S. (1993). *Dialog journal writing and the mediated development of writing: How do second language learners engaged in authentic writ-*

ing activities develop as writers? (ERIC Document Reproduction Service No. ED306849)

Vanett, L., & Jurich, D. (1990). The missing link: Connecting journal writing to academic writing. In J. K. Peyton, (Ed.), *Students and teachers writing together: Perspectives on journal writing* (pp. 21–33). Alexandria, VA: Teachers of English to Speakers of Other Languages.

Vann, R. J., Lorenz, F. O., & Meyer, D. M. (1991). Error gravity: Faculty response to errors in the written discourse of nonnative speakers of English. In L. Hamp-Lyons (Ed.), *Assessing second language writing in academic contexts* (pp. 87–107). Norwood, NJ: Ablex.

Weigle, S. C. (2002). *Assessing writing.* Cambridge: Cambridge University Press.

Weissberg, R. (1998). Acquiring English syntax through journal writing. *College ESL, 8*(1), 1–22.

Williams, J. M. (1997). *Style: Ten lessons in clarity and grace* (5th ed.). New York: Longman.

Williams, J. M., & Colomb, G. G. (1993). The case for explicit teaching: Why what you don't know won't help you. *Research in the Teaching of English, 27,* 252–264.

Wolfe-Quintero, K., Inagaki, S., & Kim, H. (1998). *Second language development in writing: Measures of fluency, accuracy, and complexity* (Technical Report No. 17). Honolulu, HI: National Foreign Language Resource Center.

Yates, R., & Kenkel, J. (2002). Responding to sentence-level errors in writing. *Journal of Second Language Writing, 11,* 29–47.

Young, R. (1978). Paradigms and problems: Needed research in rhetorical invention. In C. R. Cooper & L. Odell (Eds.), *Research on composing: Points of departure* (pp. 29–47). Urbana, IL: National Council of Teachers of English.

Zamel, V. (1976). Teaching composition in the ESL classroom: What we can learn from the research in the teaching of English. *TESOL Quarterly, 10,* 67–76.

Zamel, V. (1982). Writing: The process of discovering meaning. *TESOL Quarterly, 10,* 67–76.

Zamel, V. (1983a). The composing process of advanced ESL students: Six case studies. *TESOL Quarterly, 17,* 165–187.

Zamel, V. (1983b). Reply to Barnes. *TESOL Quarterly, 17,* 138–139.

Zamel, V. (1984). The author responds. *TESOL Quarterly, 18,* 154–158.

Zamel, V. (1985). Responding to student writing. *TESOL Quarterly, 19,* 79–102.

Zamel, V. (1987). Recent research on writing pedagogy. *TESOL Quarterly, 21,* 697–715.

Ziv, N. (1984). The effects of teacher comments on the writing of four college freshmen. In R. Beach & L. S. Bridwell (Eds.), *New directions in composition research* (pp. 362–380). New York: Guilford Press.

Chapter 4

Assessment

"[C]lassroom teachers, more than anyone else, are actively and continuously involved in evaluation." (Genesee & Upshur, 1996)

"The problem is fundamentally that any language performance that is worthy of interest will be complex and multidimensional." (Skehan, 1984)

"[T]he susceptibility of language to precise measurement seems to be in direct proportion to its fragmentation." (Horowitz, 1991)

"[T]he traditional direct test of writing, the one-hour (or less) time and the unprepared topic in the stressful conditions of the examination room, is only a partial indication of what a person can do in writing." (Hamp-Lyons, 1991d)

"No one can make a trustworthy judgment about a student's skill or ability in writing without seeing multiple pieces of writing, written on multiple occasions, in multiple genres, directed to different audiences, written in more or less realistic writing conditions." (Elbow, 1994)

"Liking and disliking seem like unpromising topics in an exploration of assessment. They seem to represent the worst kind of subjectivity, the merest accident of personal taste. But I've recently come to think that the phenomenon of liking is perhaps the most important evaluative response for writers and teachers to think about." (Elbow, 1993)

LEADING QUESTIONS

- What purposes does assessment of writing serve?
- What are some of the basic problems we face in making fair and accurate assessments of students' writing?
- What are the issues surrounding notions in writing assessment such as reliability, validity, objectivity, and subjectivity?
- What ethical issues are implicated in writing assessment, particularly of L2 students?
- What alternatives are there to traditional assessment in L2 writing classes?

Introduction to the Issues

Many of the decisions that both L1 and L2 writing teachers make in their classes revolve around assessment of students' writing. Assessment activities and schemes pervade the broader system of schooling as well. Indeed, in most countries assessment of all kinds, not just of writing, is such an inherent part of the whole enterprise of schooling that it is difficult to imagine doing without it. Because a culture of assessment is built into the schooling enterprise, teachers rarely ask whether they need to assess their students. After all, the system often starts, continues, and ends with entrance, placement, progress, and exit assessments and examinations. Not all teachers are happy about the culture of assessment they are immersed in. But regardless of individual teachers' opinions and beliefs about assessment, if students are to be given a grade or admitted into or released from a class or program, their ability or performance usually needs to be evaluated. Rather than recommending wholesale overthrow of assessment schemes, therefore, most teachers ask instead how their students can be assessed accurately and fairly. The issue of accurate and fair assessment of student writing probably constitutes the major dilemma in both the L1 and L2 writing fields, and I will discuss the specifics of some of the controversies later in this chapter. But first, let me highlight several key questions that L2 writing teachers need to consider as they reflect on their own beliefs about assessment and as they plan writing and assessment activities within their own classrooms. Most of these questions ultimately link to issues of accuracy and fairness.

Early in the decision-making process, writing teachers and administrators need to be clear about what they mean by assessment. Consider the following terms: *assessment, testing, measurement, grading, evaluating.* All are related yet refer to different aspects of assessment (perhaps the broadest of the terms). By giving some kind of *test,* we can *measure* something and then assign a *grade* or a score. We can also *evaluate* students' writing in a variety of ways that may or may not result in a grade or a score. In the general language testing field, Bachman (1990) distinguishes among the terms *measurement, test,* and *evaluation. Measurement* refers to "the process of quantifying the characteristics of persons according to explicit procedures and rules" (p. 18). A *test* is a measurement of a "specific sample of an individual's behavior" (p. 20). *Evaluation* refers to collection and perusal of information for the purpose of making decisions about people (p. 22). It is possible to evaluate without testing, just as it is possible to test without evaluating. Tests, Bachman points out, may be used as part of instructional activities, such as to motivate students or to review past lessons. Hamp-Lyons (1991c) and Bailey (1998) refer to the effects of tests on teaching as "washback." Tests become evaluative, on the other hand, when they are used to make decisions about students (Bachman, 1990, pp. 22–23). In this chapter, I use the term *assessment* in a general sense but distinguish between assessments designed for the purposes of evaluation and decision-making and those designed for descriptive and instructional purposes. The main controversies about writing assessment concern cases where decisions are made about students based on evaluations of language and writing samples.

Another major decision that writing teachers and administrators are faced with concerns what they understand the purpose(s) to be of assessing students' writing (see also Bailey's [1998] discussion of the dilemmas of conflicting purposes in language assessment). Is students' writing being assessed in order to see if the students are qualified to enter a particular school or program? In this case, writing assessment functions as a selection and sorting instrument. Is writing being assessed in order to place students in some kind of hierarchy, such as in a remedial writing class; a low-, mid-, or high-level ESL class; or an honors writing class? In this case, students are guaranteed some kind of placement, but the specifics of placement decisions may determine whether students can take other classes or get credit for their writing classes. Within writing classes, writing is assessed as well, but possibly without grades. Ongoing assessment of writing is common in process writing classes and in classes where students are asked to keep portfolios of their writing. The final portfolio may then be assessed summatively to indicate what students have learned during a term. Finally, writing assessment may take the form of an exit mechanism, as is the case on many university campuses. In some high-stakes writing assessment, students who do not pass a writing test are not allowed to graduate, in spite of passing grades in other classes.

Formal assessments of writing for purposes of deciding who enters and exits a school, class, or program are considered high-stakes in the sense that students' lives can be affected by the outcomes in major ways. Less formal assessments that evaluate proficiency and progress in writing for purposes of ongoing evaluation and feedback to students are considered low-stakes in that they do not usually affect students' lives in major and irrevocable ways. Teachers need to be aware as well that formal assessments of many kinds, not just of writing, may really be designed not to benefit students but to provide evidence to agencies and funders that a particular writing program is working; to influence changes in curriculum, through the back door as it were, by virtue of washback effects on curriculum and pedagogy (Bailey, 1996; Hamp-Lyons, 1997; Messick, 1996); or to exert some kind of social or political control (Shohamy, 1997, 2001b; Spolsky, 1997).

In short, writing teachers and administrators need to clarify for themselves and for students what the purposes are for different kinds of assessments of students' writing, particularly those on which decisions about students are based—for example, sorting before a class or program begins or ends (selective evaluation), demonstrating ongoing growth (formative evaluation), or showing achievement at the end of a course or program (summative evaluation) (Cumming, 2001). If there is a social or political agenda to writing assessment, this, too, needs to be made clear to all stakeholders (Shohamy, 2001b).

Once the purposes for assessment are clarified, the question becomes what kinds of assessment instruments will best achieve those purposes. It is here that decisions become entangled in practical, institutional, and logistical constraints in addition to challenging our beliefs and knowledge of how students' writing ability or growth can be accurately assessed. In large-scale assessment (statewide, nationwide, or throughout an entire institution), how much time and money is required for teachers, students, and administrators to do a fair assessment? In such cases, a single essay written under constraints of time and place, such as TOEFL's Writing Test (formerly TWE: Test of Written English), may be the only practical solution. (In some places large-scale portfolio assessment is being tried; see Callahan, 1997, for a description of a state-mandated portfolio assessment scheme in Kentucky, designed to reform curricula.) Similarly, raters of student placement essays and writing teachers with large classes are constrained by the difficulties of finding time to read and assess possibly hundreds of student papers. Even though a single piece of writing is no longer thought to represent accurately a student's ability, it is often not feasible to assess multiple writings, particularly in large-scale assessments. One of the biggest dilemmas in writing assessment is therefore finding an accurate, yet practical, means of assessing.

In much L1 and L2 writing assessment in recent years, particularly when a numerical score is needed for record keeping or accountability, assessment involves one or more readers evaluating actual samples of writing. In the past, indirect measures of writing that did not involve any actual writing, such as multiple-choice tests of grammar and style, were used as assessment instruments because they were considered objective and reliable and could be subjected to the psychometrician's statistical tools "proving" them to be so. Now, however, direct tests of writing, also called performance assessments, in which students actually write something, are much more widely used. Although direct assessments have face validity and authenticity to varying degrees, they have proved to be very difficult to score in ways that were traditionally considered valid and reliable. And as Messick (1994, p. 21) points out, the term *direct assessment* is a bit of a misnomer, given that it is mediated by people's judgment. The main dilemma, discussed in more detail shortly, lies in the fact that different readers rate the same essay in different ways, and students themselves do not write consistently. Writing teachers and scholars are thus hard pressed to define what they mean by a "fair and accurate" score.

Another major question asks what the assessments assess when we are not even certain if there is such a thing as "general writing ability." Is writing ability a general behavior made up of separable complex skills? If so, how do we describe those skills? Are they or are they not connected with particular domains? And if we do not see writing as consisting of a complex of skills, how do we characterize the act of writing? Questions such as these pose dilemmas for all who evaluate writing and other complex performances in school settings, and discussions in both the L1 and the L2 literature demonstrate how thorny this issue is (see the excellent discussion by Messick [1994] in which he lays out many of the controversies in performance-based educational assessment).

For instance, it is one thing to say that we wish to evaluate the quality of students' writing and quite another to define in unambiguous terms what we mean by "quality." In the case of

L2 student writing, evaluators look for evidence that students control the basic grammar and vocabulary of the language, yet every writing teacher and scholar knows that writing quality is not determined just by writers' control of the linguistic aspects of their writing. Crosscultural research shows as well that standards for "good writing" may differ across cultures and disciplines (Cai, 1999; Currie, 1994; Hamp-Lyons & Zhang, 2001; Li, 1996; see also the literature on contrastive rhetoric and, in this volume, chap. 2 and chap. 3, "Paths to Improvement"). A debate in the EAP (English for Academic Purposes) scholarship concerns whether assessment instruments (usually of reading and writing) need to deal with discipline- and domain-specific content and performance or with more general language proficiency (Clapham, 2000; Fulcher, 1999, 2000; Robinson & Ross, 1996). In all these cases, major efforts by test designers and committees of teachers therefore go into constructing "rubrics" that try to encapsulate descriptively what constitutes a strong or weak essay, or more detailed rubrics in analytic scoring that describe different dimensions of writing (e.g., coherence, logical flow of ideas, mechanics) that are then assigned a number. (See, for example, the early composition profile in Jacobs, Zinkgraf, Wormuth, Hartfiel, and Hughey, 1981, and that same profile plus additional examples in Ferris and Hedgcock, 1998, and in Weigle, 2002.)

In general, many writing teachers and scholars believe that in order to understand what we are assessing, the criteria for our assessments need to be articulated, agreed upon by assessment designers and teachers, and shared with students. But even here arguments such as those made by Peter Elbow (1993, 1994) and others (e.g., Broad, 1994; Huot, 1996; Smit, 1994) state that it is unnatural for multiple raters to agree on the quality of a piece of writing. Rather than try to train or impose agreement, they argue, we should be seeking ways to assess writing that do not depend on agreement among raters (in psychometric terms, interrater reliability). They say that natural judgments of writing quality are inherently subjective and that to try to force them into the psychometrician's conception of objectivity is to do an injustice to student writers.

Bachman (1990, p. 37) further points out that even carefully designed language tests are subjective in nearly every aspect, including development, scoring, and interpretation, in the sense that the judgments of people are represented at all stages.

Let us now look at a few of these dilemmas in more detail. The arguments flourish in L1 writing and are generally later picked up by L2 scholars, so some of the published debates I discuss will draw on L1 literature, much of which is familiar to L2 writing scholars. (See Weigle, 2002, for a more how-to perspective on assessment of writing in which some of these issues are discussed.)

Discussions in the Literature

Perhaps the most hotly debated general issue in both first and second language writing assessment (and other kinds of assessments as well), and an umbrella issue under which other controversies flourish, is that of fairness of assessment techniques and practices. As a way to move into some of the specific discussions in the literature, let us first examine what a commonsense view of a fair writing assessment might be.

A fair assessment of writing, above all, treats all students equally without bias against differences in culture, background knowledge of content, students' experience (or lack thereof) with particular assessment instruments, different conditions of writers at the time they write a piece for assessment (are they ill? fatigued?), or even different environments for writing (a stuffy or crowded classroom? a solitary cubicle or carrel?). A fair assessment, in a commonsense view, is also authentic, in the sense that it examines performance in writing rather than (for example) multiple-choice knowledge of grammar, style, or vocabulary, and in the sense that it asks students to write something that they have been taught or that they will actually need to write later. A fair assessment, furthermore, captures what it is that students can actually do in writing, so that each evaluation, whether a score or a description, describes students' abilities and writing quality in a meaningful and accurate way. This would be the case whether we believe that there is such a thing as general writing ability or that writing must be assessed within specific domains and disciplines. Fairness means as well that we acknowledge that writers are better at some kinds of writing than at others. We thus know that in fairness students should not be penalized for doing poorly on a single sample. A fair assessment is also ethical, in the sense that it does not harm writers. It seems obvious, therefore, that if we guard against different biases, we will be able to assess writing fairly. The problem with this commonsense view of writing assessment is that by capturing the complex and multidimensional nature of the activity of writing, it practically assures that no assessment instrument can ever be totally fair or accurate (Horowitz, 1991; Skehan, 1984). Many of the dilemmas teachers face in deciding how to assess their students' writing stem from our knowledge of this complexity.

Objectivity and Subjectivity/Reliability and Validity

In debates about writing assessment, a very basic argument concerns whether assessments can or should be objective, or, instead, whether what has traditionally been pejoratively labeled subjectivity is inevitable and even desirable. The arguments link to two other controversial concepts in assessment, those of reliability and validity, also the subject of debate in literature on educational measurement (e.g., Messick, 1989, 1994) and in language assessment literature as to what they mean (e.g., Bachman, 1990; Bailey, 1998; Cohen, 1994; McNamara, 1996, 2000) and how they should be applied to writing assessment (e.g., Ferris & Hedgcock, 1998; Hamp-Lyons, 1991b; Henning, 1991; Horowitz, 1991; Weigle, 2002; White, 1994). The proponents of objectivity in assessment have persuasive arguments on their side, including the weight of "science" and of the statistical tools of the powerful psychometricians who dominate traditional views of testing and evaluation. Fairness and accuracy in assessment must be protected from the vagaries of teachers' and raters' individual values, beliefs, and interpretations, the argument goes; we must find ways to interpret students' writing abilities consistently, according to criteria that lie outside the minds of individual raters. In his argument against subjectivity in portfolio assessment, for example, White (1994, p. 36) asserts that "[u]nreliable [i.e., inconsistent] measures are merely subjective impressions by disparate individuals." Our judgments of writing, he claims, must "stand up to outside scrutiny" (p. 30).

One reason that indirect tests of writing, such as multiple-choice or fill-in tests, were so attractive over the years is that they did stand up to outside scrutiny by being scored easily and without disagreement among scorers. Measuring the objective features in themselves is thought to provide a degree of fairness in evaluation not possible with fuzzier assessment instruments. The numbers are based on right and wrong answers, are not subject to multiple interpretations and so are highly reliable, and allow for easy comparison of individuals and groups. The controversy arose, beginning in the late 1970s with the communicative language teaching movement, when critics complained that assessments of writing needed to be based on actual samples of writing, not on indirect, right-wrong measures. In addition, indirect measures of writing were "invalid" because they lacked, at the very least, the face validity that makes an assessment of writing authentic. The problem with actual writing samples, which have high face validity, lay in how to make sure that the targeted aspects of writing were actually the ones being assessed and in how to generate stable scores.

Since then, proponents of objectivity in assessment have sought ways first to clarify and describe criteria by which writing samples are assessed and then to train raters to evaluate essays according to the same criteria so as to meet traditional standards of reliability (consistency) and validity (accuracy in measuring what an assessment instrument intends to measure). Early attempts at evaluating writing samples objectively looked closely at whether holistic evaluation could be "validated objectively" (Homburg [1984] decided that it could), and they depended on measures such as syntactic complexity and error-free clauses (e.g., as measured by T-units: minimal terminable units consisting of an independent clause and all attached dependent clauses and phrases; Hunt, 1977; Homburg, 1984; Perkins, 1980). This style of objective evaluation, where words, and clauses, and errors could be counted, can be criticized for describing writing quality in terms of syntactic complexity and for missing larger discourse features, as Homburg (1984) pointed out. But the search for objective ways to evaluate student writing persists (e.g., Ishikawa, 1995).

Other measures that aim for objectivity use trained readers who rate essays holistically (one numerical score per essay) and try to reach agreement or who rate numerically according to analytic criteria of different dimensions of writing, described carefully in rubrics (Brown & Bailey, 1984; Charney, 1984; Hamp-Lyons, 1991f; Jacobs et al., 1981; Sasaki & Hirose, 1999). Even the most complex and sophisticated of these methods, ones that take into account variability in writers, readers, and task, still have as a primary goal an objective, often numerically consistent and accurate assessment that is both reliable and valid (see, e.g., Hamp-Lyons, 1991f, for a discussion of multiple trait scoring, and McNamara, 1996, for justification of mathematical Rasch models for this purpose). The voices that support the belief that writing assessment should be both reliable and valid speak in unhedged terms. Hamp-Lyons (1991f, p. 252) asserts strongly: "No test can be valid without first being reliable. Only when we have stable score data to look at can we usefully go on to ask questions about validity." Her position is echoed by Ferris and Hedgcock (1998, p. 230), who address the fairness issue: "Validity is . . . as essential to meaningful and equitable writing assessment as reliability."

A different argument is made by people who feel that the psychometrician's metalanguage and goals (e.g., objectivity, reliability, validity, generalizability) need to be disposed of before we can let go of concepts that do not and cannot apply to the assessment of writing (or even to language ability in general). It will not do simply to try to fine-tune the same criteria, they claim. We need to find other ways to assess students' language ability in general and their writing in particular. Spolsky (1997, p. 246) puts it this way.

> As positivists, psychometrists have lacked the necessary scepticism, and have assumed that finer and finer tuning will make the noise go away. What we are starting to do . . . is accept the inevitable uncertainty, and turn our attention to the way tests are used, insisting on multiple testing and alternative methods, and realizing that the results need cautious and careful interpretation.

In the context of large-scale portfolio assessment, Broad (1994) asserts that we spend far too much time and money trying to achieve statistical reliability among raters (see the following section of this chapter) and that we need to "let go of the quantification of writing ability" (p. 271) in order to learn more about the "positioned readings that 'produce' those numbers" (p. 269). According to Smit (1994), it is impossible to come up with general criteria of competence in writing, because each writing sample is the product of particular assignments written in particular contexts.

One of the strongest supporters of using more local and context-rich writing assessment as opposed to standardized assessments that follow the psychometrician's notions of objectivity, reliability, and validity is Huot (1990a, 1990b, 1996; Huot & Williamson, 1997). Criteria for making decisions about students' writing cannot be separated from local contexts, he argues; it thus makes little sense to "maintain . . . procedures based on a positivist epistemology" (Huot, 1996, p. 563). Echoing Moss (1994), Huot and Williamson (1997) challenge the "traditional notion that assessment has to be reliable in order to be valid" (p. 45) and that "concepts like validity and reliability are unquestionable and theoretically necessary" (p. 44). What matters most in fair writing assessment are the very local and diverse practices that supporters of traditional "objective" assessment wish to downplay or to erase through mathematical juggling. As Elbow (1993, p. 188) puts it, "Evaluation implies the recognition of different criteria

or dimensions—and by implication different contexts and audiences for the same performance." If we adopt this view, it is
likely we will consider large-scale assessment to be inherently
unfair. Elbow, Huot, and other critics of large-scale assessment
schemes believe that fair assessment can only be done locally,
where the people, practices, and purposes involved in writing are well known.

Rater Reliability

Large-scale direct assessment of writing involves raters who
are trained to read sets of essays consistently. But even in local settings, such as in classes or programs that rely on essay
tests for placement or on portfolio assessment of writing, the
role of raters is central (see, e.g., Hamp-Lyons and Condon,
2000, and the chapter in Weigle, 2002, on portfolio assessment). As I suggested earlier, perhaps one of the most vexing
dilemmas in writing assessment concerns the inconsistency
with which different readers tend to evaluate the same piece
of writing (exacerbated by the inconsistency with which the
same writer writes at different times and for different purposes). Elbow (1993, p. 188) states the problem succinctly:
"To rank [*sic:* rate?] reliably means to give a *fair* number, to
find the single quantitative score that readers will agree on.
But readers don't agree."

Still, it is widely believed that the only fair way for writing
to be assessed by readers is if all readers agree on the scoring
criteria and then respond in ways that are similar to each
other and that are consistent within their own readings. If
raters A and B disagree on how to rate an essay, how can the
final score (e.g., an average or a total) be fair or meaningful to
the writer? Similarly, if a rater scores one way when fresh and
another when fatigued, how can a student whose paper is read
when the reader is tired be rated fairly? These two kinds of
consistency in responding are referred to in the general testing literature as interrater reliability (among raters) and intra-
rater reliability (within the same rater) and can be calculated
mathematically (see Bailey, 1998, or other books on educational

research or testing in applied linguistics). In seeking ways to learn how raters respond and how to help them respond in similar ways, such as through training or norming sessions, writing researchers have conducted various studies in both L1 and L2, with results that are not as conclusive as we might wish. Still, in the assessment debate, many support the idea that we must fine-tune our criteria (denounced by Spolsky [1997], as mentioned earlier) and find ways to train readers, in large- and small-scale assessment and in research on writing, to respond consistently to the same criteria in the papers they evaluate. Supporters of this argument believe that it is both possible and necessary to articulate criteria for assessment and that it is therefore possible to train raters to use the criteria consistently and appropriately.

Let us look at the problem of holistic scoring of single writing samples (the assigning of a single numerical score, usually between 1 and 6, to a piece of writing). Holistic scoring, widely used in large-scale formal writing assessment, is fraught with rater problems (Hamp-Lyons, 1995; Hayes, Hatch, & Silk, 2000; Huot, 1990b; Shohamy, Gordon, & Kraemer, 1992; Sweedler-Brown, 1993; Tedick & Mathison, 1995; Vaughan, 1991; Weigle, 1994). In her discussion of the complexity involved in trying to judge the many relevant influences on a piece of writing, such as a writer's knowledge of grammar, vocabulary, coherence, content, and writing processes, Hamp-Lyons (1995, pp. 760–761) states that a single holistic score cannot capture the strengths and weaknesses of a writing sample. A holistic scoring system, she argues:

> is a closed system, offering no windows through which teachers can look and researchers can enter. Scores generated holistically cannot be explained to other readers in the same assessment community; diagnostic feedback is out of the question.

Because single-sample essay testing remains a pervasive way of assessing writing, especially for entrance and exit purposes, what is needed is multiple trait assessment, or what Murphy

(1999) calls dimensional scoring, in which readers evaluate writing according to different dimensions that have been carefully described and that raters are trained, as in holistic scoring, to respond to in similar ways.

But herein lies the ongoing problem: Although the problem is far more serious with holistic scoring, even if raters score essays according to multiple, rather than overall, criteria, we still do not know precisely how they arrived at their decisions and whether they in fact were applying the criteria in similar ways (Connor-Linton, 1995b). Vaughan (1991), who used think-aloud procedures to monitor the thoughts of raters as they read different essays, found great variety in the criteria they applied. Often a salient factor in an essay, such as handwriting or grammar errors, jumps out at readers and influences the final score, overriding stated criteria (Charney, 1984; Sweedler-Brown, 1993; Vaughan, 1991). Studies also show that novice and expert readers tend to rate differently (Cumming, 1990); that L1 writing teachers, content area teachers, ESL teachers, and ESL college students respond differently to the same essays (Leki, 1995); and that native and nonnative English-speaking readers who do rate EFL university students' compositions similarly may differ in the criteria they use even though they arrive at similar numbers (Connor-Linton, 1995a; Shi, 2001). Rater agreement improves, however, through training sessions (Shohamy, Gordon, & Kraemer, 1992; Sweedler-Brown, 1993; Weigle, 1994). Supporters of holistic and multiple trait scoring therefore depend greatly on clearly described criteria and careful training of raters to ensure that raters score consistently and therefore fairly (Davidson, 1991).

The other side of the argument, expressed most persuasively by Peter Elbow in his defense of portfolio assessment and evaluation-free writing (1993, 1994) and suggested by others mentioned earlier (see, e.g., Broad, 1994; Elbow & Belanoff, 1997; Smit, 1994), states that when we get readers to agree on essay scores through training and norming procedures, we are forcing them to read in ways that alter their normal responses to writing. If it is normal for readers to respond differently to the same writings, then "the reliability in holistic scoring is not a measure of how texts are valued by real readers in natural settings, but only of how they are valued in artificial settings with imposed agreements" (Elbow, 1993, p. 189). Moreover, a valid assessment of someone's writing must include more than a single sample, given that students perform quite differently on different kinds of writings (Hayes, Hatch, & Silk, 2000). Elbow and others cautiously favor portfolio assessment for this very reason: multiple kinds of writing, at different stages of completion, reveal what students' writing ability consists of much more validly than does a single essay (Black, Daiker, Sommers, & Stygall, 1994; Calfee & Perfumo, 1996; Ferris & Hedgcock, 1998; Hamp-Lyons & Condon, 1993, 2000; Huot & Williamson, 1997; Murphy, 1999; Murray, 1994; Yancey, 1992, 1996; Yancey & Weiser, 1997). A portfolio collection, argue Elbow and Belanoff (1997), will thus be more valid, but with multiple pieces and multiple readers, the collection will probably not be scored reliably (consistently). Nor should it, they and others argue. In fact, Broad (1994) labels "portfolio scoring" a contradiction in terms, noting that the push to reach consensus on evaluations of student writing does not allow raters to value variety, richness, and diversity (p. 273). Given that not all assessments need to lead to decision making (Bachman, 1990), consistency and consensus is not a major issue. For this group of scholars, it is indeed possible to separate validity and reliability. They do not need or want stable scores to assess writing. On the contrary, they believe that stable, consensually produced scores undermine the validity of the writing assessment.

White (1994) disagrees. He supports portfolio assessment as more valid than a single essay test, but he insists we do not have to dispose of rater reliability in order to achieve validity. We should make every effort, he asserts, "to develop consistency in our judgments, not only so that our measures will be reasonably reliable (and hence support our claims for validity) but so that our students will be able to develop self-assessment by internalizing consistent criteria" (White, 1994, p. 36). The scholars in the debate appear to differ deeply on what they believe is important, and possible, in writing assessment, so the arguments continue.

Another reason that arguments persist on the connections between fairness in writing assessment and rater reliability is that it is difficult to justify diverse readings in large-scale assessment. If a schoolwide or even statewide writing test has been mandated, what are test designers and raters to do with diverse readings of students' essays? In such cases, it seems as unfair *not* to impose criteria on raters as it does to do so. This dilemma has not been solved and probably cannot be solved if large-scale standardized tests of writing continue to proliferate, as they seem inclined to do. Arguments against large-scale testing in favor of local assessment (Huot, 1996; Huot & Williamson, 1997) often fall on deaf ears of politicians and school boards, who want some accountability for how their money is being spent. On the other hand, those who argue against the control of writing assessment by concepts such as rater reliability believe that they need to be accountable primarily to students and to local stakeholders. Readers of student writing should be able to do more than provide an agreed-upon score, in other words. They should be able to provide feedback to students and to improve pedagogy as a result of their writing assessments. In the context of his own teaching, Elbow (1993, Elbow & Belanoff, 1997) argues that we need to identify only the very weakest and strongest writers in order to achieve these goals and that readers do in fact tend to agree on which writings lie at either end of this continuum. Furthermore, teachers should consider another form of judgment: liking. If we like a piece of writing or something about a piece of writing, including our own writing, it is much easier to criticize it and improve it (Elbow, 1993). Moreover, in writing classes, we assess writing all the time, mostly informally, in ways that we hope will help students improve. It is not clear how much of our assessment needs to result in a score or a grade to achieve this purpose. In short, educators like Elbow believe that too much emphasis on assessment and rater reliability undermines pedagogy.

Authenticity

Discussions of authenticity need to consider whether we believe that only activities performed outside a school context or closely modeled on them, in the so-called real world, are authentic, or whether the school context itself is its own authentic world, even if the activities there differ from those beyond classroom doors (Messick, 1994; Sternberg, 1990). Messick's (1994) arguments about the validation of performance assessments can be helpful in laying out the issues for writing teachers. In the case of portfolio assessment, for instance, we can ask whether educational assessments should be "authentic reflections of classroom work or authentic representations of real-world work" (Messick, 1994, p. 18). Writing teachers and assessment designers may have strong beliefs about what they consider to be authentic performances and assessments of writing or even about whether authenticity is important. In discussions of what "authentic writing" in a school context might mean, teachers can get bogged down in false dichotomies, of course—namely, that a writing performance that is not authentic is unauthentic and therefore, by definition, bad. Or, as Messick (1994) points out, if we believe that only direct, performance assessments are authentic and valid, we may be tempted to conclude that other forms of assessment are unauthentic (p. 14).

In a broader argument concerning authenticity and performance assessment in educational contexts, Messick (1994, pp. 14–15) asks us to consider whether a performance or a product is the target or the vehicle of an evaluation. In an arts contest or athletic competition, what counts for an evaluation is only the quality of the product or the performance. Evaluators do not need to worry about the replicability and generalizability of the artist's or athlete's onetime performance, nor do they need to make inferences about or evaluate underlying skills. Does writing fit in such a category, better characterized as a generic proficiency rather than a composite of underlying skills and constructs? If so, teachers may focus their assessment efforts on task development and not concern themselves with scoring criteria. In this view, every skill that contributes to the writing performance in a task-centered approach is considered relevant, with the result that judgments of qualities such as clarity of expression and depth of understanding cannot be separated. These judgments therefore contaminate each other (Messick, 1994, p. 17).

If, on the other hand, we view authentic writing performance as made up of a complex array of different constructs, teachers and assessment designers will wish to break down writing performance into those different skills and constructs and to describe them as thoroughly as possible. The problem for teachers who believe in this approach to authenticity in writing assessment is that, as Messick (1994) reminds us, something will always be left out (what is referred to in the literature of educational assessment as "construct underrepresentation"). If we assess by task, in contrast, without breaking a writing performance down into skills and constructs, we cannot know what a score means. As Messick (1994, p. 20) asks: "By what evidence can we be assured that the scoring criteria and rubrics used in holistic, primary trait, or analytic scoring of products or performances capture the fully functioning complex skill?" Separate skills are most difficult to untangle, he notes, from aspects of performance such as clarity and coherence (p. 20). He argues for a construct-centered approach in which scoring rubrics are designed that fall somewhere in between a task-specific description and a generic description. Messick (1994, p. 17) summarizes the dilemma as follows.

In the task-centered approach to authentic assessment, credibility depends on the simulation of as much real-world complexity as can be provided. But along with realism there comes a multiplicity of variables as well as lack of control. This puts an enormous burden on test development: It makes difficult the creation and application of criteria for scoring relevant aspects of this complexity, while at the same time jeopardizing scorer reliability and very likely limiting generalizability. The construct-centered approach makes possible a compromise by focusing on selected constructs of knowledge and skill and the conditions of their realistic engagement in task performance.

The problems associated with objectivity, rater reliability, validity, and authenticity in writing assessment will continue to be debated. However, it is important for teachers of writing to note that the dilemmas described here become most problematic when teachers themselves or administrators demand actual scores of some kind on students' writing in order to make decisions rather than to assess for other purposes. Some of these problems diminish in importance if we do not need our assessments of students' writing to result in a score or a grade. In the "Classroom Perspectives" section of this chapter, I describe some alternatives to traditional assessment that may help writing teachers escape the thorniest of these issues. But first, let me address a final set of issues that concern the ethics of assessment, some of which have been hinted at earlier.

Ethical Dilemmas

It has become increasingly common to hear arguments over the ethical uses of assessments. The arguments apply across the board to assessment of all kinds, of which writing assessment is just a small part. They concern how tests are developed, administered, scored, and interpreted and—importantly for the discussion in this chapter—how formal tests and assessments are then used. In the next section, I focus on the use of tests in the belief that even if classroom writing teachers are not involved in the development and administration of formal testing, they need to be aware of the issues related to how tests are used. Particularly in the case of language and writing assessment of L2 speakers, ethical issues are especially touchy because they concern how fairly second language speakers are treated when they are being tested in a language that is not their own and often on material that is culturally unfamiliar.

How Tests Are Used

The language testing field, as described by McNamara (2001), has been the most positivist in orientation of all areas in applied linguistics, relying, as discussed earlier, on "scientific" notions of objectivity, reliability, and validity. Influenced in recent years by discussions of postmodernism and social constructionism, language testing is now seen as a social and political activity, inseparable from values and social consequences. The work of Messick (1989, 1994, 1996), for example, has been recognized by some of the testing specialists in applied linguistics and incorporated into reconceptualizations of the traditional notion of validity. Messick, whose work spans 30 years, has helped people in language testing to understand that an essential aspect of validity concerns the social consequences of how tests are used as well as the value-laden interpretive procedures by which we understand what tests mean. He notes:

> The consequential basis of test validity includes evidence and rationales for evaluating the intended and unintended consequences of test interpretations and use in both the short and the long term. Particularly prominent is the evaluation of any adverse consequences for individuals and groups that are associated with bias in test scoring and interpretation or with unfairness in test use. (Messick, 1994, p. 21)

Indeed, well-known voices in applied linguistics are now openly discussing how important it is to consider the ethics and politics of how tests are used (Hamp-Lyons, 1997; Lynch, 1997, 2001a, 2001b; McNamara, 2001; Norton & Starfield, 1997; Spolsky, 1997; Shohamy, 2001a, 2001b). In his review of modern language testing at the turn of the century, Bachman (2000) notes that testing issues have broadened greatly, to include among other things ethical issues related to how tests are used and the meaning of professionalism in language testing (p. 15). He notes that Messick has contributed ideas on the social consequences of validity that make "validation re-search" a promising, and complex, area of investigation for the future (p. 22).

The strongest arguments on the dangers of unethical uses of tests come from Shohamy (1997, 2001a, 2001b). Part of a movement that supports a critical approach to language as-sessment (Lynch, 2001b), she is worried that tests are used in many ways that have little to do with measuring knowledge or language proficiency. Rather, she sees how tests are used to manipulate and even control stakeholders. She asks diffi-cult questions, such as who makes tests, what the political motives are of test designers, how test results are used, and what the meaning of tests is for various stakeholders, such as teachers, students, parents, and school administrators (Sho-hamy, 2001b). In her research on tests of Arabic and of English in Israel, she found that tests were used to impose a politically motivated curriculum, to force teachers to teach certain things and not others, and to "punish, exclude, gate-keep and per-petuate existing powers" (p. xii). Critical language testing, she asserts, challenges the power of tests and questions how they are used, works to involve those being tested in how tests are designed, and obligates test designers and administrators to take responsibility for ensuring that tests are used ethically (Shohamy, 2001a).

Ethics and Assessment of the L2 Writer

In L2 writing, ethical issues are closely tied to language and culture. In the most obvious case, language proficiency and writing ability interact such that it is difficult to say anything meaningful about the writing ability or content knowledge of students whose proficiency in the L2 is quite low. Norton and Starfield (1997) documented a case in South Africa in which neither students nor faculty were clear about the extent to which language proficiency influenced the assessments made on students' academic writing. It is also common for L2 edu-cators to generalize about the writing and thinking abilities of L2 students, concluding from samples written in L2 that stu-dents who do not write well cannot think well. Moreover, until recently, L2 writing researchers did not assess students' writing ability in L1, a problem that scholars such as Sasaki and Hirose (1999) are correcting. It has also been pointed out by writing scholars interested in portfolio assessment (e.g., Murray, 1994) and journal writing (e.g., Lucas, 1992) that students perform differently on different writing tasks because their cultural and educational backgrounds do not prepare them for genres that are probably familiar to L1 English speakers. Personal writing in a school setting is a comfortable genre for many speakers of Japanese, for instance, but not for speakers of Arabic, who may do better at argumentative writing (Liebman, 1992).

There are serious high-stakes ethical issues in writing assessment of L2 students as well. The primary one concerns what to do with the student who seems to be passing his or her content classes but cannot pass an English writing exit exam or required ESL class (Johns, 1991b; Schneider & Fujishima, 1995). If we believe that tests should benefit students and pedagogy, what are we to say about tests that prevent such students from continuing their studies or graduating?

Happily, ethical issues in language and writing assessment of L2 students are becoming increasingly salient to designers and users of assessment instruments. These issues highlight aspects of assessment that simply were not considered in the past. Particularly when writing assessments are used to make evaluative high-stakes decisions about L2 students, these ethical issues need to be fronted, discussed, and shared with stakeholders as part of all decision making.

Classroom Perspectives

Many of the dilemmas discussed in this chapter concern issues of assessment and testing beyond the individual classroom. Writing teachers may feel they have little control over decisions about assessment that are made, or apply to writing done, outside their own classes. Still, teachers have a responsibility to be aware of the issues and, to the extent possible, to participate in and encourage ethical assessment practices (Lynch, 2001a). They also need to be aware that many calls are being made for alternatives to traditional assessment outside the local contexts of particular classrooms even though it is generally agreed that all assessment instruments provide only partial information about students' language and writing abilities.

At the institutional level, one such attempt at alternative assessment was made at the University of Michigan, which developed a performance-based initial placement assessment for ESL students who are beginning university work (Feak & Dobson, 1996). Recognizing that the traditional single impromptu essay is unfair and invalid, in that it cannot represent what students can do in writing, and that portfolio assessment is too time-consuming and labor-intensive to be used as a placement mechanism, the English Language Institute designed a "source-based assessment" for incoming freshman ESL students. This assessment activity involved examinees' reading and synthesizing quoted passages on a single general academic topic and generating two kinds of writing: sentence completions that ask students to compare and contrast views of different authors and an essay in which students integrate their own ideas with those of the authors of the quoted passages. The assessment was designed to capture students' abilities to engage in the kinds of academic work that is typical at universities: reading, comparing and contrasting ideas, synthesizing, and commenting. These activities, moreover, paralleled those in the university's EAP classes. The problem of rater reliability remains, of course, and the authors regrettably do not comment on how they handled this problem or on what their beliefs are on this thorny issue. They summarize the strong points of the assessment activity for their university's purposes, noting that it is

> an attempt to preserve the best elements of the impromptu essay (ease of administration, ease in scoring, and a topic accessible to all examinees) within a reading-to-write test that calls on examinees to demonstrate the critically important

academic writing skills of writing from sources, synthesizing multiple texts, and going beyond knowledge telling to
knowledge transforming. (Feak & Dobson, 1996, p. 80)

Within their own classrooms, however, writing teachers are
inevitably caught in the dilemma of being both supportive
nonjudgmental readers and critical evaluators who ultimately
must assign a grade to student performance. These roles conflict. Students know they will receive grades, even if individual papers are not marked, and so tend to write for grades
rather than to develop their writing. (This conflict is especially pronounced in required classes.) Teachers thus need to
decide within the contexts of their own classes how to juggle
their conflicting roles as readers and as evaluators. In this section, I consider some ways to assess students' writing without
the need for scores, grades on papers, or interrater reliability.
My own beliefs lead me to follow what Hamp-Lyons (1994)
refers to as the interweaving of assessment and instruction in
writing classes, even though the dilemma of teacher as both
reader and evaluator cannot be completely resolved. Hamp-
Lyons discusses various ways to weave instruction and assessment within a process approach to writing instruction,
including peer commenting, process logs, self-reflective commentary, and portfolio evaluation. However, I will focus on
one type of writing activity, with examples from my own work
and that of Tillyer and Sokolik (1993; Sokolik & Tillyer, 1992).
The writing activity involves students in a project that results in a product of some kind. In my own work, I compare
this activity to the writing and research that teachers do in
their professional lives, our ongoing project work that is
evaluated not by grades and scores but by its acceptance by a
professional community—for example, in the form of a publication (Casanave, 1998). Similarly, we do not need to assess
a student project with grades and scores but, instead, can use
descriptive feedback on and evaluation of how students design and carry out the project and how well the final product
meets their goals. As Sokolik and Tillyer (1992) point out,
"[S]ince the project has a clearly-defined goal—to complete

the project—ambiguities of evaluation are frequently avoided: students either complete the task or they don't, and the decision is theirs" (p. 49).

Sokolik and Tillyer (1992, p. 47) define a project as follows.

A project is a unified piece of writing on one theme or topic having at least 3000 words and as many as 10,000. It may take a variety of forms: a research report, a novel, or a play. The project itself is a final draft, but the previous drafts or assignments pertaining to the project are available for assessment when the project is being used as an evaluation instrument.

In my own project assignments during my years of teaching in Japan, I usually did not specify a word length but tried to help students understand that if the project is designed and carried out well, the length will take care of itself. Importantly, the project was "owned" by students in the sense that they designed something that was meaningful to them. I found it useful to "begin at the end" in my project work with Japanese university students. In order to design a meaningful project, one that will involve many steps and activities during a semester, students need to have a vision of what they want to end up with. As Tillyer and Sokolik (1993) note, much of the writing teacher's work occurs in these early design stages, which can last for many weeks as they help students formulate a vision and a plan for their projects. My students, particularly undergraduates, often did not know exactly what they wanted to do or what topic or area they wished to investigate. They always began with ideas that were way too broad, and they had little idea what they wanted their end product to look like. I resisted giving them the typical essay or report format, because this looks like just another paper written for a teacher rather than for themselves. What do you need or want to learn? I asked them. What might you need to do with writing this school year or the next? How can you use this project to accomplish your (not my) goals?

As Tillyer and Sokolik (1993) point out, even low- and

intermediate-level L2 students can design and complete writing projects. In the case of low-level students who cannot do extensive reading in English, many interesting interview projects can be created. An oral family history project can be created to fit the specific case of each student. Students learn all they can about their families, drawing on photographs, phone or in-person interviews from questionnaires they have created, or written communication by mail. The language used in gathering these data is not an issue, so in the case of low-level students, the pressure to try to use English 100 percent of the time is taken off. With teacher guidance, students then need to organize their data, transforming and selecting as needed to fit a particular format for their final product. Designing an appropriate format requires careful thought on the part of teacher and students but should be done early so that data can be transformed in suitable ways. Time needs to be carefully managed; in my experience this is the most difficult aspect of project work. Students need to produce drafts of different sections of their project, revise, rewrite, and perhaps even consider doing illustrations and a cover. There is enough to do, in fact, to make the project the entire focus of a writing class. In Japan, my classes usually met only once a week, so even spending an entire semester on a project required strict time management and even then some students could not finish a polished version of their project to their satisfaction.

Other project examples from Tillyer and Sokolik (1993) are a self-portrait (especially suited for low-level students) and, for more advanced students, a student handbook that provides details of different courses, discussions of career choices and options, and interview commentary from professors or administrators and a library research project that includes an annotated bibliography. When students know that projects like these can be printed, bound, and copied for others, they invest in polishing and revising from pride of ownership rather than just to please a teacher. Whether or not such projects are ultimately given a letter or number grade, assessment of the instructional kind, including self-assessment, is built into them every step of the way as teachers and students work together to complete the projects. Assessment here is not done for traditional purposes but from pride of ownership in a well-done project.

A final example is from an elective upper-division and graduate-level writing class that I offered each semester in a Japanese university. This small class met only once a week for a semester, for a total of 13 or 14 meetings. Students' English proficiency was mixed but generally quite high (above 500 TOEFL). I explained that I gave no tests, quizzes, or even grades on papers and drafts but that any student who attended all classes and worked regularly on a writing project would easily pass with at least a B (cf. Peter Elbow's [1993] similar grading scheme). Students were from different areas of study and at different places in their academic trajectories, so for them it made little sense for me to assign a uniform project or paper that I would then grade by uniform criteria. If they were to improve their writing in ways meaningful to them, they needed to design their own projects, and I needed to help guide them to do something that could reasonably be accomplished in a short time. (By the way, I myself am not able to write a paper in one semester, as I discovered over several semesters in which I tried to complete my own writing project along with students.) Some students worked on a literature review section of a master's thesis (some students write theses in English at the Japanese university); others did background literature searches and wrote summaries and responses to readings in preparation for doing a paper or thesis later. Other students wrote a conference proposal or a long self-introduction essay as part of an application for an English-medium graduate school. Assessment happened every week, as students did short freewritings on their writing problems and progress, talked about their ideas and got feedback from me and from peers, and turned in ideas or drafts in writing and got written responses from me or shared drafts with peers. In my general assessment of the students, I also considered the extent to which they demonstrated engagement in and commitment to the project through their attendance and participation in class.

The two most difficult aspects of project teaching for me were first that I could not, in good conscience, demand a final (i.e., finished) product if I were to be true to my word about having students work on a project that contributed to work they were doing outside my class. Students' deadlines outside my class differed from my schedule as a writing teacher. A few students who were heavily invested in their unfinished projects sometimes took the same class the following semester or followed up with me after the semester was over. Second, inevitably there were students in the class who were not ready to take on their own projects. These students probably belonged in a general academic writing class, and I encouraged such students to transfer into one, although not all took my advice. I was usually able, with some frustration, to accommodate students who did not want to transfer out or who were seeking only a credit-bearing course in English or general writing practice. They, too, had to design their own "projects"— even if they had no specific purpose for writing—and to participate in activities and discussions with the more focused students.

The point for this chapter on assessment is that with term-long in-class writing projects, assessment and instruction cannot really be separated, and grades and scores diminish in importance as students gradually take control of the progress on their own projects. Assessment, importantly, eventually involves students' increasingly assessing their own work. The ultimate assessment lies in what happens with the final product: a class publication that wins praise from outsiders, a master's thesis in English, a conference paper accepted, a journal article published, an acceptance to an English-medium graduate school. Nevertheless, the project-writing alternative to assessment, no matter how satisfying as an assessment practice in the writing class, does not solve the continuing dilemmas associated with using L2 writing samples for admissions screening, placement, or exit mechanisms.

Ongoing Questions

It is likely that writing teachers hold strong beliefs about assessment. There are those who believe that assessment, and a lot of it, benefits students and curricula greatly—for example, via positive washback—and that nothing is inherently harmful in assessment practices. Even the strongest critics of unethical assessment practices (e.g., Shohamy, 1997, 2001a, 2001b) believe that assessment and testing can be conducted ethically and fairly. There are other teachers who believe that we do far too much assessment of our L2 students' language growth and writing ability. These teachers ask, what would change in my teaching and in my students' learning if I assessed and tested less? What alternatives are there, they ask as well, to traditional assessment? These teachers tend to re-conceptualize assessment as regular but informal interaction with students as they write and as a central aspect of instruction rather than of formal evaluation. Teachers who hold very different beliefs from one another about assessment will not only assess their students differently; they will also teach differently from one another, given the natural washback effect of assessment on pedagogy.

It is also possible that those involved in assessment will make different decisions according to the different beliefs they have about assessment and the different purposes they have for assessing students' writing. These decisions, as is the case for all the decisions that teachers make, can only be made in conjunction with the constraints and contexts of particular settings, and in interaction with others, including students. The central questions remain: In the context of my particular setting, do I need to assess my L2 writing students, formally or informally? If yes, for what specific purposes? To what extent are those purposes high-stakes or low-stakes for students? To what extent do I need to test students as opposed to integrating assessment and instruction? Who will design the assessments, and how will they be carried out fairly in my particular setting? What will the assessments mean to students, and how will the results be used? What influence will the assessments in my class and in my school have on my own teaching, my students' learning activities, a school or program curriculum, politicians, or someone or something else?

Hamp-Lyons (2001) notes that "third generation assessment" refers to portfolio assessment in writing research and pedagogy. Looking ahead, she predicts that "fourth generation assessment" will delve more deeply than at present into the role that technology might play in assessment, a prediction also made by Weigle (2002). It will also involve stakeholders—more than at present—in expanding their understanding of the humanistic, ethical, and political aspects of assessment. These aspects will not go away. They await the responsible involvement of all who are engaged in assessment practices.

Beliefs and Practices

Beliefs

1. What distinctions, if any, do you believe need to be made between testing and assessment of L2 writing?
2. Do you believe that L2 writers who are planning to study in English-medium universities should be required to achieve a certain score on a standardized test of writing (e.g., the TOEFL Writing Test) as part of an admissions or exit requirement? What are your beliefs about the role of English-language writing requirements in EFL contexts?
3. What are your beliefs about what a fair way to evaluate students' writing might be?
4. What do you believe are the purposes and effects of giving your L2 writing students concrete scores or grades on some or all of their writing? What might be the purposes and effects of giving no grades at all?

Practices

1. What are your own experiences with different tests and assessments of L2 writing, as an L2 writer yourself? Describe these. In what ways were (or were not) these tests or assessments fair and accurate? What do you believe would be needed to get a fair and accurate assessment of your own writing?

2. What are your experiences with different tests and assessments of L2 writing in your role as an L2 writing teacher? Describe these. In what ways were (or were not) these tests or assessments fair and accurate?

3. Have you ever assessed L2 students' writing without giving grades or scores of any kind? If so, describe what your assessment practices were, and explain why you used them.

4. In your setting, are L2 students (including possibly yourself) required to take any prerequisite writing classes or pass particular writing tests before they can take other classes or before they can graduate later? Describe the requirements, and evaluate them in light of your beliefs and understandings about assessment.

5. What experiences, if any, have you had with large-scale assessment—for example, as a writing-test developer or a reader of essays? Given your current beliefs about assessment practices, what are your reflections on those experiences?

References and Relevant Readings

Allai, S. K., & Connor, U. (1991). Using performative assessment instruments with ESL student writers. In L. Hamp-Lyons (Ed.), *Assessing second language writing in academic contexts* (pp. 227–240). Norwood, NJ: Ablex.

Bachman, L. F. (1990). *Fundamental considerations in language testing.* Oxford: Oxford University Press.

Bachman, L. F. (2000). Modern language testing at the turn of the century: Assuming that what we count counts. *Language Testing, 17,* 1–42.

Bachman, L. F., & Palmer, A. S. (1996). *Language testing in practice: Designing and developing useful language tests*. Oxford: Oxford University Press.

Bailey, K. M. (1996). Working for washback: A review of the washback concept in language testing. *Language Testing, 13,* 257–279.

Bailey, K. M. (1998). *Learning about language assessment: Dilemmas, decisions, and directions*. Pacific Grove, CA: Heinle and Heinle.

Ballard, B., & Clanchy, J. (1991). Assessment by misconception: Cultural influences and intellectual traditions. In L. Hamp-Lyons (Ed.), *Assessing second language writing in academic contexts* (pp. 19–35). Norwood, NJ: Ablex.

Belanoff, P. (1994). Portfolios and literacy: Why? In L. Black, D. A. Daiker, J. Sommers, & G. Stygall (Eds.), *New directions in portfolio assessment: Reflective practice, critical theory, and large-scale scoring* (pp. 13–24). Portsmouth, NH: Boynton/Cook.

Black, L., Daiker, D. A., Sommers, J., & Stygall, G. (Eds.). (1994). *New directions in portfolio assessment: Reflective practice, critical theory, and large-scale scoring*. Portsmouth, NH: Boynton/Cook.

Brindley, G., & Ross, S. (2001). EAP assessment: Issues, models, and outcomes. In J. Flowerdew & M. Peacock (Eds.), *Research perspectives on English for academic purposes* (pp. 148–166). Cambridge: Cambridge University Press.

Broad, R. L. (1994). "Portfolio scoring": A contradiction in terms. In L. Black, D. A. Daiker, J. Sommers, & G. Stygall (Eds.), *New directions in portfolio assessment: Reflective practice, critical theory, and large-scale scoring* (pp. 263–276). Portsmouth, NH: Boynton/Cook.

Brown, J. D., & Bailey, K. M. (1984). A categorical instrument for scoring second language writing skills. *Language Learning, 34*(4), 21–42.

Cai, G. (1999). Texts in contexts: Understanding Chinese students' English compositions. In C. R. Cooper & L. Odell (Eds.), *Evaluating writing: The role of teachers' knowledge about text, learning, and culture* (pp. 279–297). Urbana, IL: National Council of Teachers of English.

Calfee, R., & Perfumo, P. (Eds.). (1996). *Writing portfolios in the classroom: Policy and practice, promise and peril*. Mahwah, NJ: Lawrence Erlbaum.

Callahan, S. (1997). Kentucky's state-mandated writing portfolios and teacher accountability. In K. B. Yancey & I. Weiser (Eds.), *Situating portfolios: Four perspectives* (pp. 57–71). Logan: Utah State University Press.

Carlisle, R., & McKenna, E. (1991). Placement of ESL/EFL undergraduate writers in college-level writing programs. In L. Hamp-Lyons (Ed.), *Assessing second language writing in academic contexts* (pp. 197–211). Norwood, NJ: Ablex.

Carlson, S. B. (1991). Program evaluation procedures: Reporting the program publicly within the political context. In L. Hamp-Lyons (Ed.), *Assessing second language writing in academic contexts* (pp. 293–320). Norwood, NJ: Ablex.

Casanave, C. P. (1998). Procedural and conceptual parallels between student and teacher product-driven writing projects. *JALT Journal, 20,* 90–103.

Charney, D. (1984). The validity of using holistic scoring to evaluate writing. *Research in the Teaching of English, 18,* 65–81.

Clapham, C. (2000). Assessment for academic purposes: Where next? *System, 28,* 511–521.

Cohen, A. (1994). *Assessing language ability in the classroom* (2nd ed.). Boston: Heinle and Heinle.

Connor, U. (1991). Linguistic/rhetorical measures for evaluating ESL writing. In L. Hamp-Lyons (Ed.), *Assessing second language writing in academic contexts* (pp. 215–225). Norwood, NJ: Ablex.

Connor-Linton, J. (1995a). Crosscultural comparison of writing standards: American ESL and Japanese EFL. *World Englishes, 14,* 99–115.

Connor-Linton, J. (1995b). Looking behind the curtain: What do L2 composition ratings really mean? *TESOL Quarterly, 29,* 762–765.

Cooper, C. R., & Odell, L. (Eds.). (1999a). *Evaluating writing: The role of teachers' knowledge about text, learning, and culture.* Urbana, IL: National Council of Teachers of English.

Cooper, C. R., & Odell, L. (1999b). Introduction: Evaluating student writing—What can we do, and what should we do? In C. R. Cooper & L. Odell (Eds.), *Evaluating writing: The role of teachers' knowledge about text, learning, and culture* (pp. vii–xiii). Urbana, IL: National Council of Teachers of English.

Crusan, D. (2002). An assessment of ESL writing placement assessment. *Assessing Writing, 8,* 17–30.

Cumming, A. (1990). Expertise in evaluating second language compositions. *Language Testing, 7*, 31–51.

Cumming, A. (2001). ESL/EFL instructors' practices for writing assessment: Specific purposes or general purposes? *Language Testing, 18*, 207–224.

Cumming, A. (2002). Assessing L2 writing: Alternative constructs and ethical dilemmas. *Assessing Writing, 8*, 73–83.

Cumming, A., & Berwick, A. (Eds.). (1996). *Validation in language testing.* Clevedon, England: Multilingual Matters.

Currie, P. (1994). What counts as good writing? Enculturation and writing assessment. In A. Freedman & P. Medway (Eds.), *Teaching and learning genre* (pp. 63–79). Portsmouth, NH: Boynton/Cook.

D'Aoust, C. (1992). Portfolios: Process for students and teachers. In K. B. Yancey (Ed.), *Portfolios in the writing classroom: An introduction* (pp. 39–48). Urbana, IL: National Council of Teachers of English.

Davidson, F. (1991). Statistical support for training in ESL composition rating. In L. Hamp-Lyons (Ed.), *Assessing second language writing in academic contexts* (pp. 155–164). Norwood, NJ: Ablex.

de Jong, J. H. A. L., & Stevenson, D. K. (Eds.). (1990). *Individualizing the assessment of language abilities.* Clevedon, England: Multilingual Matters.

Delpit, L. (1988). The silenced dialogue: Power and pedagogy in educating other people's children. *Harvard Educational Review, 58*, 280–298.

Douglas, D. (2001). Three problems in testing language for specific purposes: Authenticity, specificity and inseparability. In C. Elder, A. Brown, E. Grove, K. Hill, N. Iwashita, T. Lumley, T. McNamara, & K. O'Loughlin (Eds.), *Experimenting with uncertainty: Essays in honour of Alan Davies* (pp. 45–52). Cambridge: Cambridge University Press.

Douglas, D., & Chapelle, C. (Eds.). (1993). *A new decade of language testing research.* Alexandria, VA: Teachers of English to Speakers of Other Languages.

Elbow, P. (1993). Ranking, evaluating, and liking: Sorting out three forms of judgment. *College English, 55*, 187–206.

Elbow, P. (1994). Will the virtues of portfolios blind us to their potential dangers? In L. Black, D. A. Daiker, J. Sommers, & G. Stygall (Eds.), *New directions in portfolio assessment: Reflective practice, critical theory, and large-scale scoring* (pp. 40–55). Portsmouth, NH: Boynton/Cook.

Elbow, P., & Belanoff, P. (1997). Reflections on an explosion: Portfolios in the '90s and beyond. In K. B. Yancey & I. Weiser (Eds.), *Situating portfolios: Four perspectives* (pp. 21–33). Logan: Utah State University Press.

Elder, C., Brown, A., Grove, E., Hill, K., Iwashita, N., Lumley, T., McNamara, T., & O'Loughlin, K. (Eds.). (2001). *Experimenting with uncertainty: Essays in honour of Alan Davies.* Cambridge: Cambridge University Press.

Faigley, L., Cherry, R. D., Jolliffe, D. A., & Skinner, A. M. (1985). *Assessing writers' knowledge and processes of composing.* Norwood, NJ: Ablex.

Feak, C., & Dobson, B. (1996). Building on the impromptu: A source-based academic writing assessment. *College ESL, 6*(1), 73–84.

Ferris, D., & Hedgcock, J. (1998). *Teaching ESL composition: Purpose, process, and practice.* Mahwah, NJ: Lawrence Erlbaum.

Freedman, W. S. (1993). Linking large-scale testing and classroom portfolio assessments of student writing. *Educational Assessment, 1*(1), 27–52.

Fulcher, G. (1999). Assessment in English for academic purposes: Putting content validity in its place. *Applied Linguistics, 20,* 221–236.

Fulcher, G. (2000). The "communicative" legacy in language testing. *System, 28,* 483–497.

Genesee, F., & Upshur, J. A. (1996). *Classroom-based evaluation in second language education.* New York: Cambridge University Press.

Hamp-Lyons, L. (Ed.). (1991a). *Assessing second language writing in academic contexts.* Norwood, NJ: Ablex.

Hamp-Lyons, L. (1991b). Basic concepts. In L. Hamp-Lyons (Ed.), *Assessing second language writing in academic contexts* (pp. 5–15). Norwood, NJ: Ablex.

Hamp-Lyons, L. (1991c). Issues and directions in assessing second language writing in academic contexts. In L. Hamp-Lyons (Ed.), *Assessing second language writing in academic contexts* (pp. 323–329). Norwood, NJ: Ablex.

Hamp-Lyons, L. (1991d). Pre-text: Task-related influences on the writer. In L. Hamp-Lyons (Ed.), *Assessing second language writing in academic contexts* (pp. 87–107). Norwood, NJ: Ablex.

Hamp-Lyons, L. (1991e). Reconstructing "academic writing proficiency." In L. Hamp-Lyons (Ed.), *Assessing second language writing in academic contexts* (pp. 127–153). Norwood, NJ: Ablex.

Hamp-Lyons, L. (1991f). Scoring procedures for ESL contexts. In L. Hamp-Lyons (Ed.), *Assessing second language writing in academic contexts* (pp. 241–276). Norwood, NJ: Ablex.

Hamp-Lyons, L. (1991g). The writer's knowledge and our knowledge of the writer. In L. Hamp-Lyons (Ed.), *Assessing second language writing in academic contexts* (pp. 51–68). Norwood, NJ: Ablex.

Hamp-Lyons, L. (1994). Interweaving assessment and instruction in college ESL writing classes. *College ESL, 4*(1), 43–55.

Hamp-Lyons, L. (1995). Rating nonnative writing: The trouble with holistic scoring. *TESOL Quarterly, 29,* 759–762.

Hamp-Lyons, L. (1997). Washback, impact and validity: Ethical concerns. *Language Testing, 14,* 295–303.

Hamp-Lyons, L. (2001). Fourth generation writing assessment. In T. Silva & P. K. Matsuda (Eds.), *On second language writing* (pp. 117–127). Mahwah, NJ: Lawrence Erlbaum.

Hamp-Lyons, L., & Condon, W. (1993). Questioning assumptions about portfolio-based assessment. *College Composition and Communication, 44,* 176–190.

Hamp-Lyons, L., & Condon, W. (2000). *Assessing the portfolio: Principles for practice, theory, and research.* Cresskill, NJ: Hampton Press.

Hamp-Lyons, L., & Kroll, B. (1996). Issues in ESL writing assessment: An overview. *College ESL, 6*(1), 52–72.

Hamp-Lyons, L., & Zhang, B. W. (2001). World Englishes: Issues in and from academic writing assessment. In J. Flowerdew & M. Peacock (Eds.), *Research perspectives on English for academic purposes* (pp. 101–116). Cambridge: Cambridge University Press.

Hayes, J. R., & Hatch, J. (1999). Issues in measuring reliability: Correlation versus percentage of agreement. *Written Communication, 16,* 354–367.

Hayes, J. R., Hatch, J. A., & Silk, C. M. (2000). Does holistic assessment predict writing performance? Estimating the consistency of student performance on holistically scored writing assignments. *Written Communication, 17,* 3–26.

Henning, G. (1991). Issues in evaluating and maintaining an ESL writing assessment program. In L. Hamp-Lyons (Ed.), *Assessing second language writing in academic contexts* (pp. 279–291). Norwood, NJ: Ablex.

Homburg, T. (1984). Holistic evaluation of ESL compositions: Can it be validated objectively? *TESOL Quarterly, 18,* 87–107.

Horowitz, D. (1991). ESL writing assessments: Contradictions and resolutions. In L. Hamp-Lyons (Ed.), *Assessing second language writing in academic contexts* (pp. 71–85). Norwood, NJ: Ablex.

Howe, K. R. (1994, November). Standards, assessment, and equality of educational opportunity. *Educational Researcher, 23,* 27–33.

Huerta-Macías, A. (1995). Alternative assessment: Responses to commonly asked questions. *TESOL Journal, 5*(1), 8–11.

Hunt, K. W. (1977). Early blooming and late blooming syntactic structures. In C. R. Cooper & L. Odell (Eds.), *Evaluating writing: Describing, measuring, judging* (pp. 91–106). Urbana, IL: National Council of Teachers of English.

Huot, B. (1990a). The literature of direct writing assessment: Major concerns and prevailing trends. *Review of Educational Research, 60,* 237–263.

Huot, B. (1990b). Reliability, validity, and holistic scoring: What we know and what we need to know. *College Composition and Communication, 41,* 201–213.

Huot, B. (1996). Toward a new theory of writing assessment. *College Composition and Communication, 47,* 549–566.

Huot, B., & Williamson, M. M. (1997). Rethinking portfolios for evaluating writing: Issues of assessment. In K. B. Yancey & I. Weiser (Eds.), *Situating portfolios: Four perspectives* (pp. 43–56). Logan: Utah State University Press.

Ishikawa, S. (1995). Objective measurement of low-proficiency EFL narrative writing. *Journal of Second Language Writing, 4,* 51–69.

Jacobs, H. L., Zinkgraf, S. A., Wormuth, D. R., Hartfiel, V. F., & Hughey, J. B. (1981). *Testing ESL composition: A practical approach.* Rowley, MA: Newbury House.

Jennings, M., Fox, J., & Graves, B. (1999). The test-takers' choice: An investigation of the effect of topic on language test performance. *Language Testing, 16,* 426–456.

Johns, A. (1991a). Faculty assessment of ESL student literacy skills: Implications for writing assessment. In L. Hamp-Lyons (Ed.), *Assessing second language writing in academic contexts* (pp. 167–179). Norwood, NJ: Ablex.

Johns, A. (1991b). Interpreting an English competency examination. *Written Communication, 8,* 379–401.

Johnson, R. L., Penny, J., & Gordon, B. (2001). Score resolution and the interrater reliability of holistic scores in rating essays. *Written Communication, 18,* 229–249.

Leki, I. (1995). Good writing: I know it when I see it. In D. Belcher & G. Braine (Eds.), *Academic writing in a second language: Essays on research and pedagogy* (pp. 23–46). Norwood, NJ: Ablex.

Li, X. (1996). *"Good writing" in cross-cultural context.* Albany: State University of New York Press.

Liebman, J. D. (1992). Toward a new contrastive rhetoric: Differences between Arabic and Japanese rhetorical instruction. *Journal of Second Language Writing, 1,* 141–166.

Linn, R. L., Baker, E. L., & Dunbar, S. B. (1991). Complex performance-based assessment: Expectations and validation. *Educational Researcher, 20*(8), 15–21.

Lucas, T. (1992). Diversity among individuals: Eight students making sense of classroom journal writing. In D. E. Murray (Ed.), *Diversity as resource: Redefining cultural literacy* (pp. 202–232). Alexandria, VA: Teachers of English to Speakers of Other Languages.

Lynch, B. K. (1997). In search of the ethical test. *Language Testing, 14,* 315–327.

Lynch, B. K. (2001a). The ethical potential of alternative language assessment. In C. Elder, A. Brown, E. Grove, K. Hill, N. Iwashita, T. Lumley, T. McNamara, & K. O'Loughlin (Eds.), *Experimenting with uncertainty: Essays in honour of Alan Davies* (pp. 228–239). Cambridge: Cambridge University Press.

Lynch, B. K. (2001b). Rethinking assessment from a critical perspective. *Language Testing, 18,* 351–372.

Maher, J. C. (2001). The unbearable lightness of being a native speaker. In C. Elder, A. Brown, E. Grove, K. Hill, N. Iwashita, T. Lumley, T. McNamara, & K. O'Loughlin (Eds.), *Experimenting with uncertainty: Essays in honour of Alan Davies* (pp. 292–303). Cambridge: Cambridge University Press.

McNamara, T. F. (1996). *Measuring second language performance.* Harlow, England: Addison Wesley Longman.

McNamara, T. (2000). *Language testing.* Oxford: Oxford University Press.

McNamara, T. (2001). Language assessment as social practice: Challenges for research. *Language Testing, 18,* 333–349.

Messick, S. (1989). Meaning and values in test validation: The science and ethics of assessment. *Educational Researcher, 18*(2), 5–11.

Messick, S. (1994). The interplay of evidence and consequences in the validation of performance assessments. *Educational Researcher, 23*(2), 13–23.

Messick, S. (1996). Validity and washback in language testing. *Language Testing, 13,* 241–256.

Moss, P. (1994). Can there be validity without reliability? *Educational Researcher, 23*(2), 5–12.

Murphy, S. (1997). Teachers and students: Reclaiming assessment via portfolios. In K. B. Yancey & I. Weiser (Eds.), *Situating portfolios: Four perspectives* (pp. 72–88). Logan: Utah State University Press.

Murphy, S. (1999). Assessing portfolios. In C. R. Cooper & L. Odell (Eds.), *Evaluating writing: The role of teachers' knowledge about text, learning, and culture* (pp. 114–135). Urbana, IL: National Council of Teachers of English.

Murray, D. E. (1994). Using portfolios to assess writing. *Prospect, 9*(2), 56–69.

Norris, J. M., Brown, J. D., Hudson, T., & Yoshioka, J. (1998). *Designing second language performance assessments.* Manoa, HI: University of Hawai'i.

Norton, B., & Starfield, S. (1997). Covert language assessment in academic writing. *Language Testing, 14,* 278–294.

Perkins, K. (1980). Using objective methods of attained writing proficiency to discriminate among holistic evaluations. *TESOL Quarterly, 14,* 61–67.

Polio, C. G. (1997). Measures of linguistic accuracy in second language writing research. *Language Learning, 47,* 103–143.

Raimes, A. (1990). The TOEFL test of written English: Causes for concern. *TESOL Quarterly, 24,* 427–442.

Robinson, P., & Ross, S. (1996). The development of task-based assessment in English for academic purposes programs. *Applied Linguistics, 17,* 455–475.

Santos, T. (1988). Professors' reactions to the academic writing of nonnative-speaking students. *TESOL Quarterly, 22,* 69–90.

Sasaki, M., & Hirose, K. (1999). Development of an analytical rating scale for Japanese L1 writing. *Language Testing, 16,* 457–478.

Schneider, M., & Fujishima, N. K. (1995). When practice doesn't make perfect: The case of an ESL graduate student. In D. Belcher & G. Braine

(Eds.), *Academic writing in a second language: Essays on research and pedagogy* (pp. 3–22). Norwood, NJ: Ablex.

Shepard, L. A. (2000). The role of assessment in a learning culture. *Educational Researcher, 29*(7), 4–14.

Shi, L. (2001). Native- and nonnative-speaking EFL teachers' evaluation of Chinese students' English writing. *Language Testing, 18,* 303–325.

Shohamy, E. (1994). The validity of direct versus semi-direct oral tests. *Language Testing, 11,* 99–123.

Shohamy, E. (1997). Testing methods, testing consequences: Are they ethical? Are they fair? *Language Testing, 14,* 340–349.

Shohamy, E. (1998). Critical language testing and beyond. *Studies in Education, 24,* 331–345.

Shohamy, E. (2001a). Democratic assessment as an alternative. *Language Testing, 18,* 373–391.

Shohamy, E. (2001b). *The power of tests: A critical perspective on the uses of language tests.* Harlow, England: Pearson Education.

Shohamy, E., Gordon, C. M., & Kraemer, R. (1992). The effect of raters' background and training on the reliability of direct writing tests. *Modern Language Journal, 76,* 27–33.

Skehan, P. (1984). Issues in the testing of English for specific purposes. *Language Testing, 1,* 202–220.

Smit, D. W. (1994). A WPA's nightmare: Reflections on using portfolios as a course exit exam. In L. Black, D. A. Daiker, J. Sommers, & G. Stygall (Eds.), *New directions in portfolio assessment: Reflective practice, critical theory, and large-scale scoring* (pp. 303–313). Portsmouth, NH: Boynton/ Cook.

Sokolik, M., & Tillyer, A. (1992). Beyond portfolios: Looking at student projects as teaching and evaluation devices. *College ESL, 2*(2), 47–51.

Song, B., & August, B. (2002). Using portfolios to assess the writing of ESL students: A powerful alternative? *Journal of Second Language Writing, 11,* 49–72.

Spolsky, B. (1995). *Measured words.* Oxford: Oxford University Press.

Spolsky, B. (1997). The ethics of gatekeeping tests: What have we learned in a hundred years? *Language Testing, 14,* 242–247.

Sternberg, R. J. (1990). T & T is an explosive combination: Technology and testing. *Educational Psychologist, 25,* 201–222.

Sweedler-Brown, C. O. (1993). The effects of ESL errors on holistic scores assigned by English composition faculty. *College ESL, 3*(1), 53–69.

Tedick, D. J., & Mathison, M. A. (1995). Holistic scoring in ESL writing assessment: What does analysis of rhetorical features reveal? In D. Belcher & G. Braine (Eds.), *Academic writing in a second language: Essays on research and pedagogy* (pp. 205–230). Norwood, NJ: Ablex.

Tillyer, A., & Sokolik, M. (1993). Beyond portfolios: A practical look at student projects as teaching and evaluation devices (part 2). *College ESL, 3*(1), 80–87.

Valdés, G., & Sanders, P. A. (1999). Latino ESL students and the development of writing abilities. In C. R. Cooper & L. Odell (Eds.), *Evaluating writing: The role of teachers' knowledge about text, learning, and culture* (pp. 249–278). Urbana, IL: National Council of Teachers of English.

Vann, R. J., Lorenz, F. O., & Meyer, D. M. (1991). Error gravity: Faculty response to errors in the written discourse of nonnative speakers of English. In L. Hamp-Lyons (Ed.), *Assessing second language writing in academic contexts* (pp. 181–195). Norwood, NJ: Ablex.

Vaughan, C. (1991). Holistic assessment: What goes on in the raters' minds? In L. Hamp-Lyons (Ed.), *Assessing second language writing in academic contexts* (pp. 181–195). Norwood, NJ: Ablex.

Weigle, S. C. (1994). Effects of training on raters of ESL compositions. *Language Testing, 11,* 197–223.

Weigle, S. C. (1998). Using FACETS to model rater training effects. *Language Testing, 15,* 263–287.

Weigle, S. C. (2002). *Assessing writing.* Cambridge: Cambridge University Press.

White, E. M. (1994). Portfolios as an assessment concept. In L. Black, D. A. Daiker, J. Sommers, & G. Stygall (Eds.), *New directions in portfolio assessment: Reflective practice, critical theory, and large-scale scoring* (pp. 25–39). Portsmouth, NH: Boynton/Cook.

White, E. M., Lutz, W. D., & Kamusikiri, S. (Eds.). (1996). *Assessment of writing: Politics, policies, practices.* New York: Modern Language Association of America.

Williamson, M., & Huot, B. (Eds.). (1993). *Validating holistic scoring for writing assessment: Theoretical and empirical foundations.* Cresskill, NJ: Hampton Press.

Wolcott, W., with Legg, S. M. (1998). *An overview of writing assessment: Theory, research, and practice.* Urbana, IL: National Council of Teachers of English.

Yancey, K. B. (Ed.). (1992). *Portfolios in the writing classroom: An introduction.* Urbana, IL: National Council of Teachers of English.

Yancey, K. B. (1996). Dialogue, interplay, and discovery: Mapping the role and rhetoric of reflection in portfolio assessment. In R. Calfee & P. Perfumo (Eds.), *Writing portfolios in the classroom: Policy and practice, promise and peril* (pp. 83–102). Mahwah, NJ: Lawrence Erlbaum.

Yancey, K. B., & Weiser, I. (Eds.). (1997). *Situating portfolios: Four perspectives.* Urbana, IL: National Council of Teachers of English.

Chapter 5

Interaction

"One important controversy currently engaging scholars and teachers of writing involves the role of audience in composition theory and pedagogy. How can we best define the audience of a written discourse? What does it mean to address an audience? To what degree should teachers stress audience in their assignments and discussions?" (Ede & Lunsford, 1994)

"In a number of senses, all writing is social and even shot through with the words and thoughts of others. Nevertheless, writers often fit their words better to outside readers when they put those readers out of mind for a while and write privately to try to make sure their words fit themselves and their own experience of things." (Elbow, 1999)

"Teachers, especially of composition and foreign languages, must do more to inform themselves about the cultural differences between themselves and their students—differences that left unexamined can give rise to charges of 'plagiarism' and 'intellectual dishonesty,' when the disagreements usually arise from different theories of knowledge, patterns of discourse, and cultural values." (Dryden, 1999)

"Unfortunately, some of the cultural stereotypes associated with ESL students have led to oversimplification in teaching about plagiarism." (Bloch, 2001)

"For all composition teachers, the proliferation of electronic texts has meant both that there are more opportunities for students to conduct research and that there are more opportunities for them to copy texts and pass them off as their own." (Bloch, 2001)

LEADING QUESTIONS

- What kinds of interactions take place in L2 writing classes, for example, with texts and with people, and what issues are associated with those interactions, such as audience considerations and peer interaction?
- What kinds of real and imagined audiences do we intend L2 writing students to interact with?
- What kinds of decisions do teachers need to make about interactive writing practices such as textual borrowing?
- What are some of the cultural issues surrounding the Western concept of plagiarism?

Introduction to the Issues

Interaction is a word we often see associated with studies of second language acquisition, a common belief being that children and adults learn a second language in great part by interacting with other people. Through these interactions, they receive input, negotiate and construct meaning, acquire sociolinguistic competence, and develop strategies for communication even when their language proficiency is low. These kinds of interactions are quite transparent to observers and to learners themselves.

In L2 writing, the concept of interaction is somewhat less transparent, if only because it is so common to consider writing a solitary act—a writer alone with only a pen, pencil, or word processor. However, a great deal of research in both first and second language writing has shown the many ways that writing is an interactive social practice (Nystrand, 1989; Thompson, 2001), involving interactions of many kinds. These interactions happen with present and absent others through discussion and reading and with oneself in different guises as well (e.g., planner, reader, critic, autobiographical and historical self). Teachers of L2 writing need to understand the social

and interactive aspects of writing in order to make good decisions about how to help their students improve and in order
to understand the challenges and problems they face along
the way, particularly in a school setting. All literacy practices
in school settings involve interactions of some kind: readers
with authors, writers with imagined and real audiences, writers with other collaborators and peers, writers with evaluators
and critics. Researchers of L2 writing, too, need to factor into
their research plans the interactive nature of writing. Not all
aspects of a social, interactive view of L2 writing are controversial, of course, so in this chapter I discuss only two areas
in which some controversy exists and around which L2 writing teachers face difficult decisions. These areas concern issues
of audience and of plagiarism.

A major dilemma in classroom writing contexts concerns
audience—an interaction between writers and someone who
reads what we write. Good writing teachers help their students understand the importance of audience, without a clear
vision of which we don't know how to advise students about
their writing. But who is the audience for classroom L2 writing? It is certainly the teacher—the one who reads everything,
marks some or all of students' drafts, and gives some kind of
grade or score, if not on individual pieces of writing, then at
the end of a term. Students know this well and will naturally
try to figure out how to write for particular teachers in order
to get the grades they need or want. Teachers, however, often
emphasize to students that they need to imagine other audiences and to write to suit the needs and knowledge of the
imagined audience. Accomplished writers, in fact, are quite
good at imagining their audiences. However, students tend to
know who their real audience is—their own teacher. Finding
authentic audiences outside the writing class is a solution to
this dilemma, but one that may not be feasible in all contexts.
In writing classes, many teachers arrange for real readers by
having students share and comment on each other's writing.
Opinions differ about the value of peer reading in writing
classes (Carson & Nelson, 1996; Jacobs, Curtis, Braine, & Huang,
1998; Zhang, 1995). What we can say is that peers can certainly

be real readers, but under conditions that are usually contrived by the teacher. Again, the students know who their real audience is.

The second area of controversy deals with how writers interact with the words of others, namely, those of published authors or of writers of unpublished manuscripts and essays whose words or ideas a writer wishes to incorporate into his or her own text. If a writer uses the words of others as though they were his or her own, academic regulations in many English-medium contexts call this plagiarism—an academic crime. But plagiarism and ownership of words are relatively recent concepts in Western countries and may have no clear parallel in other cultures (Pennycook, 1996). All academic writers use "textual borrowing" (Pennycook, 1996), but few of them intentionally plagiarize. In order to make fair and ethical decisions about how to teach and treat textual borrowing in their writing classes, L2 writing teachers need to understand these distinctions and to recognize that what they call plagiarism may not exist in the cultures of some of their students. In the next section, I discuss issues of audience and textual borrowing in more detail.

Discussions in the Literature

Audience

In setting up writing activities, L2 writing teachers face decisions about who the audience will be for their students' writing. In general, there is not much controversy about the importance of having L2 students write for some kind of audience (although see the argument against audience by Elbow [1994], discussed later in this chapter). Unlike in the past, when L1 and L2 students alike wrote essays that only their writing teachers ever looked at, more recent views stress how central a concept of authentic or realistic audience is in helping students construct a piece of writing. Writing, so the argument goes, is fundamentally an interactive relationship between authors and readers such that the more we know about who our readers are, the easier it will be to know what to write and how to revise. As I mentioned in the introduction to this chapter, in L2 writing instruction, the dilemmas arise when we try to decide who the audiences for L2 writers can or should be, given that the writing teacher is usually the bottom-line reader and that he or she is also likely to be a language teacher. In this section, I discuss various real, imagined, and imaginary audiences with whom L2 writing students might interact, demonstrating the wide array of choices that teachers need to decide about within their particular writing classes. I follow this discussion with a brief argument against audience.

Real and Imagined Audiences:
Seen and Unseen

By "real audience" I mean the people who actually read, or are intended to actually read, students' writing for purposes other than language correction. Some of these readers are visible and present, such as the writing teacher or classmates, and others are unseen and imagined, such as raters who read essay examinations. Given the reality that the writing teacher is ordinarily the bottom-line reader and evaluator, teachers need to decide whether they will openly acknowledge this role or disguise or underplay this interaction between themselves and their student writers in the interest of designing activities with other kinds of audiences. As I mentioned in the introduction to this chapter, students are not easily deceived into dismissing the all-powerful teacher as their main reader. If teachers decide to front their own sometimes high-stakes interactions with their students, or if students need to learn to write essays that will be read by raters for assessment purposes (see chap. 4), teachers can be involved in carefully designing writing prompts (Horowitz, 1986, 1991) and can then explicitly teach their students how to respond to them. They can also help their students understand what the evaluation criteria are so that students can write directly to audience expectations. When the evaluating audience is unseen and not present, we know that L2 and nonmainstream students do not necessarily understand what readers expect on essay examinations (Johns, 1991; Mlynarczyk, 1998). The criteria may also be elusive to L2 writing teachers who are outside the testing loop.

If the classroom writing teacher is the bottom-line evaluator, students at least have the opportunity to interact in person with their real audience, asking questions as needed. In such cases, teachers may need to help students learn how to interact with them like this, given that it is not considered appropriate for students in some cultures to ask questions of their teachers (Leki, 1992). Also, many students have no experience interacting with teachers about writing at the draft stage, such as in writing conferences (Goldstein & Conrad, 1990; Patthey-Chavez, & Ferris, 1997). Teachers who decide to make their evaluation criteria explicit to students also need to unveil hidden or tacit criteria that they themselves may not be fully aware they are using when they read students' writing. Students, for their part, need to figure out what their writing teachers really want, not just what they say they want.

Many L2 writing teachers believe, however, that students benefit from having a real audience for their writing besides their writing teacher-evaluators and essay exam raters (Belcher, 1989; Mittan, 1989; Starks, 1996). One of the core beliefs expressed in the journal-writing literature, for example, is that teachers can be real, nonjudgmental readers of their students' writing. In dialogue journal writing and other ungraded journal writing in particular, teachers and students interact not just in their roles as teacher or student but as interested participants in ongoing conversations (Casanave, 1993; Peyton, 1990; Peyton & Staton, 1991; see, in the present book, chap. 3, "Paths to Improvement"). This kind of interactive journal writing is also thought to benefit students' academic writing by helping students develop a sense of real audience, explore ideas and topics, and reflect on readings and issues in interaction with a responsive teacher-reader (Casanave, 1995; Mlynarczyk, 1991; Steer, 1988; Vanett & Jurich, 1990). In the case of academic journal writing, students are interacting with a real reader (the writing teacher) in preparation for interacting with other academic readers later. Students also may interact with each other, as present or absent readers and writers, as is the case when students write to members of a different group within or outside the students' school or even to unidentified participants within the same class (Green & Green, 1993). My own students in Japan enjoyed sitting with a small group of classmates and reading and discussing parts of their journals aloud with each other, while still handing their journals in to me as the main reader.

However, not all teachers and students find such interactions appropriate in school settings. In addition to some strong reactions against personal and expressive writing in academic settings, including journal writing (see Leki & Carson, 1997, and the discussion in the present book in chap. 3), some L2 writing scholars have raised questions about whether peer reading activities are appropriate for L2 students, particularly those from non-Western cultures (Carson & Nelson, 1994, 1996; Leki, 1990; Leki & Carson, 1994; Zhang, 1995). The "contrarian" journal writer Dang, for instance, wanted help not from peers but from his teachers for the purpose of grammar correction (Holmes & Moulton, 1995), even in his journal writing. Carson and Nelson (1996) found that the three Chinese students in their interview study were not comfortable criticizing their peers' work, lending credence to the depiction of Far East Asian students as seekers of group harmony. In such cases, even if students acknowledge that peers provide them with a real audience, they cannot provide each other with credible linguistic feedback, whatever the reason may be. Zhang (1995) found in an either-or choice questionnaire that ESL students preferred teacher feedback over peer feedback or self-feedback by a large margin. This finding reflects students' interest in help with language. It may be that students' development of language and of audience awareness needs to be handled in separate kinds of activities.

Others have found that ESL students appreciate the chance to interact with peers about their writing (Leki, 1990; Mangelsdorf, 1992; Liu & Hansen, 2002). For instance, Jacobs et al. (1998) specifically criticized Zhang (1995) for not posing a more sensible choice in the questionnaire to students—that of a preference for peer feedback as one type of feedback among others, including teacher feedback. In a one-item questionnaire, an overwhelming 93 percent of 121 students in Hong Kong and Taiwan said they preferred feedback from other students rather than no peer feedback at all. Other strong arguments, in addition to affective benefits, have been made in favor of peer interactions. Mittan (1989) notes the following theoretical and practical advantages: Theoretically, language use and language learning are fundamentally social and interactive processes, meaning that "the social context created by peer interaction is more realistic, and therefore the feedback more powerful [than that provided by teachers alone]" (p. 209). In a practical sense, peers are authentic readers, not "numbed by the experience of reading stacks of papers" (p. 209). Moreover, peer reading provides students with feedback from multiple sources. Student writers also benefit by gaining an understanding of what readers need—a skill they can apply to their own writing as well as to that of their peers. They can additionally boost their confidence and that of their peers by sharing difficulties and problems in writing. Finally, Mittan notes that writing teachers may save a bit of time by having multiple readers respond to student papers (pp. 209–211). Ferris and Hedgcock (1998) provide a review of some of the peer response literature and offer suggestions for peer response activities. Reviewing the arguments and evidence from research can help L2 writing teachers decide whether and how to use peer interactions in their classes.

In deciding what kinds of authentic audience interactions their students might benefit from, teachers do not need to limit audiences to themselves and peers. In her New Zealand ESL class, Starks (1996) had her adult students do a project that involved students' setting up their own interviews with unknown people by writing letters of request, taping the interviews, writing a report, and writing a follow-up thank-you letter. Other very real audiences for students' writing consist primarily of unseen readers. These include those that L2 writers interact with over email and in electronic chat groups; the imagined readers of Letters to the Editor in newspapers and newsletters; readers of professional writings such as journal articles, conference papers, or proposals; readers of college admissions letters and essays; and readers of student publications such as essays, stories, and school guidebooks. In all these cases, very real (not just realistic) writing activities can be designed in which students are writing to audiences outside their classrooms. (See the discussion of Judy Noguchi's letter-writing activity under "Classroom Perspectives" in this chapter.) In most such cases, little controversy exists over whether these unseen audiences benefit students, except in cases where there seems to be an overt teacher-imposed political agenda for students' writing (see chap. 6, "Politics and Ideology"). Rather, teachers need to make decisions about audiences for their students based on goals, needs, and time. However, questions arise about the value and impact of electronic communication and composing for L1 and L2 students alike.

Electronic Audiences

Much of the literature on technology and writing focuses on the potential advantages and disadvantages to students' composing processes (see, e.g., the reviews in Ferris and Hedgcock, 1998, and Pennington, 1993). In this chapter, however, I am more interested in the questions surrounding the interactive side of electronic communication and composing for second language and nonmainstream students. Even though electronic communication such as email has been described as sharing features of oral and written language (Murray, 1991, 2000), I include such communication in my discussion because it requires that students represent their ideas in alphabetic or ideographic form rather than in sound. Electronic composing, unlike oral communication, may be done in relative solitude, but writing teachers also use computer technology to set up collaborative writing and revising among students (see more on this in the section "Plagiarism and Textual Borrowing" that follows), to communicate with students about revisions, and to exchange journals.

One of the major benefits of electronic communication is thought to be its capacity for disguising the identities of the interactants, thereby making it easier for students who are normally silent in class to participate in conversations and writing activities. In chat groups, students can disguise their identities fully and take on roles that they would never risk taking on in person (see Sherry Turkle's [1984, 1995] ground-breaking work in this area and the more detailed discussion in the present book in chap. 6). In writing classes, women, shy students, hearing-impaired students, and other students who feel reluctant to speak out in class can potentially communicate without fear in the electronic medium and get some sort of writing practice at the same time.

In my own case, some years ago, as part of my job teaching English in Japan, a colleague and I were charged with helping a severely hearing-impaired student, Shuuichi, through his required English course. This experience is described in more detail in chapter 6, under "Classroom Perspectives," and in Casanave, McCornick, and Hiraki, 1993. Suffice it to say here that we thought that electronic journal exchanges among the three of us would be an ideal medium for our student Shuuichi to explore ideas, write extensively, and get plenty of English input from his two teachers. They were, and we found that Shuuichi was able to take on the identity of a confident and assertive writer. He taught us about his education in Japan as a deaf student, corrected what he thought were our misperceptions of what the deaf needed and wanted, and argued with my colleague about philosophy and religion. In person, Shuuichi was shy and formal in his behavior, and communication was slow and limited to written notes. As my colleague said, after a semester of email exchanges, he forgot that Shuuichi was a young, undergraduate deaf student. But as satisfying as these written interactions were, something was missing. Yes, the email interactions brought out an identity of our student that we could not have imagined. Yet we were left after this intensive electronic interaction not having any idea who Shuuichi was, and I am guessing he had little idea who we were. We were not present in each other's interactions; we could not see who we were communicating with. Later, when I reviewed the printouts of our communications, I was astonished at the amount of language that Shuuichi produced and received, but I was disarmed by the distance I felt from him as a person.

In another case of electronic communication and identity, Matsuda (2003) found that as a young graduate student he was able to participate in some rather powerful written interactions about contrastive rhetoric in an electronic discussion group. He chose to hide the fact that he was a graduate student and not to advertise that he was a nonnative English speaker, so he was not treated like a student in the communications. Hiding his student identity gave him confidence to participate in discussions as a knowledgeable interlocutor: "On the screen, my discursive voice must have painted the image of me as a competent scholar/teacher with many, many years of experience . . . ; at the computer desk in my one-bedroom apartment, however, I was an insecure MA student desperately trying to impress other people on the list" (p. 44). His authoritative-sounding written interactions soon brought him an offer from one of the discussants to collaborate on a research project. At that point, as a first-year MA student lacking experience in research and publication, he "freaked out" and deleted the message without responding. Matsuda was also caught up in the highly emotional debates over contrastive rhetoric (see chap. 2 in the present book), and like those he was debating, he ended up overstating his claims and falling into the trap of dichotomies. Although he no doubt benefited greatly from these written interactions, which pulled him into the professional arena just as he was beginning graduate school, he eventually found that he needed to do a different kind of writing in order to make and support his points: He needed to write journal articles. Through the writing of journal articles, he would still be interacting with professionals, though at a greater distance, and would be able to write "longer texts, replete with all the supports and qualifications to present, justify, and defend my perspective" (p. 46). He was not able to build this professional identity in a chat group. Later, in another study of identity and interaction, Matsuda (2002; see also chap. 6 in the present book) examined 200 email messages in Japanese electronic discussions among Japanese professional English teachers. In these discussions, in the absence of strong linguistic criteria for establishing hierarchies of identity and power, differences in power were negotiated over time as it became clear who seemed to possess more knowledge than others. A teacher-learner distinction emerged, and interaction proceeded accordingly.

In chapter 6, I discuss the dilemma of power in electronic interaction in more detail. The dilemma I introduce here is the unresolved question as to whether electronic communication will enhance the opportunities of discussants to participate equally in their online interactions, assuming that they have equal access to computer technology to begin with. They often do not, as Murray (2000) has pointed out. Therefore, even though very real audiences of many kinds can be established in electronic communication, dilemmas of power and access plague our decisions about whether and how to use computer technology in L2 writing classes.

A final question to be discussed in this section on electronic interaction in writing classes asks whether interactive writing online results in better writing than that produced in less interactive ways. Braine (2001) examined just this question in a study of Cantonese-speaking EFL students in Hong Kong. He compared the holistic scores of first and final drafts done over a three-week period by students who wrote through interactions in a local-area network (LAN) and by those who wrote in traditional writing classes. In the LAN system, multiple computers are linked by a server, allowing all students in a group to participate in discussions in a variety of ways (depending on the software). Braine noted, as did Faigley (1992), that a LAN allows students to participate actively who otherwise remain silent in the traditional oral class (Sullivan & Pratt, 1996), that it generates motivation, and that partici-

pants produce a great deal of language. From a sample tran-
script of some of Braine's L2 writing students, we can concur
with him that "perhaps the most remarkable and attractive
features of LANs in writing classes are the large quantity of
writing and the degree of interaction" (Braine, 2001, p. 278).

Braine's (2001) study looked at the writing of 87 undergraduates, advanced users of English who also had keyboard
skills. Half were taught on the LAN and half in a traditional
process-oriented class (drafting, discussion, revision, etc.),
where computers were used only as word processors. He
analyzed the quality of writing on a six-point holistic scale
(TWE: Test of Written English) of first and final drafts of the
first assignment of the course. Although the first drafts done
in the LAN class were rated slightly higher than those done
in the traditional class and although both groups of papers
improved in the final draft, the papers in the traditional class
improved more than did those in the LAN group (traditional:
$4.12 \rightarrow 4.54$; LAN: $4.25 \rightarrow 4.45$). Braine's explanation for his
results cannot be considered conclusive, but he speculates that
the LAN discussions were too disjointed and overwhelming
in terms of the amount of language generated for students to
benefit from peer interactions. Examples from peer interactions
on the LAN and in the traditional class support his contention
that the traditional face-to-face interactions were more or-
derly, focused, and beneficial. Braine notes that peer review
activities "provide second and foreign language learners with
the most opportunity for interaction and collaboration" because of the "nonthreatening environment of small groups,
the mutually beneficial and dependent nature of the task, the
pressure to provide useful feedback within a time limit, and
the 'real' communicative nature of the activity" (Braine, 2001,
p. 286). However, his study concludes that LAN classes hold
no advantages over traditional peer interaction activities in an
L2 writing class. His findings contradict those of Sullivan and
Pratt (1996). Their analysis of the writing and interactions done
in two ESL writing environments, one computer-mediated
and the other oral, showed that computer-mediated peer
comments were more focused and those in the oral classroom

more numerous and that the writing quality produced in the computer environment improved while that in the oral classroom decreased over a 15-week semester. However, Braine's (2001) review of this and other studies on the quality of writing done on LANs and in traditional classrooms showed mixed results, with no clear advantage for writing done on LANs.

Electronic communication and composing are here to stay in spite of the controversies surrounding them. In making decisions about what kinds of audiences and modes of interaction are suitable for their students, L2 writing teachers need to consider the pros and cons of technology in helping students develop their writing. We do not yet have enough evidence either to condemn or wholeheartedly to support technology in the L2 writing class. At the very least, institutions need to decide cautiously whether they will invest in expensive, inconclusively beneficial computer systems for writing classes. Other decisions about audience, whether they are best set up as authentic, realistic, imagined, or even purely imaginary ("Imagine that you are writing to a . . . ;" "Imagine that you are a . . . ") are needed as well, but these decisions do not entail the financial risks of converting classes to electronic forums.

Against Audience

To conclude this section on audience, I summarize the arguments of Elbow (1994, 1995, 1999) against audience. An L1 educator, Elbow's ideas have influenced people in L2 writing for many years, as is indicated by the numerous references to him in this book. As he has done throughout his career, Elbow believes in something that he calls "private writing"—writing done without concern for audience. Distinguishing between writers and academics, Elbow (1994, 1995) claims that academics write for audiences and that students definitely need to develop audience awareness for this purpose and for any revising they might do. Writers, however, have different goals and may be exploring ideas for themselves. Keeping readers in mind at all times may constrain or distort their ideas or intimidate writers into not taking beneficial risks in their writing. Audience awareness, in other words, can get in the way of writing.

In his 1994 article (a conference talk first published in *College English* in 1987), Elbow offers the following arguments for ignoring audience. He begins with the clarification that he is not suggesting that "writers should never think about their audience"; the question is, rather, when (p. 259). First, Elbow notes that some audiences intimidate writers, such as when students are writing for teachers who will judge and grade them, causing writers to think in defensive and confusing ways. In composition, students are expected to create new meaning in their writing, but "[i]t's often difficult to work out new meaning while thinking about readers" (p. 261). Second, Elbow claims that writers who ignore audience sometimes produce better writing, not worse, from the beginning. If writers, both novice and professional, worry excessively about audience, they may be "thinking too much about how their readers will receive their words" (p. 261), and they may produce writing that is both weak and dull. Finally, Elbow argues against the idea that writing done with readers in mind is automatically more mature than writing done without audience awareness. Mature professional writers often write to and for themselves as a way of working out ideas that will later be revised with an audience in mind, so novice writers should be encouraged to do similar exploratory writing. This kind of individualism has been criticized either as theoretically impossible or as culturally ethnocentric (Bakhtin, 1981; Ramanathan & Atkinson, 1999), but Elbow (1999, p. 156) believes that "[s]elf-exploration usually increases people's ability to identify with others."

Elbow is a writer who wants to help his students come to see themselves as writers, not just as students and academics. He wants them to develop a sense of confidence and authority in their writing that will then carry over into writing done for an audience. Ignoring audience at certain times, he believes, can contribute to this goal. L2 writing teachers need to decide whether this stance suits their and their students' goals in the L2 writing class.

In sum, questions about interactions with audience in L2 writing classes linger at several different levels. If the L2 writing teacher is always the bottom-line audience for students' writing, it is not clear how to instruct students in realistic ways about the importance of other kinds of audience interaction. Email and Internet chat-group audiences are certainly authentic, but it is not clear how such discussions contribute to students' writing or what the role, if any, of a writing instructor should be. Writing for no audience at all beyond the self, as advocated by Elbow, may benefit students greatly, but we are still not sure which students benefit most or whether cultural beliefs about writing and writing instruction might interfere or merge comfortably with such a practice.

Plagiarism and Textual Borrowing

When students write from published or unpublished sources, they are interacting with other authors, with textual material, and possibly with disciplinary communities. Even though many kinds of writing do not require such interactions, in academic settings it is important for students in many fields to learn how to write from published sources. Learning how to do this is challenging and fraught with pitfalls for both L1 and L2 students, with the result that plagiarism, usually inadvertent, is common; "borrowing" from unpublished sources is common as well (Barks & Watts, 2001; Bloch, 2001; Buranen, 1999; Campbell, 1990; Dryden, 1999; Pecorari, 2001). L2 students in particular may have little sense of why unattributed textual borrowing is considered an academic "crime" in Western academic contexts or may not know how to write from sources without committing what many educators believe to be this crime. Students need specific guidelines in how to incorporate the voices of others in their own work (Barks & Watts, 2001; Leki, 1992; Swales & Feak, 1994). Moreover, teachers will benefit from knowing something about the historical roots of the Western concept of plagiarism, which appeared as a "logical outgrowth of the creation of intellectual property" (Halbert, 1999, p. 111; Pennycook, 1996).

For L2 writing teachers, a number of questions arise from this seemingly black-and-white issue. First, we don't know how widespread plagiarism is (in its Western sense). Second, it has been extremely difficult to define plagiarism in a way that can be taught unambiguously to students. Third, cultural differences in how source material is used complicate the efforts of L2 writing teachers to help their students write acceptable multivocalic texts. Finally, the growth of electronic communication and information sources makes it easier for students to "cut and paste" but also adds questions to the academic community about how to draw a line between plagiarism and a new kind of textual multivocality.

Is Plagiarism Widespread?

Many teachers in English-medium colleges and universities suspect that plagiarism is widespread, particularly if writing assignments are not carefully designed to discourage copying, cutting, and pasting. Our evidence, however, is primarily anecdotal (Pecorari, 2001). In her historical look at plagiarism in U.S. colleges in the 19th century, Simmons (1999, p. 41) claims that "[w]ith the requirement to write papers came student plagiarism," particularly with canned paper topics. Even though there were admonitions against cheating, students who felt little ownership of their papers and whose primary goal was just to get through school saw no reason not to copy, use "fraternity files," or purchase papers (p. 50). More recently, Buranen (1999, p. 64) notes that in a teleconference it was reported "that cheating was more widespread among students than we would like to believe." She herself had had "occasional" experiences of L1 and L2 students turning in plagiarized papers. In a telephone interview study of 20 faculty at her U.S. university, Roy (1999) was told by only two of the interviewees that plagiarism was a large problem in their classes. Several more said that the problem was moderate. In a focused study of attitudes toward and practices of plagiarism in Japan, LoCastro and Masuko (1997) examined several senior theses written in Japanese and English and 30 other student papers and found that the theses and more than half the student papers contained large quantities of unattributed material from other sources. My own undergraduate students in Japan revealed to me that cutting and pasting from Internet sources was routine at report time. Pennycook (1996) reported on a student from Hong Kong who wrote a memorized essay about Abraham Lincoln, a story that one of my own students from China also had to memorize, prompting him to ask whether this should be considered plagiarism. In Japan, Dryden (1999) noted that there is a great deal of unattributed translation from English to Japanese in the writing of graduate students and faculty. In addition, faculty mentors routinely list their names on work produced solely by their students. I observed both these practices while I was in Japan. Recognizing instances of plagiarism, however, requires that we define plagiarism in an unambiguous way, a task that has proved challenging.

Defining Plagiarism

The concept of plagiarism presumes that people can own words and ideas and that words and ideas can be original—that they can be authored. In the absence of the idea of intellectual property and the legal notion of copyright, it is not possible to plagiarize. These notions are all relatively modern in the West. As Swearingen (1999, p. 19) points out, "Western notions of intellectual property, and the related ideas of copyright and plagiarism, are less that [sic] three hundred years old."

In academic settings, both individual faculty and the institution itself need to have an idea of what they mean by plagiarism in order to advise, decide how to instruct, and perhaps punish students. In her interview study, Roy (1999) found that faculty tended to define plagiarism either as stealing or taking someone else's work without giving credit or as misrepresenting someone else's ideas as one's own. Plagiarism, in other words, consisted either of stealing or of deceiving. In her international survey of 54 universities, Pecorari (2001), too, found a great deal of consistency in how documents characterized plagiarism. Although details differed, it was generally described as unattributed use of the work of others, through copying or paraphrase, in work that was submitted for assessment. Most universities in her survey treated plagiarism as an academic crime.

Students themselves may have mixed or confused ideas about what plagiarism consists of (Kroll, 1988; Deckert, 1993). In an interesting study of peer writing groups, for example, Spigelman (1999) found that L1 students' ideas and values about appropriating ideas, words, and phrases from their peers differed from student to student. Still, all the students in her study considered plagiarism to be a form of "personal misrepresentation," including the "unacknowledged appropriation of student texts" (Spigelman, 1999, pp. 234–235). One student distinguished between ideas that peers gave him in peer discussion groups and ideas that were taken without someone's knowledge or permission. Another student defined plagiarism as direct copying, word for word, but considered it legitimate appropriation if he reshaped the words and ideas from the original. Students disagreed as well about whether it was possible to own ideas. The dilemma arises when we hold the view that knowledge is socially constructed and when we set up peer writing groups in accordance with this belief but adhere to definitions of plagiarism that demand "original" work from students (Spigelman, 1999, p. 239). Clark (1999), in her discussion of writing centers, where students get direct help from others, concurs, asserting:

> if writing centers were freed from concerns about plagiarism, they could be more honest in their pedagogy, no longer requiring students to maintain a standard that they themselves do not observe. All of us who write and publish habitually receive commentary from colleagues and editors that frequently result in extensive changes in a text. Yet, hypocritically, our concern about plagiarism forbids us to make similar suggestions to our students. (Clark, 1999, p. 167)

Another dilemma was revealed in Roy's (1999) study of faculty attitudes toward plagiarism. Does plagiarism include both the intentional and the unintentional use of the words or ideas of another as one's own? If a student does not intend to deceive anyone in his or her textual borrowing (a less negative term than *plagiarism*) should the practice be treated as a case of plagiarism? Pecorari (2001) asserts that much student plagiarism, particularly that by international (L2) students, is probably inadvertent and due to lack of knowledge of citation rules, carelessness, or a developmental linguistic and writing stage that L2 writers pass through. Moreover, there are gray areas in deciding what is considered plagiarism such that we need to do much more than advise students how to cite source materials properly (Pecorari, 2001, p. 241). For these reasons, she believes that inadvertent plagiarism must be treated not as a crime but as an opportunity to educate students.

But even educating students to employ Western practices can be difficult and delicate, as Pennycook (1996) pointed out. In his important article on the links among textual ownership, textual borrowing, and memory, he found numerous examples in the writing of Western scholars that could be considered plagiarized if we do not apply nuanced definitions to the concept. After all, in academic writing we are supposed to use the words and ideas of others, integrate them into our own texts, and still manage to be original. As Campbell (1990, p. 211) noted, using background material in our own writing requires "reading, understanding, learning, relating, planning, writing, revising, editing, and orchestrating." It also involves blending the style of language from sources with our own, a skill that the L2 writers in her study found more difficult than the L1 writers did. Indeed, many L2 writing teachers suspect plagiarism if the style of students' writing shifts suddenly between polished and nonstandard language. If the practice of writing from source materials is difficult for L1 writers to conceptualize and learn, and if the concept of plagiarism is not as black-and-white as many institutions present it, the complications multiply when we look at textual borrowing from a cross-cultural perspective.

Cultural Issues in Textual Borrowing

Related to how we define plagiarism is the thorny issue of cultural differences in how writers treat source material and conceptualize the idea of authorship (Barks & Watts, 2001; Bloch, 2001; Buranen, 1999; Deckert, 1993; Dryden, 1999; Pecorari, 2001; Pennycook, 1996; Scollon, 1995; Swearingen, 1999). Much of the work in this area concerns the writing of Chinese students.

For example, following Kroll's (1988) survey of L1 college students on their views of plagiarism, Deckert (1993) conducted a survey of 170 first-year and 41 third-year students at his university in Hong Kong. He found that the first-year students had little ability to detect plagiarism or to sense why it was wrong except that it hampered their learning. Their attitudes differed from Kroll's (1988) L1 students, who showed awareness of the idea that writers can own words and that they need to be able to do independent work. Deckert's third-year students, on the other hand, showed more concern for the original author. Deckert believes that his students' educational experiences are to blame. His experience in Hong Kong and the results of his survey lead him to claim that "most Chinese students overuse source material through an innocent and ingrained habit of giving back information exactly as they find it" (Deckert, 1993, p. 133).

Not only do inexperienced Chinese writers view source material in different ways from Western writers. Differences can also be found at the professional level. Bloch and Chi (1995) studied how Chinese and English-speaking academic writers use citations when they write in their own languages. They analyzed 60 articles each in Chinese and English from the physical and social sciences and found that the Chinese writers used older citations more often than did the English-language writers. The authors explain that this difference could be due to the Chinese writers' reliance on older texts, as part of a Confucian respect for tradition, or that the Chinese writers simply had less access to newer texts. They found as well that the writers used citations somewhat differently, both across languages and within the Chinese texts but across disciplinary areas. English-language writers used more citation strategies than did the Chinese writers, but the Chinese writers, unlike the stereotype suggesting that they are not good at making critical commentary, used critical citations in both the physical science and social science articles. However, they tended not to place them in the introduction. Bloch and Chi also discussed at length the possible influences of cultural and rhetorical traditions from Chinese history, with the intention of dismantling the myth that Chinese culture and rhetoric are based on simple collectivist ideas of social harmony: "Chinese rhetoric, rather than being monolithic, encompasse[s] a variety of forms of thought, often reflecting the divergence of philosophical inquiry in Chinese society" (Bloch & Chi, 1995, p. 267).

Others have explained the problem as stemming from Chinese students' reliance on literary traditions based on imitation of authorities (Matalene, 1985), on the influence of Confucian and neo-Confucian rhetoric, and on the historical influence of the Chinese civil service exams, which emphasized memorization (Bloch & Chi, 1995). However, it is not necessarily the case that L2 students from Asia are relying on ancient cultural traditions. Students may also be employing developmental and compensatory strategies due to their low language proficiency (Bloch & Chi, 1995). Case studies of ESL writers have shown that what might be labeled plagiarism served as a successful survival strategy for the undergraduate L2 writers, who lacked both confidence in their language ability and time to prepare their written work in more acceptable ways (Currie, 1998; Spack, 1997). Novice L1 writers as well use techniques that Howard (1995) has labeled "patchwriting" to construct pieces of academic writing. Graduate students are under extra pressure to write "original" work (a concept that Pennycook [1996] reminds us is difficult to define) as well as to incorporate the words and ideas of others in their writing—to situate their work within a disciplinary community (Swales, 1990).

There is at least some evidence suggesting that graduate ESL students' conceptions of textual borrowing do not differ greatly from those of L1 students, leading Barks and Watts (2001) to ask whether ignorance and lack of experience, rather than culture, lead to unorthodox textual borrowing. It is likely, too, that writing tasks that are perceived as meaningless to students encourage plagiarizing. As research evidence builds, in other words, it has become increasingly difficult to attribute L2 students' plagiaristic practices to cultural traditions.

In short, from the mid-1990s and early 2000s, our understanding of plagiarism and of cultural influences on how L2 writers interact with the work of others became more complex as L1 and L2 scholars provided us with historical and cultural information about authorship, the ambiguities in the Western notion of plagiarism, and about other possible reasons why students plagiarize (Bloch, 2001; Bloch & Chi, 1995; Howard, 1995; Pennycook, 1996; Stearns, 1999). In the L2 writing field, Pennycook (1994, 1996) has helped us see some of the complexities and inconsistencies of textual borrowing practices within Western culture and to raise questions about our black-and-white definitions of plagiarism. He suggests that by treating what looks like plagiarism by L2 students as a crime, we are unfairly imposing an oversimplified Western notion of authorship on a complex cross-cultural phenomenon that is as ideological as it is textual (Scollon, 1995). The other side of this position is expressed by Deckert (1994), who insists that students who write in English for an international research audience need to protect themselves from any writing practices that could be labeled as plagiaristic. Deckert's position, labeled reductionist and ethnocentric by Pennycook, captures the pragmatic view of many L2 writing teachers that their main job is to help students' survive in settings where strong sanctions apply to writers who are perceived as plagiarizing. (See the discussion in chap. 6 on the clash between pragmatist and critical perspectives in EAP.)

Most writers now agree that cases of unintentional plagiarism by novice writers, both L1 and L2, should not automatically be treated as academic crimes but should be taken as evidence that students need more instruction, more practice, and more understanding from their teachers. L2 writing teachers who ask their students to write academic pieces using source materials thus need to make careful decisions about how to ease students into writing practices that all novice writers find challenging and confusing (see the suggestions for graduate students in Barks and Watts, 2001 [discussed in the "Classroom Perspectives" section that follows], and in Swales and Feak, 1994).

Electronic Communication and Plagiarism

To conclude this discussion of plagiarism, I refer briefly to the growing dilemma facing educators in developed and developing countries—that of the proliferation of opportunities for students of all kinds to construct their writing from sources drawn from the Internet. Because we still do not have clear guidelines as to whether electronic and print texts should be treated similarly in copyright and plagiarism cases (Bloch, 2001), educators face difficult decisions in guiding students to use Internet sources in ways that fit existing legal and ethical notions of writing in academic settings.

> The increase in on-line information, usenet groups, news lists, and electronic journals adds a new dimension to this discussion of plagiarism. These new electronic resources provide a vast new supply of texts that can be added to the network of texts available for student use; at the same time, however, their rhetorical value is unclear, since their status in the academic world has yet to be determined. (Bloch, 2001, pp. 221–222)

In addition to postmodern views on "the death of the author" (Pennycook, 1996), we do not yet know how to conceptualize authorship in an age of electronic multiliteracies (Cope & Kalantzis, 2000). Has the traditional view of an author as someone who creates his or her own ideas and words disappeared (Lunsford & West, 1996; Woodmansee & Jaszi, 1995)? Bloch makes an interesting argument that if we do away with the idea of the solitary and original author, our idea of authorship might more closely resemble that in China, where the idea of original authorship is less prevalent than it is in the West (Bloch, 2001, p. 224). If we develop a more collaborative view of writing, how will this affect our L2 writing pedagogies?

Bloch (2001) offers us two scenarios. The conservative view is that electronic text is treated the way we treat print text, with the result that L2 students (and others) will need to learn traditional rules about how to use source materials in their writing. A more radical view is that "cyberspace will have different rules regarding what is public and what is private" (p. 225). For students from cultures where there is a "healthy respect for intertextuality," such as those from China, the task of integrating source material may not be so problematic. In either case, argues Bloch, L2 writing teachers need to decide whether they see themselves as language teachers or writing teachers—choices that he insists are not mutually exclusive. They need as well to consider the possibility that "the Internet can . . . become a place where Chinese (and other) students, with their long and varied traditions of authorship and intertextuality, may feel more at home than in traditional classrooms" (Bloch, 2001, p. 226).

The main point to be taken from this section on plagiarism is that the concept is both complex, even within Western cultures, and culturally loaded. L2 writing teachers may not easily be able to answer the many questions that surround the practice of textual borrowing, except in clear cases of intentional deception when large amounts of text are copied in work that is submitted for evaluation. However, before assigning writing tasks that require students to write from sources, teachers are advised first to consider whether they hold pragmatist, accommodationist beliefs or ones that are more critical and questioning of the status quo (see also chap. 6). They then need to think through some of the issues, discuss them with colleagues, learn what institutional regulations exist, and plan how to approach the issue from a positive, educational perspective with students. Should L2 students never copy? It may be that at some early point in writing instruction, copying words, phrases, and even passages is a technique that could contribute to students' linguistic and rhetorical development. How do new concepts of "multiliteracies" influence our attitudes toward authorship and ownership of print, electronic, and graphic texts (Cope & Kalantzis, 2000)? At the very least, if teachers are able to design meaningful writing activities for their students and to raise students' awareness of cross-cultural practices of authorship, plagiarism may not arise as a serious problem.

Classroom Perspectives

Clever teachers can no doubt come up with wonderful ideas for helping students learn about audience and textual borrowing. I mention just two here. The first example comes from a colleague in Japan, Judy Noguchi.[1] For her English class, she designed a writing task that simultaneously addresses the issues of audience and of plagiarism. The second set of examples comes from Barks and Watts (2001), who discuss ways to help graduate students understand English language practices of textual borrowing.

Briefly, in Judy's class, her students read about and discuss issues from a current-issues section of a newspaper published in English in Japan that has a monthly Readers' Forum section, with themes announced each month for the following month. Then, they compose letters to the editor, drafting and revising with feedback from each other. Finally, they send the letters to the newspaper. Much to the delight of both students and teacher, some of the letters get published. Students have written to a real audience, about recent issues that interest

---

1. At the time of this writing, Judy Noguchi taught at Mukogawa Women's University and part-time at Osaka University. She has been especially interested in ESP (English for Specific Purposes) courses that use authentic materials and tasks rather than language textbooks. I am grateful to her for granting me permission to describe her class activities and to refer to examples of her students' work from 1999–2002.

them (recency helps prevent plagiarism), for an authentic purpose—to try to get their voices heard by the public readership of the paper. In addition to helping students learn about audience and avoid plagiarism, this task contributes to students' reading and critical-thinking skills and to their skills at making reasoned, supported arguments.

Judy's students at the time she communicated with me (2002) were primarily second-year university students in the human sciences. She had up to 30 students in a class. Her class was not a writing class but an oral communication class on issues of current interest. The class met once a week. Grades for the class were based on participation, including feedback to the other students, oral presentations, and completion of assignments. Students had to discuss and present their views orally on a regular basis in response to the issue chosen by the newspaper as the theme for the following month. Although all students also had to write responses to issues they had read about in the form of a letter to the Readers' Forum section, they submitted their letters to the newspaper on a volunteer basis. About one-third to one-half of the students submitted letters in a given month. The topics of discussion for the following month's Readers' Forum were announced each month, giving students time to build their knowledge and to discuss and present their ideas.

Judy prepared her students for this activity carefully. Following her guidelines, they first studied the Readers' Forum section in the newspaper, answering questions such as how many letters were published, how many seemed to be written by foreigners living in Japan, how many paragraphs the letters tended to be, and what kinds of information appeared to be located in different parts of the letters. She also asked her students to observe how the authors of the published letters tried to persuade readers of their opinions, such as through references to authorities, rhetorical questions, examples, and comparisons. She then asked students to look ahead to the next month's theme for the Readers' Forum and to collect information on it for oral presentation in the following week's class. Students gathered information from sources such as the

Internet, magazines, and personal interviews. The week after students' oral presentations, they prepared the first draft of their letters for the Readers' Forum and presented them either to a small group of peers or to the whole class. The first readers of their letters, in other words, were their classmates, who filled out simple evaluation sheets for each other and provided feedback on main points and suggestions for improvements. Judy's role as instructor in this exercise was not as editor or language teacher but as one of the many class evaluators. She did collect copies of the students' letters, but only to check that they had been written. Students who wished to do so then sent their letters to the newspaper, without having them edited by the teacher. This decision allowed Judy to be a real reader, not a teacher-evaluator, although students' whose letters were published would receive extra points. After the letters were sent in, Judy then sometimes did some editing exercises with the class.

At this point, the writing done by Judy's students was out of her hands. Other readers were taking over, in the form of editors of the Readers' Forum section of the newspaper. Those letters that were published were edited by newspaper staff, allowing students to compare their originals with the published versions. Judy reports that between 1999 and 2002, in nine different monthly Readers' Forums where a total of eight to nine letters were published each month, several of Judy's students' letters appeared. The students who contributed letters benefited from at least two sets of interactions with real readers: one with their classmates and teacher and one with editors at the newspaper. Those students whose letters were published interacted as well with a third audience, the unseen, unknown, but very real audience of newspaper readers. All who did this task benefited from the satisfaction of writing in their second language in an authentic writing task. Judy's writing activity shows how authentic, interactive writing tasks can be effectively carried out in EFL contexts.

In the second example, two writing teachers discuss a variety of ways to familiarize L2 graduate students with textual borrowing practices (Barks & Watts, 2001). They first critique the limited ways that textbooks tend to address this issue. Textbooks, they say, tend to present black-and-white definitions of plagiarism, then warn students about how serious the "crime" of plagiarism is in Western contexts, and finally introduce exercises in paraphrase, summary, and quotation (p. 252). Barks and Watts claim that such a simplistic approach is both pedagogically unsound and (following Pennycook, 1996) intellectually arrogant (Barks & Watts, 2001, p. 253).

The authors then present a variety of instructional strategies culled from the literature and from their own teaching materials for developing students' understanding of and skill at textual borrowing. First, they suggest ways to discuss with students the complexities of authorship, notions of originality and plagiarism, and cross-cultural practices of textual borrowing. Noting that students and teachers are easily attracted to simple explanations and unambiguous definitions, they encourage teachers not to settle for the easy way out but to engage students in lively, if difficult, discussion—the kind of interaction and intellectual engagement "that ultimately lead to greater understanding" (p. 254). To spur this discussion, Barks and Watts present a list of true-false statements to be responded to twice, once for the context of students' countries and once for the United States (the context of the authors' teaching), such as "It is acceptable to copy passages from a source text and use them in your paper without attribution" (p. 255). In a second discussion activity, the authors pose open-ended questions about students' practices of using source texts and their own definitions of terms such as *author* and *intellectual property*. A third example borrowed from Swales and Feak (1994) asks students to consider the purposes of citation practices in English-language academic contexts and to compare these practices with their own understandings. With exercises like these, the authors raise students' awareness of the issues surrounding textual borrowing and build a foundation for instruction in the practices themselves.

Students who write in academic contexts need to learn how to integrate the voices of the authors they read into their own work. In their next set of exercises, adapted from the ideas of

Howard (1995), Barks and Watts recommend helping students with the intermediary step of textual borrowing, which Howard calls patchwriting. Patchwriting includes textual borrowing techniques that would technically be labeled plagiarism, such as copying, paraphrasing without attribution, and using short phrases to compose a paragraph. Students then need to cross the line from patchwriting to acceptable borrowing techniques. Swales and Feak (1994) show how students can paraphrase appropriately by retaining all technical terms from their sources, relieving students of the worry of not knowing how to find synonyms for technical vocabulary. Barks and Watts then cite an example from the 1984 book on academic writing by Arnaudet and Barrett, on how to simplify detailed definitions of technical words in short summaries. Finally, they mention how students can appropriate stock phrases used in academic writing without fear of plagiarizing (a technique I also discuss in Casanave, 2003). Phrases that express a function such as framing a paper, introducing results or findings, and signaling arguments can all be used directly in students' writing. The examples from Barks and Watts (2001, p. 260) include "The data show that . . . "; "One explanation for this may be . . . "; and "It should be noted that . . . "

Barks and Watts then ask students to take an "ethnographic approach," recommended by Hirvela (1997), Johns (1997), and others. In this approach, students examine the interactive literacy practices in their chosen fields by analyzing various features of published articles. They examine, for example, how and why citations are used, interview faculty about their practices of textual borrowing, and analyze how they themselves, their peers, and their own teachers use citations. These investigations then feed into students own writing and their reflections on their writing.

Barks and Watts conclude with an important dilemma, one that has plagued my own teaching for many years: the separation of courses for L2 students into reading and writing courses. Both reading and writing are considered closely linked interactive practices in academic writing but are still often considered separate skills. For example, in Japan I was assigned to teach "professional English" courses to graduate students who wished to improve their reading and writing in English. The courses in reading and writing were listed separately, and most students had no time to take both of these labor-intensive courses at the same time. In some cases, separating reading and writing courses may be justified, but in graduate-level EAP instruction, reading and writing are two aspects of the same interactive practice. We cannot teach L2 students about audience or textual borrowing without involving them deeply in reading activities. In making decisions about how to help students with academic writing, administrators, curriculum developers, and teachers themselves are advised to merge reading and writing courses whenever possible.

Ongoing Questions

Writing is considered an interactive practice in many ways. Only two have been discussed in this chapter: interaction between writers and audiences and interactions that occur as writers draw on the words and ideas of others in the construction of their texts. Among the many decisions that L2 writing teachers must make are those concerning whom their students will write to and for and how students will be expected to incorporate source material into their writing.

A basic decision concerns whether teachers believe that audience awareness is centrally important to the development of students' writing or whether it is possible and advisable to ignore audience in the interest of other aspects of writing. If audience is important, who shall the audiences be? Is it possible to eliminate the teacher as the primary audience in a classroom setting and to arrange for students to write for someone else? What possibilities exist for real audiences in the L2 writing class? Do we deceive students if we set up imagined or imaginary audiences, when students know their writing teachers are the bottom-line evaluators? If teachers and students interact through journal writing, what (potentially contradictory) roles do teachers play in this activity, and what benefits accrue to students?

Many L2 students need to learn to write academic essays, reports, and theses. In all of these cases, they will be asked to draw on published and Internet sources to build and support ideas and arguments. In the limited time that L2 writing teachers usually have with students, how do we raise students' awareness of conventions for doing this in the context of their home cultures, their L2 cultures, and their goals for future writing? If we insist that students strictly follow Western conventions for textual borrowing and citation, are we arrogantly imposing ethnocentric cultural norms, as Pennycook (1994, 1996) suggests? How are cultural norms of textual borrowing in non-Western cultures changing as scholarship becomes increasingly international and multiliterate? What roles, if any, are there for copying and imitation in the L2 writing class? And how are practices and expectations for multivocalic texts changing as a result of electronic technology?

Beliefs and Practices

Beliefs

1. In what ways do you believe that writing is an interactive practice? What kinds of interactions do you believe characterize writing?
2. Do you believe that there is such a thing as solitary or private writing, as Elbow claims, or that all writing is inevitably a social practice? What arguments and examples can be presented to support both views?
3. What are your beliefs about the value of helping L2 students develop a sense of audience awareness?
4. Before reading this chapter, what were your beliefs about and definitions of plagiarism? If your beliefs have changed, describe the changes.
5. Do you believe that intentional and unintentional plagiarism should be handled similarly or differently at the institutional level? At the classroom level?
6. Do you believe that intentional and unintentional pla-

giarism should be handled similarly or differently in Western ESL settings and in non-Western EFL settings?

Practices

1. In your own experiences learning to write in an L1 and L2 (and L3 etc.), what kinds of real or imagined audiences have you written for? In what ways has an awareness of audience helped you, or in what ways could it have helped you, learn to write? Are there ways in which audience awareness hindered you?

2. In your teaching experiences, how have you incorporated a sense of audience into your writing activities? How do you help students understand the concept of audience? What do your students seem to understand about this concept? If you are not yet teaching, speculate about these questions.

3. What stories, if any, have your students or colleagues told you about the practice of plagiarism at your school? What written or unwritten institutional or departmental regulations exist to define and control plagiarism?

4. If you have experiences dealing with a plagiarism problem in class, or if you provide guidelines for your students, describe these and compare them with those of your colleagues. Construct guidelines for the future if you are not yet teaching.

5. If you, your colleagues, or your students are from non-Western cultures, compare your views on copying, imitation, and memorization as (a) instructional techniques in the writing class and (b) practices that are or are not allowed in academic writing.

6. Try designing a writing task for a group of L2 students that you are currently working with or hope to work with in which you decide about and specify the authentic aspects of the task (if any), the real or imagined audience(s), and the means by which you will attempt to prevent intentional or unintentional plagiarism.

References and Relevant Readings

Bakhtin, M. M. (1981). *The dialogic imagination: Four essays* (C. Emerson & M. Holquist, Trans.; M. Holquist, Ed.). Austin: University of Texas Press.

Barks, D., & Watts, P. (2001). Textual borrowing strategies for graduate-level ESL writers. In D. Belcher & A. Hirvela (Eds.), *Linking literacies: Perspectives on L2 reading-writing connections* (pp. 246–267). Ann Arbor: University of Michigan Press.

Belcher, D. (1989). Is there an audience in the advanced EAP composition class? (ERIC Document Reproduction Service No. ED316028)

Blakeslee, A. M. (1997). Activity, context, interaction, and authority: Learning to write scientific papers in situ. *Journal of Business and Technical Communication, 11*(2), 125–169.

Bloch, J. (2001). Plagiarism and the ESL student: From printed to electronic texts. In D. Belcher & A. Hirvela (Eds.), *Linking literacies: Perspectives on L2 reading-writing connections* (pp. 209–228). Ann Arbor: University of Michigan Press.

Bloch, J. (2002). Student/teacher interaction via email: The social context of Internet discourse. *Journal of Second Language Writing, 11,* 117–134.

Bloch, J., & Chi, L. (1995). A comparison of the use of citations in Chinese and English academic discourse. In D. Belcher & G. Braine (Eds.), *Academic writing in a second language: Essays on research and pedagogy* (pp. 231–274). Norwood, NJ: Ablex.

Braine, G. (2001). A study of English as a foreign language (EFL) writers on a local-area network (LAN) and in traditional classes. *Computers and Composition, 18,* 275–292.

Buranen, L. (1999). "But I *wasn't* cheating": Plagiarism and cross-cultural mythology. In L. Buranen & A. M. Roy (Eds.), *Perspectives on plagiarism and intellectual property in a postmodern world* (pp. 63–74). Albany: State University of New York Press.

Campbell, C. (1990). Writing with others' words: Using background reading text in academic compositions. In B. Kroll (Ed.), *Second language writing: Research insights for the classroom* (pp. 211–230). Cambridge: Cambridge University Press.

Carson, J. G., & Nelson, G. L. (1994). Writing groups: Cross-cultural issues. *Journal of Second Language Writing, 3,* 17–30.

Carson, J. G., & Nelson, G. L. (1996). Chinese students' perceptions of ESL peer response group interaction. *Journal of Second Language Writing, 5,* 1–19.

Casanave, C. P. (Ed.). (1993). *Journal writing: Pedagogical perspectives.* Keio University SFC Monograph No. 3. (ERIC Document Reproduction Service No. ED423682)

Casanave, C. P. (1995). Journal writing in college English classes in Japan: Shifting the focus from language to education. *JALT Journal, 17,* 95–111.

Casanave, C. P. (2003). Multiple uses of applied linguistics literature in a multidisciplinary graduate EAP class. *ELT Journal, 57,* 43–50.

Casanave, C. P., McCornick, A. J., & Hiraki, S. (1993). Conversations by E-mail: A study of the interactive writing experiences of a Japanese deaf student and two English teachers. *SFC Journal of Language and Communication, 2,* 145–175.

Clark, I. L. (1999). Writing centers and plagiarism. In L. Buranen & A. M. Roy (Eds.), *Perspectives on plagiarism and intellectual property in a postmodern world* (pp. 155–167). Albany: State University of New York Press.

Cope, B., & Kalantzis, M. (Eds.) (2000). *Multiliteracies: Literacy learning and the design of social futures.* London: Routledge.

Currie, P. (1998). Staying out of trouble: Apparent plagiarism and academic survival. *Journal of Second Language Writing, 2,* 131–148.

Deckert, G. D. (1992). A pedagogical response to learned plagiarism among tertiary-level ESL students. *Guidelines, 14*(1), 94–104.

Deckert, G. D. (1993). Perspectives on plagiarism from ESL students in Hong Kong. *Journal of Second Language Writing, 2,* 131–148.

Deckert, G. D. (1994). Author's response to Pennycook's objections. *Journal of Second Language Writing, 3,* 285–289.

De Guerrero, M. C. M., & Villamil, O. S. (2000). Activating the ZPD: Mutual scaffolding in L2 peer revision. *Modern Language Journal, 84,* 51–68.

Dryden, L. M. (1999). A distant mirror or through the looking glass? Plagiarism and intellectual property in Japanese education. In L. Buranen & A. M. Roy (Eds.), *Perspectives on plagiarism and intellectual property in a postmodern world* (pp. 75–95). Albany: State University of New York Press.

Ede, L., & Lunsford, A. (1994). Audience addressed/audience invoked: The role of audience in composition theory and pedagogy. In G. Tate, E. P. J. Corbett, & N. Myers (Eds.), *The writing teacher's sourcebook* (3rd ed., pp. 243–257). New York: Oxford University Press.

Elbow, P. (1994). Closing my eyes as I speak: An argument for ignoring audience. In G. Tate, E. P. J. Corbett, & N. Myers (Eds.), *The writing teacher's sourcebook* (3rd ed., pp. 258–276). New York: Oxford University Press.

Elbow, P. (1995). Being a writer vs. being an academic: A conflict in goals. *College Composition and Communication, 46,* 72–83.

Elbow, P. (1999). In defense of private writing: Consequences for theory and research. *Written Communication, 16,* 139–170.

Eldred, J., & Hawisher, G. (1995). Researching electronic networks. *Written Communication, 12,* 330–359.

Faigley, L. (1992). *Fragments of rationality: Postmodernism and the subject of composition.* Pittsburgh: University of Pittsburgh Press.

Ferris, D., & Hedgcock, J. (1998). *Teaching ESL composition: Purpose, process, and practice.* Mahwah, NJ: Lawrence Erlbaum.

Geisler, G. (1990). The artful conversation: Characterizing the development of advanced academic literacy. In R. Beach & S. Hynds (Eds.), *Developing discourse practices in adolescence and adulthood* (pp. 93–109). Norwood, NJ: Ablex.

Goldstein, L. M., & Conrad, S. (1990). Student input and the negotiation of meaning in ESL writing conferences. *TESOL Quarterly, 24,* 443–460.

Green, C., & Green, J. M. (1993). Secret friend journals. *TESOL Journal, 2*(3), 20–23.

Halbert, D. (1999). Poaching and plagiarizing: Property, plagiarism, and feminist futures. In L. Buranen & A. M. Roy (Eds.), *Perspectives on plagiarism and intellectual property in a postmodern world* (pp. 111–120). Albany: State University of New York Press.

Hirvela, A. (1997). "Disciplinary portfolios" and EAP writing instruction. *English for Specific Purposes, 16,* 83–100.

Holmes, V. L., & Moulton, M. R. (1995). A contrarian view of dialogue journals: The case of a reluctant participant. *Journal of Second Language Writing, 4,* 223–251.

Horowitz, D. (1986). Essay examination prompts and the teaching of academic writing. *English for Specific Purposes, 5,* 107–120.

Horowitz, D. (1991). ESL writing assessments: Contradictions and resolutions. In L. Hamp-Lyons (Ed.), *Assessing second language writing in academic contexts* (pp. 71–85). Norwood, NJ: Ablex.

Howard, R. (1995). Plagiarisms, authorships, and the academic death penalty. *College English 57,* 788–805.

Hyland, K. (1999). Academic attribution: Citation and the construction of disciplinary knowledge. *Applied Linguistics, 20,* 341–367.

Jacobs, G. M., Curtis, A., Braine, G., & Huang, S.-Y. (1998). Feedback on student writing: Taking the middle path. *Journal of Second Language Writing, 7,* 307–317.

Johns, A. M. (1991). Interpreting an English competency exam: The frustrations of an ESL science student. *Written Communication, 8,* 379–401.

Johns, A. M. (1997). *Text, role, and context: Developing academic literacies.* Cambridge: Cambridge University Press.

Kroll, B. M. (1988). How college freshmen view plagiarism. *Written Communication, 5,* 203–221.

Leki, I. (1990). Potential problems with peer responding in ESL writing classes. *CATESOL Journal, 3,* 5–19.

Leki, I. (1992). *Understanding ESL writers: A guide for teachers.* Portsmouth, NH: Boynton/Cook Heinemann.

Leki, I., & Carson, J. G. (1994). Students' perceptions of EAP writing instruction and writing needs across the disciplines. *TESOL Quarterly, 29,* 81–101.

Leki, I., & Carson, J. (1997). "Completely different worlds": EAP and the writing experiences of ESL students in university courses. *TESOL Quarterly, 31,* 39–69.

Liu, J. & Hansen, J. (2002). *Peer response in second language writing classrooms.* Ann Arbor: University of Michigan Press.

LoCastro, V., & Masuko, M. (1997, March). *Plagiarism and academic writing of NNS learners.* Paper presented at the 31st International Conference of the Teachers of English to Speakers of Other Languages, Orlando, FL. (ERIC Document Reproduction Service No. ED409724)

Lunsford, A. A., & West, S. (1996). Intellectual property and composition studies. *College Composition and Communication, 47,* 383–411.

Mangelsdorf, K. (1992). Peer reviews in the ESL composition classroom: What do the students think? *ELT Journal, 46,* 274–284.

Matalene, C. (1985). Contrastive rhetoric: An American writing teacher in China. *College English, 47,* 789–808.

Matsuda, P. K. (2002). Negotiation of identity and power in a Japanese online discourse community. *Computers and Composition, 19,* 39–55.

Matsuda, P. K. (2003). Coming to voice: Publishing as a graduate student. In C. P. Casanave & S. Vandrick (Eds.), *Writing for scholarly publication:*

Behind the scenes in language education (pp. 39–51). Mahwah, NJ: Lawrence Erlbaum.

Mittan, R. (1989). The peer review process: Harnessing students' communicative power. In D. M. Johnson & D. H. Roen (Eds.), *Richness in writing: Empowering ESL students* (pp. 207–219). New York: Longman.

Mlynarczyk, R. W. (1991). Is there a difference between personal and academic writing? *TESOL Journal, 1*(1), 17–20.

Mlynarczyk, R. W. (1998). *Conversations of the mind: The uses of journal writing for second-language learners.* Mahwah, NJ: Lawrence Erlbaum.

Murray, D. E. (1988). The context of oral and written language: A framework for mode and media switching. *Language in Society, 17,* 351–373.

Murray, D. E. (1991). *Conversation for action: The computer terminal as medium of communication.* Amsterdam: John Benjamins Publishing Company.

Murray, D. E. (2000). Protean communication: The language of computer-mediated communication. *TESOL Quarterly, 34,* 397–421.

Myers, S. (1998). Questioning author(ity): ESL/EFL, science, and teaching about plagiarism. *TESL-EJ, 3*(2), 1–20.

Nystrand, M. (1989). A social-interactive model of writing. *Written Communication, 6,* 66–85.

Patthey-Chavez, G. G., & Ferris, D. R. (1997). Writing conferences and the weaving of multi-voiced texts in college composition. *Research in the Teaching of English, 31,* 51–90.

Pecorari, D. (2001). Plagiarism and international students: How the English-speaking university responds. In D. Belcher & A. Hirvela (Eds.), *Linking literacies: Perspectives on L2 reading-writing connections* (pp. 229–245). Ann Arbor: University of Michigan Press.

Pennington, M. (1993). A critical examination of word processing effects in relation to L2 writers. *Journal of Second Language Writing, 2,* 227–255.

Pennycook, A. (1994). The complex contexts of plagiarism: A reply to Deckert. *Journal of Second Language Writing, 3,* 277–284.

Pennycook, A. (1996). Borrowing others' words: Text, ownership, memory, and plagiarism. *TESOL Quarterly, 30,* 201–230.

Peyton, J. K. (Ed.). (1990). *Students and teachers writing together: Perspectives on journal writing.* Alexandria, VA: Teachers of English to Speakers of Other Languages.

Peyton, J. K., & Staton, J. (Eds.) (1991). *Writing our lives: Reflections on dialogue journal writing with adults learning English*. Englewood Cliffs, NJ: Prentice-Hall Regents.

Porter, D., & O'Sullivan, B. (1994). *Writing for a reader: Does the nature of the reader make a difference?* Paper presented at the annual meeting of the Southeast Asian Ministers of Education Organization Regional Language Center Seminar, Singapore. (ERIC Document Reproduction Service No. ED403780)

Ramanathan, V., & Atkinson, D. (1999). Individualism, academic writing, and ESL writers. *Journal of Second Language Writing, 8,* 45–75.

Roy, A. M. (1999). Whose words these are I think I know: Plagiarism, the postmodern, and faculty attitudes. In L. Buranen & A. M. Roy (Eds.), *Perspectives on plagiarism and intellectual property in a postmodern world* (pp. 55–61). Albany: State University of New York Press.

Scollon, R. (1995). Plagiarism and ideology: Identity in intercultural discourse. *Language in Society, 24,* 1–28.

Simmons, S. C. (1999). Competing notions of authorship: A historical look at students and textbooks on plagiarism and cheating. In L. Buranen & A. M. Roy (Eds.), *Perspectives on plagiarism and intellectual property in a postmodern world* (pp. 41–51). Albany: State University of New York Press.

Spack, R. (1997). The acquisition of academic literacy in a second language: A longitudinal case study. *Written Communication, 14,* 3–62.

Spigelman, C. (1999). The ethics of appropriation in peer writing groups. In L. Buranen & A. M. Roy (Eds.), *Perspectives on plagiarism and intellectual property in a postmodern world* (pp. 231–240). Albany: State University of New York Press.

Starks, D. (1996). Audience in language teaching and learning. *TESL Canada Journal, 13*(2), 26–32.

Stearns, L. (1999). Copy wrong: Plagiarism, process, property, and the law. In L. Buranen & A. M. Roy (Eds.), *Perspectives on plagiarism and intellectual property in a postmodern world* (pp. 5–17). Albany: State University of New York Press.

Steer, J. (1988, March). *Dialogue journal writing for academic purposes.* Paper presented at the 22nd International Conference of Teachers of English to Speakers of Other Languages, Chicago, IL. (ERIC Document Reproduction Service No. ED295479)

Sullivan, N., & Pratt, E. (1996). A comparative study of two ESL writing environments: A computer-assisted language classroom and a traditional oral classroom. *System, 29,* 491–501.

Swales, J. (1987). Utilizing the literatures in teaching the research paper. *TESOL Quarterly, 21,* 41–68.

Swales, J. M. (1990). *Genre analysis: English in academic and research settings.* Cambridge: Cambridge University Press.

Swales, J. M., & Feak, C. B. (1994). *Academic writing for graduate students: Essential tasks and skills.* Ann Arbor: University of Michigan Press.

Swearingen, C. J. (1999). Originality, authenticity, imitation, and plagiarism: Augustine's Chinese cousins. In L. Buranen & A. M. Roy (Eds.), *Perspectives on plagiarism and intellectual property in a postmodern world* (pp. 19–39). Albany: State University of New York Press.

Thompson, G. (2001). Interaction in academic writing: Learning to argue with the reader. *Applied Linguistics, 22,* 58–78.

Turkle, S. (1984). *The second self: Computers and the human spirit.* New York: Simon and Schuster.

Turkle, S. (1995). *Life on the screen: Identity in the age of the Internet.* New York: Simon and Schuster.

Vanett, L., & Jurich, D. (1990). The missing link: Connecting journal writing to academic writing. In J. K. Peyton, (Ed.), *Students and teachers writing together: Perspectives on journal writing* (pp. 21–33). Alexandria, VA: Teachers of English to Speakers of Other Languages.

Woodmansee, M., & Jaszi, P. (1995). The law of texts: Copyright in the academy. *College English, 57,* 769–787.

Yan, L., & Zancong, S. (2002). Enhancing an English writing class via integration of available technological resources. *TESL Reporter, 35*(1), 17–30.

Zhang, S. (1995). Reexamining the affective advantage of peer feedback in the ESL writing class. *Journal of Second Language Writing, 4,* 209–222.

Chapter 6
Politics and Ideology

"[A]ll forms of ESL instruction are ideological, whether or not educators are conscious of the political implications of their instructional choices." (Benesch, 1993)

"A prime example of what I consider extreme in critical theory and pedagogy is the premise that everything is political and ideological." (Santos, 2001)

"Common to all critical approaches is interrogating assumptions on which theory and practice are based. This means questioning, or problematizing, what had been previously taken for granted." (Benesch, 2001a)

"[I]f minority people are to effect the change which will allow them to truly progress we must insist on 'skills' within the context of critical and creative thinking." (Delpit, 1986)

"L2 student writers, given their respective sociocultural and linguistic socialization practices, are more likely than native English speaking (NES) students to encounter difficulty when being inducted into CT [critical-thinking] courses in freshman composition classes; they are not 'ready' for CT courses in either L1 or L2 writing classrooms." (Ramanathan & Kaplan, 1996b)

"[C]ritical thinking appears to be something more universally relevant than just a social practice. If some cultures differ in their present ability to appropriate the tools of critical thinking, it is probably only a difference in the degree to which critical thinking is tolerated in certain spheres of life." (Davidson, 1998)

"Critical Multiliteracies . . . requires student debate and understanding of the political and material consequences of technological change. How will IT change

our lives? Who will benefit? Who will be the advantaged?" (Luke, 2000)

"No technology is neutral or value free." (Murray, 2000b)

LEADING QUESTIONS

- What aspects of L2 writing instruction, if any, might be considered political or ideological?
- To what extent do L2 writing teachers have an obligation to help their students learn to follow existing writing conventions or to question, critique, and change those conventions?
- What will the role of Internet technology be in L2 writing classes in the coming years? In what ways will Internet technology affect the "digital divide"?

Introduction to the Issues

A number of unresolved issues concerning the politics and ideology of language teaching face L2 writing teachers as they make decisions about how best to design and carry out instructional activities. In this chapter, I discuss three of them: *critical and pragmatist stances toward academic writing; the contested meaning and role of the cultural nature of critical thinking in L2 writing classrooms;* and *the looming influence of Internet technology on all of our educational practices.* All of these issues are inextricably tied to larger questions of power and influence in the L2 writing class: Who determines students' purposes for writing and the kinds of writing they will do? What are students' and teachers' relationships with the dominant discoursal and cultural practices of literacy?

The first of the emotionally loaded issues in L2 writing that I discuss in this chapter concerns the politics and ideology of L2 writing and of English language education more generally.

In a nutshell, one side of the argument holds that all education is political and ideological, whether or not we realize it in the day-to-day practices of our teaching (Benesch, 1993; Canagarajah, 2002; Pennycook, 1989, 1994; Shor, 1992). English language education in particular is fraught with political minefields, given that English is a dominant international language associated with economic and political power, subjugation of minorities, injustice, and globalization (Canagarajah, 1999; Pennycook, 1994; Phillipson, 1992). The language of research publications in print and on the Internet is also predominantly English, thus limiting the participation of non-English users in international research communication (Gibbs, 1995; Murray, 2000b; Swales, 1997). Teachers who hold strong beliefs about the inseparability of language and politics claim that L2 writing students need not only to be aware of the ways that the English language is implicated in issues of power but also to recognize that they have the right, or perhaps the obligation, to question, resist, and challenge the status quo (Benesch, 2001a, 2001b). They believe as well that our teaching can be neither neutral nor objective. All choices we make in the classroom are therefore laden with political and ideological implications.

The other side claims that writing teachers are entrusted with a very pragmatic goal—that of assisting students to develop the language and writing proficiency they need to survive in the environments in which they will be using their second language, such as an English-medium academic institution or an international company. In this view, students need to learn prevailing discourse conventions as efficiently as possible, including lexical, syntactic, and rhetorical norms of the discourse communities they will participate in (Horowitz, 1986; Santos, 1992, 2001). Teachers who ascribe to this accommodationist view, as it is sometimes called, do not necessarily deny that political and ideological issues lurk behind every educational corner. Rather, they believe that teachers must concern themselves with kinds of language and writing that students need to succeed, must avoid imposing particular political agendas in classrooms, and must work to maintain neutrality and objectivity to the extent possible in how and what they teach. They also believe that "in essence teaching is not primarily about power or politics" but about something else (for Johnston [1999, p. 561] this would be the "moral relation between teachers and students").

Another related area of dispute in L2 classes concerns the role of culture in the kinds of topics and activities that teachers design for their students. One view is that writing teachers should beware of imposing aspects of a dominant (usually English-language) Western culture such as notions of individual voice or critical thinking on L2 students, particularly on those from non-Western cultures (Atkinson, 1997; Ramanathan & Kaplan, 1996b). Another view is that the decision not to teach practices such as critical thinking is itself a political choice and that teachers have a responsibility to help all students learn to question the status quo, a fundamental characteristic of critical thinking (Benesch, 1999b).

The third issue asks questions about the rapidly growing influence of Internet technology on literacy education, from how we conceptualize literacy to how we teach and how students learn to write, think, and use language (Murray, 2000a, 2000b; Warschauer, 1999, 2000). One argument is that technology is a "great equalizer," serving to diminish the divisions between dominant majorities and those whose voices tend not to be seen in print media or heard in classroom discussion. Some educators suspect, however, that the spread of Internet technology is increasing the divide between the haves and the have-nots.

Writing teachers need to be fully aware of these issues, to reflect regularly on their own stances, and to remain open to discussion and opposing views. As is the case with most of the other issues in this book, there are no right and wrong solutions on which teachers can base decisions about what to teach in L2 writing classes or how to design and carry out lessons. However, the positions that different educators take involve moral and ethical issues about what we believe is right, fair, just, and culturally appropriate (Hafernik, Messerschmitt, & Vandrick, 2002). Passions can therefore run high as we struggle to understand the links among politics, ideology, culture, technology, and language. Whatever stances we take, they influence greatly what we do in the classroom.

Therefore, as is the case for other issues raised in this book, teachers need to ask how each set of arguments applies to their particular local contexts and purposes of teaching. It is possible, for example, that issues and arguments about politics, ideology, and cultural constructs such as critical thinking apply differently to populations of immigrant students in ESL settings than they do to international students who plan to return to their home countries after being educated in an English-medium academic environment or to students learning English in the context of their home cultures. In other words, even though teachers may hold strong beliefs about these sensitive issues, how they enact their beliefs will depend in part on local circumstances, making it difficult for teachers to make unambiguous decisions based on published materials or books on method. Teachers' decisions flow from the specifics of their local contexts in conjunction with their beliefs and their understandings of the issues. As I have done throughout this book, I urge teachers to continue expanding their understanding of issues in L2 writing by career-long reading.

Discussions in the Literature

Accommodationist Pragmatism and Critical Pedagogy

L2 writing teachers in both second and foreign language settings, especially in the subarea called English for Academic Purposes (EAP), probably agree that their main goal in the L2 writing class is to help students succeed in the writing they need to do. In schools, this usually means helping students pass essay exams, write school reports and essays within their subject matter classes, and perhaps write creatively and expressively as well in L1 English or ESL/EFL classes. The argument between educators with a pragmatist orientation and a critical orientation is not that one group wishes to help L2 writing students and the other does not. It concerns what kinds of help we believe students need and, more broadly, what our educational goals are for all students. It also concerns deeply held and contradictory beliefs: on the one hand, that "English language teaching cannot be isolated from the cultural and political contexts in which it is embedded" (Pennycook, 1994, p. 692), and on the other hand, that it is falsely reductive to assert that education and human relations are nothing but political (Santos, 2001). In the TESOL field, these debates have been most openly undertaken between Terry Santos and Sarah Benesch and those who have responded to their original articles.

In the first issue of the *Journal of Second Language Writing,* Santos (1992) laid out what she considered to be a major distinction between L1 and L2 composition. L1 composition, for historical reasons, she said, sees itself as more ideological than does L2 composition, which, again for historical reasons, has constructed itself in much more pragmatic ways. L2 writing, with its background in the scientific traditions of applied linguistics and TESOL, has historically had little interest in sociopolitical concerns, unlike L1 composition, which has a long tradition of influence by critical literary theories. According to Santos (1992, p. 12), "[u]nderstanding what is involved in learning and teaching a second language or dialect should lead to greater emphasis on the cognitive, academic, and pedagogical rather than on the sociopolitical."

This article triggered a number of responses, including Benesch's 1993 article. At the time she wrote this article, Benesch agreed that critical sociopolitical analysis had not yet been carried out in EAP. However, she also argued that all teaching is ideological and that EAP's ideology was accommodationist. In other words, the goal of EAP was to efficiently help students learn the norms and conventions of academic writing, not to question or resist those norms. Important for her argument was the fact that she was writing from her perspective as an educator in an urban university in New York, where students were working-class immigrants rather than privileged elites (Vandrick, 1995) or EFL students outside the United States. Severino (1993) published at about the same time her own rejoinder to Santos (1992), claiming with Benesch that L2 pedagogy is just as politically charged as is L1 pedagogy but that the political and ideological aspects of L2 writing had not yet been openly discussed. Similarly, McKay (1993) discussed what she called "L2 composition ideology," noting that it is important for L2 writing teachers to ask not only what we want students to achieve (e.g., knowledge of Western academic discourse?) but why: "What is gained by asking students to master the social practices of Western academic discourse that support a particular orientation toward knowledge?" (McKay, 1993, p. 76). Like Benesch and other critical educators (e.g., Pennycook, 1997), she worried about the possibility that Western academic discourse would become oppressive rather than liberating.

In a counteropinion, however, Allison (1994) not only defended EAP's pragmatist stance but claimed that many ideological aspects of EAP had indeed been discussed in the literature. The list he provided—for example, debates about communicative language teaching, methodologies, teacher and learner goals, ethical issues in testing (pp. 620–621)—did not refer, however, to issues of power, which was Benesch's main concern, as she pointed out in her response to Allison's 1994 article (Benesch, 1994). Claiming that the discourse concerning ideology in EAP is itself ideological, and describing himself as a "pragmatically inclined EAP practitioner," Allison (1994, p. 618) boldly stated that he chose "to resist what I see as a current bid on the part of ideologist discourse to invade EAP discourse." Pragmatically oriented EAP educators, he asserted, "have not avoided ideologically laden debates and conflicts in order to fabricate some monolithic and all-encompassing account of the way things must remain in EAP and all education" (p. 622). He later accused critics of EAP pragmatism of quashing dissenting voices (Allison, 1996), and he urged educators to consider issues of pragmatism and ideology empirically and only within particular contexts.

In a response to Allison (1996), Pennycook (1997) continued

the debate by arguing that he and Allison understood the issues quite differently partly because they were using different
discourses to discuss them. He cites Cherryholmes's (1988)
description of "vulgar pragmatism" as unexamined functional
efficiency and of "critical pragmatism" as encompassing evaluation and choice, to make the point that "[EAP] is almost
always a vulgar rather than a critical pragmatism" (Pennycook,
1997, p. 256). He disagrees with Allison (1996) that EAP is
already a critical and diversely ideological field, and like Benesch, he believes that EAP needs to see language as political,
in both local and international contexts. He claims that numerous "discourses of neutrality" make it possible to characterize
EAP as having pragmatic, rather than political, agendas. For
example, English as an international language is sometimes
seen as more "neutral" than local languages, the scientific
foundations of EAP and applied linguistics are described as
universal and therefore acultural, and universities are seen as
neutral sites that are independent of "social and political environments" (Pennycook, 1997, pp. 261–262). Pennycook
contests all of these views. Universities, the language they
use, and the knowledge they produce and disseminate are not
neutral; on the contrary, "a more critical view of the global
context of tertiary education suggests that universities are key
sites of cultural and epistemological invasion, where inap-
propriate and irrelevant forms of Western culture and knowledge are thrust upon an unwitting student population" (p. 262).

   In a strong rebuttal to critical approaches to L2 writing,
Santos (2001) argued that it is the responsibility of university
teachers to "help students become as proficient as possible in
the conventions of academic discourse" (p. 183) and that not
to do so would be unethical. Students first need to become
proficient in conventional academic discourse in order to be
able to challenge those conventions "should they wish to do
so" (p. 184). In this argument, Santos implies that critical EAP
educators may not be paying enough attention to what students themselves believe they need and want and that in most
cases in her experience this is to learn the norms of academic
writing that will enable them to succeed in their studies. In

L1 composition, Smith (1997) argues similarly that critical pedagogical educators who aim to emancipate students and redress power imbalances are not asking students what they want. Gatekeeping and hierarchies, he points out, are facts of life, and many students wish to learn how to enter corporate worlds that are characterized by such hierarchies. If students do not wish to resist (and many do not, both he and Santos claim), then teachers are ethically obligated to further students' goals, not their own political agendas. Santos (2001), too, points out that university education itself is an elitist enterprise by definition—that the very nature of academic work involves us in inequalities. Provided that students can become competent in the language of the academy, most of which occurs as writing, students can choose to accommodate or resist, but the choice should be theirs. Santos's (2001) argument is based not only on strong ethical beliefs about what L2 writing teachers should and should not be doing in the classroom but also on the belief common to science that some approaches to knowledge are indeed more neutral and objective than others.

The critical pedagogues in L2 writing reject this latter belief altogether. Knowledge, education, and discourse can never be neutral, they claim, and L2 writing teachers are thus ethically obligated to recognize, and to help students recognize, their political and ideological natures. Who established the conventions of academic writing, they ask, and for whose purposes? Benesch (2001b, p. 165) continues to argue that "opponents of critical L2 composition claim neutrality for their choice to take a pragmatic position and accuse those who are not strictly pragmatic of imposing a social agenda on students." She rejects "the myth that some types of discourse are freer of cultural contamination than others and do not, therefore, impose on students" (p. 166). Like Pennycook (1997), Benesch (2001a, 2001b) believes that a critical pragmatism can be promoted in L2 academic writing classes whereby students can be prepared for what they need in their academic settings and at the same time can be encouraged to "question the status quo" (Benesch, 2001b, p. 167). Canagarajah (1999,

2002) refers to this approach as a *negotiation* model of critical academic writing.

This brings us to a final difficult issue, which concerns whether L2 writing teachers should or should not encourage social change as a way to rectify injustice and power inequities in society. Benesch (2001a, 2001b), following the work of Paolo Freire (1970, 1973, 1994), believes deeply that it is the responsibility of educators to do more than train students in various skills. Rather, it is their duty to help raise students' awareness of inequities in society and to provide them means for challenging, questioning, and resisting. L2 writing teachers need to ask whether and how this stance applies to their own classrooms, which may be quite different from Benesch's U.S.-based inner-city context. Benesch, in ESL classes linked to subject matter classes, helped her students negotiate syllabuses and assignments and learn to ask questions of their professors. She also provided students with a topic in psychology that she felt was not fully covered in the regular psychology course syllabus (anorexia), a topic that Santos (2001) criticized for being a social agenda imposed by Benesch. Although Benesch concedes that it might have been desirable, as Santos suggested, to offer students choices of topics, she argues that the main point is to help students learn to participate actively in their classes in such a way that if they choose to do so, they can request changes or at least explanations from those in authority.

What should be our stance on teaching L2 writing for social change in EFL contexts or in ESL contexts where international students intend to study English or get a graduate degree and then return to their home countries? Swales (1990; Swales & Feak, 1994, 2000) has worked with international graduate students for many years and generally takes an accommodationist, pragmatic approach to L2 writing. Even though he no longer sees the EAP field as a "culturally and politically neutral enterprise" (Swales, 1997, p. 377) and hopes that languages other than English will come to be used more than they are now for research and publication, he is primarily concerned with helping students become aware of the conventions of written language that will help them participate in scholarly discourse forums in English. For Swales the issue is to help international students contribute to the construction and dissemination of disciplinary knowledge in their fields and to learn the secondary genres, such as negotiations with journal editors, that go hand in hand with research writing. In this sense his approach is pragmatic and accommodationist. It can be argued that the populations of international students that Swales works with, or that many L2 students learning English within their own countries, are not oppressed in the way Benesch's students are, leading us to ask whether it is appropriate to promote social change in these cases. However, Swales (1997) and others (see, e.g., Canagarajah, 1999, 2002; Pennycook, 1994; Phillipson, 1992) admit that the English language and Western scholarship as promoted by North America and Britain dominate and oppress minority languages and cultures worldwide. Should writing teachers be teaching students outside Western contexts to resist the dominance of English, challenge existing norms and authority, and contribute to social change? Or is it sufficient to encourage students to be aware of these political realities (Clark & Ivanič, 1997; Fairclough, 1992) and to critique and analyze the genres they use (Luke, 1996)? On the other hand, in the interest of time, efficiency, and cultural appropriateness, should teachers in some or all L2 writing contexts simply instruct students in dominant rhetorical and linguistic conventions of writing, whatever those might be, in the belief that some kind of political and ideological neutrality should be our goal?

The Cultural Politics of Critical Thinking

Another debated ideological topic in L2 writing concerns the role of culturally constructed notions such as critical thinking, individualism, and "voice" in the kinds of writing activities teachers ask students to do and the ways that teachers expect students to write and talk about their ideas. In this section, I review only some of the ideas on critical thinking, but I urge interested readers to delve into the debates on "voice" and "individualism" as well (see, e.g., Atkinson, 1999, 2000; Atkinson & Ramanathan, 1995; Elbow, 1994, 1999; Ivanič & Camps, 2001; Ramanathan & Atkinson, 1999; Ramanathan & Kaplan, 1996a; Stapleton, 2002; and the special issue on voice in the *Journal of Second Language Writing, 10*[1–2]). In making decisions about whether some aspect of critical thinking (or voice) will be built into L2 writing activities, L2 writing instructors need to consider what they, their students, and indeed the cultures in which writing instruction is taking place believe about the concept of critical thinking and its role in education. In Western educational settings, teachers may take it for granted that all students need to learn to think critically in order to succeed in school and in later life. But what do we mean by "critical thinking"? Is it something that can and should be taught? And if so, to whom?

Expressed in the simplest terms, the debate about critical thinking pits two sets of beliefs against one another. The first set of beliefs constructs critical thinking as a culture-specific construct, taken for granted as an analytical skill that people develop as they are socialized and educated in particular cultures, such as Anglophone Western cultures. People who hold this belief question whether L2 educators should be imposing this uniquely Western way of thinking on L2 students. The second set of beliefs constructs critical thinking in broader ways, characterizing it as a basic human survival mechanism used by all societies, even if applied minimally in some educational settings. Those who hold this set of beliefs argue that all students, particularly those who are minorities or speakers of a nondominant language, need to develop the critical-thinking skills of questioning and analyzing in order to understand and resist dominance and injustice, as well as to solve problems at home, school, and the workplace. Let us review these arguments in more detail.

Arguing that critical thinking is a peculiarly Western construct, characteristic of middle-class (U.S.) socialization practices, Dwight Atkinson, Vai Ramanathan, and Robert Kaplan (Atkinson, 1997; Atkinson & Ramanathan, 1995; Ramanathan & Atkinson, 1999; Ramanathan & Kaplan, 1996a, 1996b) have all urged TESOL educators, and L2 writing teachers in particular, to consider whether the kinds of critical-thinking activities often found in L1 classrooms are suitable for L2 populations. Perhaps one of the strongest statements in this regard, a quote introducing this chapter, appeared in an article by Ramanathan and Kaplan (1996b, p. 232).

> L2 student-writers, given their respective sociocultural and linguistic socialization practices, are more likely than native English speaking (NES) students to encounter difficulty when being inducted into CT [critical-thinking] courses in freshman composition classes. They are not "ready" for CT courses in either L1 or L2 writing classrooms.

The following year, Atkinson (1997) published his much discussed critique of critical thinking in TESOL. In this article, he laid out four major points, all of which, he argues, suggest that TESOL educators refrain from unthinkingly adopting critical-thinking pedagogies in their classrooms. He first notes that critical thinking is a social practice in which "an individual is automatically immersed by virtue of being raised in a particular cultural milieu and which the individual therefore learns 'through the pores'" (p. 73). For this reason, critical thinking is especially difficult to define, although educators seem to have a felt sense of what it is. In response to the evidence that U.S. children lack critical-thinking skills, Atkinson notes that "mainstream schools have become progressively more accessible to nonmainstream groups over the past 30 years," thus provoking a sense of crisis (p. 77). In other words, because the nonmainstream students cannot think critically, they are skewing the assessment of critical-thinking skills in the United States. Atkinson suggests here that because critical-thinking skills result from early socialization, they are probably impossible to teach. Second, Atkinson describes critical thinking as "exclusive and reductive" (pp. 77–79). When critical-thinking skills are reduced to (in)formal logic and argumentation, as they seem to be in some L1 composition textbooks (Ramanathan & Kaplan, 1996b), many groups—

such as women, who may not be comfortable with adversarial thinking (Belcher, 1997)—are left behind. Third, he points out that thinking styles of L2 writers have been shown to differ from Western ideas about the values of individualism, self-expression, and language as a tool for learning (see Fox, 1994). Finally, he asks whether critical-thinking skills are generalizable and transferable and finds little evidence that they are, other than perhaps within very similar domains and tasks. Atkinson then suggests that a possible solution is to teach critical-thinking skills only within specific disciplines, using a cognitive apprenticeship approach in which experts and novices work together to learn what skills are needed in that context (Lave & Wenger, 1991). He refers to such an approach as "pan-cultural" (p. 89).

Such a discipline-specific approach is also promoted by Ramanathan and Kaplan (1996b), who found that the approaches to critical thinking in the 12 freshman composition textbooks they analyzed do not suit L2 writers. In those textbooks, the authors claim that emphases on informal logic, creating knowledge, taking a stand, and developing awareness of public issues in U.S. contexts will create special problems for L2 writers. These problems are exacerbated by the questionable transferability of critical-thinking skills. Learning thinking skills within academic disciplines, on the other hand, is not only more "situated" (Brown, Collins, & Duguid, 1989), but it is also a more culturally neutral approach, given that disciplines are "freer of cultural constraints" and have relatively language-neutral ways of analyzing problems according to the "paradigms of the discipline" (Ramanathan & Kaplan, 1996b, p. 242–243).

Not surprisingly, these articles sparked vigorous debate among more "critically" oriented L2 specialists. There has been wide agreement that critical thinking should not be a buzzword that refers to a bandwagon fad but that it deserves thoughtful analysis and application (Davidson, 1998). However, other aspects of the argument against critical thinking have garnered much criticism. In the first place, Davidson (1998) points out that without the tool of critical thinking,

Atkinson (1997) could never have made his own critique of its use with L2 learners. Davidson also disagrees with Atkinson's view that useful definitions of critical thinking do not exist. Most definitions share a focus on reasoned, reflective, and skeptical thinking (Davidson, 1998, p. 121). Davidson also rejects the portrayal of critical thinking as cold, masculinist, and Western, citing his own observations of the "basic rationality of Japanese people" (p. 121). He also points out that if, indeed, students from countries such as Japan have not been trained to question, critique, and analyze to the extent that students from Western countries have, then this is all the more reason for explicitly offering such students the tools for thinking that will allow them to participate in international communications (p. 122).

In another response to Atkinson (1997), Gieve (1998) makes an important distinction between two kinds of critical thinking, only one of which he claims Atkinson refers to. Critical thinking that is characterized as informal logic, and that is the target of criticisms by Atkinson (1997) and Ramanathan and Kaplan (1996b), is labeled a *monological* view by Gieve. A second type is labeled *dialogical* critical thinking and is inherent to the kind of discourse that people engage in when they uncover and examine "the taken-for-granted assumptions and presuppositions that lie behind argumentation" (p. 125). In a later article, Benesch (1999b) takes up Gieve's (1998) distinction between monological and dialogical critical thinking to argue why and how dialogical critical thinking might be taught in L2 classes. In short, according to Gieve, by restricting their argument to a narrowly (and culturally stereotyped?) perspective of cross-cultural academic writing, Atkinson and others

> deny the enormous power of this [dialogical] use of language and the power that it brings to those capable of using it for their own ends. Analytical precision and critical insight massively enhance the power of dissent, whether the argument is against the location of a nuclear power station in the U.S. by local citizens or against human rights abuses

in China or Iraq by aggrieved minorities, and the critical
attitude is by no means restricted to the West. (Gieve, 1998,
p. 125)

Finally, Gieve claims to be puzzled by numerous contradictions in Atkinson's (1997) arguments, including his assertion
that a cognitive apprentice approach within disciplines is
somehow more culturally neutral or "universalist." If cultures
differ so radically, and if socialization happens from earliest
childhood, then it makes little sense, according to Gieve, to
argue for a "pan-cultural" approach to critical thinking. (I
might add here that disciplinary practices themselves, far from
being culturally neutral, evolved out of Western traditions of
intellectual and educational practices and that disciplinary
thinking is nothing if not critical.) In the end, Gieve (1998)
was unsure what Atkinson was suggesting: Should L2 students be given different kinds of writing instruction than L1
students? Do we eschew debate and analysis in favor of students' culturally preferred modes of learning and thinking,
assuming we know what these are? And, I would add, is anyone asking the students what they want?

In her response to Atkinson (1997), Hawkins (1998) speaks
from the U.S. context and argues that it is precisely because
critical-thinking skills are expected to be displayed by participants in U.S. culture that they need to be taught, if only by
apprenticeship, to nonmainstream students. Hawkins (1998,
p. 131) asserts that "[b]y denying access and exposure to students already marginalized by virtue of not having mainstream
language and cultural behaviors, teachers are complicit in ensuring their failure." Like Benesch (1999b, 2001a, 2001b),
Hawkins (1998) wants L2 teachers to help "render . . . transparent the workings of status and power through cultural and
educational practices, language use, and behaviors" (p. 132).
This does not mean either denying L2 students their own cultures or supplanting their cultural practices with ones foreign
to them. The critical-thinking game is a both-and endeavor. It
can include many different ways of knowing (e.g., Belcher,
1997) across cultures. As Canagarajah (2002, p. 101) points

out, "everyone has agency to rise above their culture and social conditions to attain critical insights into their human condition."

The debate on what the place of critical thinking should be in L2 writing classes, and indeed what critical thinking consists of, continues. Atkinson (1998) asks how teachers can teach something that they cannot define explicitly, but we can find evidence everywhere in educational settings where teachers do this all the time. (I recall a sociology class I had once in which a key sociological concept, "power," could not be defined clearly at all, yet it was the focus of much research and discussion, as it is in the critical approaches to literacy in the TESOL field.) The needs and wants (and rights: see Benesch, 1999a) as well as the thinking abilities of L2 students in ESL versus EFL settings have not been fully explored, nor have the deeply (Western) cultural literacy practices of different disciplines. As Benesch (1999b, p. 579) reminds us, "[t]he current debate about critical thinking is not a harmless academic exchange but a political discussion with serious implications about what should and should not be taught in EAP and L2 composition classes." Many questions remain. Is it patronizing, stereotyping, or disempowering to portray L2 writers as a single group whose members are not "ready" to think critically in either L1 or L2 (Ramanathan & Kaplan, 1996b)? Are they really so different from millions of U.S. students who also need to learn to "think critically"? And what kinds of decisions do L2 writing teachers arrive at based on their considerations of these dilemmas?

The Politics of Internet Technology

The final dilemma to be reviewed in this chapter concerns the debate about whether technology in the writing class and in educational settings more broadly is working to equalize power imbalances between the privileged and less privileged or whether it is perpetuating deeper divisions by creating a "digital divide." One reality about which there is little disagreement is that computer-mediated communication (CMC) and

Internet technology are here to stay and that they are profoundly affecting our educational, social, and literacy practices (Cope & Kalantzis, 2000; Gee, 2000; Faigley, 1997; Luke, 2000). This technology increasingly reaches into more and more aspects of our lives. Nowhere is this influence more obvious than in educational settings, where computers are thought to be essential learning tools from elementary school through university. In language teacher education programs in the TESOL field, training in computer literacy is coming to be considered indispensable (Kamhi-Stein, 2000; Kamhi-Stein et al., 2002; Nunan, 1999).

A powerful argument in favor of computer literacy for all students, regardless of age, cultural background, or economic status, is that it has the potential of being a great equalizer in educational settings, including writing classes. Shy students can express their ideas freely; "foreign" accents disappear, as do physical characteristics and even gender if the users wish; and students from all parts of the world can communicate instantly. Identities become blurred, created, and negotiated as participants in CMC transcend obstacles that silence many students in traditional classrooms (Hawisher & Selfe, 2000b; Lam, 2000; Turkle, 1995). Inside L1, L2, and language teacher education classrooms, electronic conversations can balance contributions by native and nonnative English speakers, by teachers and students, and among students themselves (Belcher, 1999; Cooper & Selfe, 1990; Kamhi-Stein, 2000). Faigley (1992, p. 167) discusses the "achieved utopia of the networked class," in which the dream of "equitable sharing of classroom authority, at least during the duration of a class discussion, has been achieved." He cites Hawisher and Selfe (1990, p. 8) from a special issue of *Computers and Composition* in which they offer their vision, as editors of that journal, of computer-supported classrooms "in which students are active, engaged, central, and one in which technology is helping teachers address racism, sexism, inequitable access to education and other disturbing social/political problems now operative in our educational system" (Faigley, 1992, p. 167). Cooper and Selfe (1990), too, writing from the perspective of L1 composition, believe that students who engage in computer conferencing can learn to "reexamine the authoritarian values of the classroom, to resist their socialization into a narrowly conceived form of academic discourse, to learn from the clash of discourses, to learn through engaging in discourse" (p. 867).

Another argument in favor of technology in the writing class is that students with Internet connections have access to vast amounts of information, regardless of whether there are libraries available locally. Online distance education, according to promoters, can offer educational experiences to many kinds of people who cannot easily find their way to college campuses. In her review of demographic research on distance learning, Murray (2000b) found that in the United States, even traditional students are tending not to live on campus and study full-time. Internet use among international students and in many countries of the world continues to expand rapidly, if not completely equitably (Hawisher & Selfe, 2000b; Pelgrum, 2001; Taylor, Jamieson, & Eignor, 2000).

A third argument in favor of writing classes with computer connections is that writing, discussions of reading and writing, and feedback from teacher and peers can potentially enrich the quality and efficiency of academic reading and writing experiences for students, in addition to equalizing the power between teacher and students. Although CMC is considered a hybrid form of communication, somewhere between writing and oral language, students still are required to read and write extensively in order to communicate in a networked classroom or on the Internet (Cooper & Selfe, 1990; Faigley, 1992). For L2 students in particular, extending their reading and writing experiences through online discussions and exchanges of drafts of assignments can provide students with both more input and more output than they could possibly obtain in a traditional classroom. In her graduate seminar on ESL composition methods, for example, Belcher (1999) found that her mixed class of L1 and L2 speakers was able to create a kind of mini-cyberutopia in online discussions of class readings that allowed a number of previously silent students to contribute confidently to the newsgroup.

In spite of many obvious benefits to bringing technology into L2 writing classes, many educators in both L1 and L2 fields caution that nothing inherent in technology itself will redress power imbalances and information gaps between privileged and less privileged students or will ensure equity of participation (Janangelo, 1991; Murray, 2000b). Technology can also be used in ways that perpetuate traditional styles of interacting in classrooms, particularly if teachers are uncomfortable sharing, or even giving up, their authority (Cooper & Selfe, 1990; Hawisher & Selfe, 1990 as cited in Faigley, 1992). The dangers of "technooppression" involving abuses of power in composition classes both between teachers and students and among teachers have been vividly portrayed by Janangelo (1991). In a broader sense, the romanticized myth of technology as a neutral, apolitical medium of communication has been dispelled by many critics, including those who continue to be strong supporters of the role of Internet use in L1 and L2 education (Gee, 2000; Hawisher & Selfe, 2000a, 2000b, 2000c; Luke, 2000; Murray, 2000b; Warschauer, 2000). L2 writing teachers who use and promote technology in their classrooms thus need to do so reflectively, paying particular attention to the politics of technology throughout the world. I here review two cautionary arguments, one concerning general Internet use and the "global-village narrative" and the other concerning issues of power and authority in writing classes themselves.

The "global-village narrative" as described by Hawisher and Selfe (2000c) has been promoted in the West, particularly by the United States, since the 1990s. In this narrative, computer technology is characterized as a neutral medium of communication and information transmission that can help unite a divided world, equalize influence among haves and have-nots, and promote global democracy, free-market enterprise, and freedom of expression.

The narrative articulates the popular American belief that technology will serve to join the various peoples of the world in a global network, a cyberlandscape that will diminish current geopolitical boundaries and erase differences among cultures even as it restores a shared community of international spirit. (Hawisher & Selfe, 2000c, pp. 5–6)

Pertinent to discussions of L2 writing is Hawisher and Selfe's point that American computer users rarely question the fact that English is the dominant language of communication throughout the computer-using world or that Western perspectives on authorship, text representation, and the value of a free market are taken for granted. However, as Hawisher and Selfe's (2000b) collection of articles from many countries of the world demonstrates, many people and many large segments of the world population find this global-village narrative far from culturally neutral. On the contrary, it can be seen as another version of colonial expansionism designed to disseminate Western culture and values. On a more positive note, Hawisher and Selfe (2000a) conclude that the Web is developing into a dynamic site where local and global values clash and interact and where hybrid, transgressive local identities are developing within global cyberspace (p. 280). Moreover, as "cracks and fissures" become more apparent in the global-village myth (e.g., increased divisions between rich and poor, the spread of questionable consumer-oriented values, the spread of transnational crime), it is increasingly clear that this myth will not apply to much of the world in the 21st century (p. 286). The authors believe that in a postmodern "redrawing of the Web landscape" that recognizes the local vitality and hybridity of online identities, a global identity will continue to develop, but without the colonial overtones of the past (pp. 287–288).

Other very real cautions about the role of electronic technology in worldwide education concern the fact that both hardware and software are now, and will continue to be, distributed unequally among the world's populations (Murray, 2000b; Pelgrum, 2001), with the result that Internet use "is even more skewed than consumption of the world's energy resources" (Faigley, 1997, p. 39). It is also likely that the continual need for basic equipment as well as upgrades in the market- and innovation-driven computer industry will be prohibitively expensive for many individuals and educational systems in developing countries. Additionally, in an increasingly networked society in which "new capitalism" demands flexibility and innovation, even disciplinary expertise goes out of date before individuals have a chance to retool and develop the multiliteracy skills they need to keep pace with the times (Gee, 2000). What are the rights of students in such a world? According to Gee (2000, p. 67), every child has the right to four kinds of integrated instruction: a great deal of situated practice, explicit instruction (cf. Delpit, 1986, 1988), critical framing (Gee's "coming to know where in the overall system you stand"), and the right to produce and transform knowledge, not just consume it. In short, hardware, software, and the kind of education that helps students think critically about power and justice need to be equitably accessible to all learners and teachers. It is not clear whether such equal access will reach into all corners of the world anytime soon.

Within specific classrooms, questions have also been raised about the roles of technology. Some years ago, Cuban (1993, p. 205) wondered whether extensive computer use in children's education might not be best for their learning and development or for teacher-student relationships. He also found resistance to computer use in many classrooms, not just because funds were sparse and teachers were unprepared, but also because computer instruction tends to alter what many teachers believe proper teaching and learning consists of. In his Japanese classroom, Swanson (1998) found the same kind of resistance from himself as a teacher, although his students overwhelmingly wanted to use computers in their language classes. Is teacher resistance part of the problem? When students are able to access the Internet for all the knowledge they need to write a report, and when discussion groups among classmates and with other people around the world diminish the authoritative role of the teacher, teachers fundamentally need to reconceptualize their own roles in the networked classroom.

Faigley (1992), for example, found some of the changes in

his own L1 writing classroom disturbing: Students indeed were taking on authority in their online discussions of their readings, but some of the male students tended to violate what he called "politeness conventions" during discussions where opinions differed (p. 190). At the same time, the electronic format permitted some of the women in the class to contribute opinions where they might not have in oral discussion. More recent work, however, shows that women are less likely than men to join or stay in electronic discussion groups (Belcher, 1999; Herring, 2000). This is partly because the more agonistic style of communication of men has made mixed-gender electronic discussion problematic for many women, who use different rules of politeness, as they tend to do in face-to-face interaction (Herring, 2000). Whatever the reasons, if women choose not to even log on, as happened with some of the women in Belcher's class (Belcher, 1999), then some voices in the classroom will continue not to be heard.

In Faigley's class (Faigley, 1992), an equally disturbing phenomenon was the undoing of some of his most treasured convictions about education, namely, that some kind of external authoritative values help us construct and evaluate our knowledge and that one value of writing is that it produces a lasting product upon which students can reflect. Students seemed to flit from topic to topic and argument to argument in their electronic discussion without even necessarily remembering who said what in their interactions. (The use of pseudonyms during one of his classes contributed to the lack of politeness and engagement with known people.) Messages were produced quickly and discarded equally quickly, and there was little depth to some of the discussions. Faigley wondered about his role in helping students learn to think and write. "Networked writing," he noted, "displaces the modernist conception of writing as hard work aimed at producing an enduring object" and displaces the idea of a single author at the center of writing (Faigley, 1992, p. 191). Other educators, such as Belcher (1999), have found that electronic discussions indeed seem to contribute to lengthy and thoughtful discussion. More recently, the idea of writing as words alone has been replaced by the concept of multiliteracies (Cope & Kalantzis, 2000) where writing teachers need to help students learn how to produce and analyze images as well as written text (Faigley, 1997). Both L1 and L2 writing teachers are left to wrestle with many difficult political and educational issues surrounding electronic written discussions and production of text.

L2 writing teachers clearly need to interrogate their own stances toward and uses of Web technology in their teaching, as well as those of their students. Issues of identity and power, once thought to be neutralized by electronic communication and text production, have become increasingly complex and subject to investigation by writing scholars and educators. For example, even when the language of electronic communication is relatively neutral, as Matsuda (2002) found in his examination of an online discussion in Japanese among Japanese teachers and graduate students in the TESOL field, participants still have ways of establishing power hierarchies, such as by the amount of knowledge they display and the subsequent mentor-mentee roles that develop. In short, the "politics of pedagogy arising from electronic discussions" have no easy conclusions, according to Faigley (1992, p. 199), a conclusion that is as true today as it was in the early 1990s. Whether L2 writing teachers believe in the potential of electronic communication as a culturally neutral and equalizing force in the 21st century or hold that it can never fulfill its "global-village" dream, it is their obligation to reflect deeply on the implications of electronic technology in the contexts of their own teaching and continued professional development.

Classroom Perspectives

This chapter on politics and ideology has covered a number of key issues, all of which could be exemplified in classroom practices. Although I will focus on only one classroom experience in this section, I urge readers to consult Benesch (2001a) and Shor (1992) for examples of critical pedagogy and to consult the textbooks for graduate student writers by Swales and

Feak (1994, 2000) for a pragmatic approach to academic writing. My own example combines a number of pragmatic, political, and technology issues, without providing a clear-cut solution to the pedagogical problem I present.

The Case of Shuuichi

The case of Shuuichi, a prelinguistically hearing-impaired Japanese undergraduate studying English at a Japanese university, began as an experiment in how email conversation between teacher and student could be used in place of regular classroom experiences in English language instruction (Casanave, McCornick, & Hiraki, 1993). Looking back at this case study of writing in an EFL setting, I was struck by the extent to which it is really a story of identity and authority, not just of the student, Shuuichi, but also of the two teachers he was communicating with by email for more than a semester, a colleague and me.

My colleague Alan and I agreed to conduct a semester-long email conversation with Shuuichi, who had been enrolled in a regular required English class of about 35 students with another teacher. Shuuichi was a fluent writer of Japanese and English; a user of Japanese sign language, though not natively; and an articulate and motivated student interested in computer science and also widely read in history, religion, and philosophy compared to other Japanese students we had worked with. Alan and I met with him individually, communicated with him by writing notes, and set up the terms of the class. I was to be the teacher of record, needing to give Shuuichi a grade, so I asked him to watch the same films my class watched and do the same readings and to use email to write responses to me and Alan. Alan participated as an interested communication partner, and all of our email was shared by all three of us. Over the semester, each of us wrote approximately 30 messages, from several lines to more than 1,000 words. Shuuichi initiated nine topics, four of which concerned issues from class readings or films and five of which were personal. Alan and Shuuichi continued communicating in the summer on topics of religion and philosophy. Seen as practice in L2 writing, this experience provided Shuuichi with more written language input, output, and teacher response than we could provide to any of our other students.

Seen as a study of writing and identity, the email exchanges show how identities and authority were being negotiated among interlocutors who differed greatly in terms of their power and authority. My comments tended to be those of an instructor who hoped to engage a student in reflection on class topics, to nurture along a student whom I took to be shy and reserved from our first face-to-face visit, and to make sure that enough "work" got done so that I could give Shuuichi a good grade. I expressed my power and authority by being directive and teacherly, encouraging Shuuichi to think critically, questioning what I saw as stereotypes of Japan and the West in some of his commentary (e.g., "Westerners cannot really understand Eastern religions because Westerners, as Christians, fear hell, which prevents them from real understanding"). Alan, in it for the conversation and not the teaching, challenged Shuuichi at every opportunity and responded to his generalizations about culture and religion with long discursive critiques, full of nuanced and complex ideas from his own extensive reading and teaching over two decades in cultural studies. Shuuichi would change topics, would write about something from Eastern religion or from his personal experience, but Alan still came back at him, challenging, pushing. Shuuichi would change topics again.

When Alan finally asked him why he did not continue the conversations they had started—was he interested in another topic or did he not want "to challenge my challenge"—Shuuichi wrote: "I changed the topic because I COULD NOT challenge your challenge. . . . I was overwhelmed by the quantity of your TOO KEEN remarks and questions" (Casanave, McCornick, & Hiraki, 1993, p. 172). But this same Shuuichi, seemingly overpowered by the language, knowledge, and authority of a professor, also wrote authoritatively of his own experiences as a deaf student and of his responses to films and readings. He asserted that electronic communication allowed people to communicate "without prejudice" because we cannot see our partners. Indeed, in email, Shuuichi sometimes took it upon himself to challenge our ideas and to instruct us, his professors, that not all deaf people want to communicate by email and that not all Japanese people want to communicate in a "Western style" of conversation. On the topic of how to communicate with the deaf, Shuuichi told us:

> I think sometimes [my two teachers] had fixed ideas about deaf students. Some deaf students, I think, would try to attend the class and get what you say with his or her limited hearing abilities. Other deaf students would refuse to attend class and deny the value of e-mail as well. And some deaf students might even request that you learn ASL (or JSL) to communicate with them and other students. (Casanave, McCornick, & Hiraki, 1993, pp. 157–158)

Shuuichi's authoritative self was hidden behind his conservative in-person self, the one who lowered his eyes in our presence and bowed deeply on leaving our offices and who shyly showed me photographs of himself standing proudly in kimono in the doorway of his traditional Japanese family home in Kyoto.

It is not only Shuuichi's identity that is revealed in a sociopolitical interpretation of these email conversations. We learn something about Alan and me too. Alan, for example, recognized his power.

> I had to recognize that I had the power, both in my role as teacher by means of my native-speaker control of the language, to back him into corners, make him feel he was being attacked, judged, condemned. I didn't want to lose him this way. I didn't want to stop the learning. (Casanave, McCornick, & Hiraki, 1993, p. 163)

Alan noted his surprise at the multiple identities that had emerged over the first two months of the email correspondence. We see both him and at least two of Shuuichi's identities in the following excerpt, in which Alan recalls a visit by Shuuichi to his office.

> Here he was in my office and he was deaf. I had forgotten. Here was the awkward Shuuichi I had met that first day, the one who I had written notes back and forth with. He had gently made fun of my handwriting. Here he was bowing to me, assuring me that he was grateful for my time, sorry for intruding. This was the kid I had met two months before, but not the Shuuichi I had come to know through my computer screen. The e-mail Shuuichi who called me a victim of imperialistic propaganda, who told me to check my facts, who suggested, "I wonder if you are a little confused!" Shuuichi in person. Shuuichi on the computer screen. Not the same person. (Casanave, McCornick, & Hiraki, 1993, pp. 164–165)

In my own reflections, I discover my interest in using email to get to know an interesting individual who happens to be deaf, and I question my ostensible commitment to finding ways to help hearing-impaired and hearing students find ways to communicate as a goal that would benefit the deaf. Perhaps this is my mission, not theirs, I speculate (Casanave, McCornick, & Hiraki, 1993, p. 169).

What the email record of a semester-plus communication experience between two professors and an undergraduate L2 English student tells us is that the written dialogue itself reveals multiple identities over time. The identities we see both reinforce the power imbalances between teacher and student identities and equalize the imbalances. In email, Shuuichi challenged us in ways he could not do in person. In email, his professors tended to forget that Shuuichi was a young deaf student using English as his second (third?) language and tended to treat him like an equal. But I also revealed myself as a teacher with ultimate decision-making power over his grades, and Alan revealed himself as a powerful senior professor who could challenge every assertion that Shuuichi made. If I could change anything about this experience now,

I would have tried to engage Shuuichi and Alan in a three-way discussion of these power issues. But in the early 1990s, we were not wrestling with issues of power and identity in L2 writing classes the way we are today.

Ongoing Questions

Whatever L2 writing teachers believe about the politics and ideology of L2 writing, the questions surrounding the decisions of writing teachers will somehow involve stances on issues of power, culture, and identity in an era that is increasingly dominated by electronic multiliteracy practices. What is the relationship of L2 writing teachers themselves to the goals and activities of second and foreign language writing classes; to student writers of different ages, statuses, and nationalities; and to the new discourses and technologies that are threatening to leave many of us behind?

Perhaps all L2 writing teachers have a set of pragmatic goals, but where did those goals come from? Does the educational system in which L2 writing teachers work provide the time and the encouragement for students and teachers to explore and question the kinds of writing they are being asked to do and the purposes of that writing? Are L2 writing teachers doing L2 students a service or disservice by asking them to question, critique, analyze, and doubt? In L2 writing classrooms, what happens when students resist and challenge their own writing teachers' decisions and authority? Will teachers be able to distinguish between resistance (a positive educational activity) and opposition (a choice not to participate) (Cooper & Selfe, 1990)? In L2 writing classrooms, what is lost and gained in terms of writing processes, depth of thought, collegial support and communication, teacher-student relationships, and eventual production of different kinds of texts in the wired classroom and in the face-to-face classroom? Importantly, in what ways should the decisions of L2 writing teachers on issues of politics and ideology differ according to the kinds of students they are working with and the settings for their writing instruction? Finally, what do students want, and do they fully understand the consequences of their choices? What do teachers want, and do they understand the consequences of their choices as well?

Beliefs and Practices

Beliefs

1. What is your own stance on the question of whether all education is political and ideological? In discussions with colleagues, do you find that this topic is a contested and emotional one? Why might this be so?
2. Where do your beliefs about the place of politics and ideology in education come from? To what extent do beliefs among your colleagues seem to differ according to cultural or educational background?
3. What kinds of L2 writing activities do you believe are steeped in cultural baggage from English-dominant cultures? To what extent do writing teachers have a responsibility to avoid imposing the norms of a dominant culture and to contextualize their writing activities within the local cultures of students? On the other hand, should it be the job of writing teachers to thoroughly familiarize students with dominant discoursal and cultural norms? How do your responses differ when you consider ESL or EFL settings?
4. Should the L2 writing class be a place where students and teachers work together to address social and institutional injustices and to promote change?
5. What are your beliefs about the political aspects of Internet technology? How are the literacy practices of L2 writing students from different parts of the world affected by this evolving technology? Is electronic multimedia technology a great equalizer, or has it created a "digital divide" in which the privileged and wealthier classes and the male gender, once again, dominate?

Practices

1. Within your own L2 writing classes in your role either as student or as teacher of writing, what writing experiences have you had that could be termed "accommodationist-pragmatist" (following dominant and mainstream conventions)? What experiences have you had in which students are encouraged to resist, doubt, and challenge prevailing conventions of writing or prevailing institutional practices?

2. Design a set of activities for L2 writing students in a local context of your choosing in which the goal is to address a social or institutional injustice that you are familiar with. How can you carry out this set of writing tasks in a way that does not impose your own political agenda but that leaves students with authentic choices?

3. Design a set of activities for L2 writing students in a local context of your choosing in which the goal is to help students acquire the conventional written discourse that they need in order to succeed in their local institutional setting (e.g., in a freshman composition class or on an essay exam or science report). If you believe it is your responsibility to help students understand the political nature of accommodating to institutional norms, how will you foster their awareness without undermining your accommodationist goals?

4. If you and your students or current classmates have access to full Internet technology both inside and outside the classroom, what differences do you notice among your own students, by country of origin, social background, and gender, as to how they use Internet technology? Do you see any evidence of a "digital divide"?

5. In your own classroom and educational institution, which medium seems to be the most powerful and influential form of literacy: the print medium or the electronic medium? Give examples.

6. In your setting and in your role as either student or teacher, what evidence do you see of shifts in literacy practices toward institutional acceptance of work that is more electronic, visual, and generally multimedia and less print-oriented? What issues arise for you, such as those of originality, plagiarism (see chap. 5), assessment (see chap. 4), and equality of access?

References and Relevant Readings

Allison, D. (1994). Comments on Sarah Benesch's "ESL, ideology, and the politics of pragmatism": A reader reacts. *TESOL Quarterly, 28,* 618–623.

Allison, D. (1996). Pragmatist discourse and English for academic purposes. *English for Specific Purposes, 15,* 85–103.

Alptekin, C. (2002). Towards intercultural communicative competence in ELT. *ELT Journal, 56,* 57–64.

Atkinson, D. (1997). A critical approach to critical thinking in TESOL. *TESOL Quarterly, 31,* 71–94.

Atkinson, D. (1998). The author responds. *TESOL Quarterly, 32,* 133–137.

Atkinson, D. (1999). TESOL and culture. *TESOL Quarterly, 33,* 625–654.

Atkinson, D. (2000). On Peter Elbow's response to "Individualism, academic writing, and ESL writers," by Vai Ramanathan and Dwight Atkinson. *Journal of Second Language Writing, 9,* 72–76.

Atkinson, D., & Ramanathan, V. (1995). Cultures of writing: An ethnographic comparison of L1 and L2 university writing/language programs. *TESOL Quarterly, 29,* 539–568.

Auerbach, E. (1991). Politics, pedagogy, and professionalism: Challenging marginalization in ESL. *College ESL, 1,* 1–9.

Auerbach, E. (1994). Participatory action research. *TESOL Quarterly, 28,* 693–697.

Auerbach, E. R. (1995). The politics of the ESL classroom: Issues of power in pedagogical choices. In J. W. Tollefson (Ed.), *Power and inequality in language education* (pp. 9–33). Cambridge: Cambridge University Press.

Belcher, D. (1997). An argument for nonadversarial argumentation: On the relevance of feminist critique for academic discourse to L2 writing pedagogy. *Journal of Second Language Writing, 6,* 1–21.

Belcher, D. (1999). Authentic interaction in a virtual classroom: Leveling the playing field in a graduate seminar. *Computers and Composition, 16,* 253–267.

Benesch, S. (1993). ESL, ideology, and the politics of pragmatism. *TESOL Quarterly, 27,* 705–717.

Benesch, S. (1994). The author responds. *TESOL Quarterly, 28,* 623–624.

Benesch, S. (1996). Needs analysis and curriculum development in EAP: An example of a critical approach. *TESOL Quarterly, 30,* 723–738.

Benesch, S. (1999a). Rights analysis: Studying power relations in an academic setting. *English for Specific Purposes, 18,* 313–327.

Benesch, S. (1999b). Thinking critically, thinking dialogically. *TESOL Quarterly, 33,* 573–580.

Benesch, S. (2001a). *Critical English for academic purposes: Theory, politics, and practice.* Mahwah, NJ: Lawrence Erlbaum.

Benesch, S. (2001b). Critical pragmatism: A politics of L2 composition. In T. Silva & P. K. Matsuda (Eds.), *On second language writing* (pp. 161–172). Mahwah, NJ: Lawrence Erlbaum.

Brown, J. S., Collins, A., & Duguid, P. (1989). Situated cognition and the culture of learning. *Educational Researcher, 18*(1), 32–42.

Canagarajah, A. S. (1993). Critical ethnography of a Sri Lankan classroom: Ambiguities in student opposition to reproduction through ESOL. *TESOL Quarterly, 27,* 601–626.

Canagarajah, A. S. (1999). *Resisting linguistic imperialism in English teaching.* Oxford: Oxford University Press.

Canagarajah, A. S. (2001). Addressing issues of power and difference in ESL academic writing. In J. Flowerdew & M. Peacock (Eds.), *Research perspectives on English for academic purposes* (pp. 117–131). Cambridge: Cambridge University Press.

Canagarajah, A. S. (2002). *Critical academic writing and multilingual students.* Ann Arbor: University of Michigan Press.

Carlson, S. B. (1991). Program evaluation procedures: Reporting the program publicly within the political context. In L. Hamp-Lyons (Ed.), *Assessing second language writing in academic contexts* (pp. 293–320). Norwood, NJ: Ablex.

Casanave, C. P., McCornick, A. J., & Hiraki, S. (1993). Conversations by E-mail: A study of the interactive writing experiences of a Japanese deaf student and two English teachers. *SFC Journal of Language and Communication, 2,* 145–175.

Chapelle, C. (1996). CALL—English as a second language. *Annual Review of Applied Linguistics, 16,* 139–157.

Chapelle, C. (1997). CALL in the year 2000: Still in search of research paradigms? *Language Learning & Technology, 1*(1), 19–43. Available at <http://llt.msu.edu>

Clark, R., & Ivanič, R. (1997). *The politics of writing.* London: Routledge.

Cooper, M. M., & Selfe, C. L. (1990). Computer conferences and learning: Authority, resistance, and internally persuasive discourse. *College English, 52,* 847–869.

Cope, B., & Kalantzis, M. (Eds.). (2000). *Multiliteracies: Literacy learning and the design of social futures.* London: Routledge.

Crump, E. (1998). At home in the MUD: Writing centers learn to wallow. In C. Haynes & J. R. Holmevik (Eds.), *High wired: On the design, use, and theory of educational MOOs* (pp. 177–191). Ann Arbor: University of Michigan Press.

Cuban, L. (1993). Computer meets classroom: Classroom wins. *Teachers College Record, 95,* 185–210.

Cummins, J. (2000a). Academic language learning, transformative pedagogy, and information technology: Towards a critical balance. *TESOL Quarterly, 34,* 537–548.

Cummins, J. (2000b). *Language, power, and pedagogy: Bilingual children in the crossfire.* Clevedon, England: Multilingual Matters.

Davidson, B. W. (1998). Comments on Dwight Atkinson's "A critical approach to critical thinking in TESOL": A case for critical thinking in the English language classroom. *TESOL Quarterly, 32,* 119–123.

Delpit, L. D. (1986). Skills and other dilemmas of a progressive Black educator. *Harvard Educational Review, 56,* 379–385.

Delpit, L. D. (1988). The silenced dialogue: Power and pedagogy in educating other people's children. *Harvard Educational Review, 58,* 280–298.

Edelsky, C. (1986). *Writing in a bilingual program: Había una vez.* Norwood, NJ: Ablex.

Elbow, P. (1994). What do we mean when we talk about voice in texts? In K. Yancey (Ed.), *Voices on voice: Perspectives, definitions, inquiry* (pp. 1–35). Urbana, IL: National Council of Teachers of English.

Elbow, P. (1999). Individualism and the teaching of writing: Response to Vai Ramanathan and Dwight Atkinson. *Journal of Second Language Writing, 8,* 327–338.

Ellsworth, E. (1989). Why doesn't this feel empowering? Working through the repressive myths of critical pedagogy. *Harvard Educational Review, 59*, 297–324.

Faigley, L. (1992). *Fragments of rationality: Postmodernism and the subject of composition.* Pittsburgh: University of Pittsburgh Press.

Faigley, L. (1997). Literacy after the revolution. *College Composition and Communication, 48,* 30–43.

Fairclough, N. (1992). Introduction. In N. Fairclough (Ed.), *Critical language awareness* (pp. 1–29). London: Longman.

Fox, T. (1990). *The social uses of writing: Politics and pedagogy.* Norwood, NJ: Ablex.

Fox, H. (1994). *Listening to the world: Cultural issues in academic writing.* Urbana, IL: National Council of Teachers of English.

Freiermuth, M. R. (1998). Small group online chat: The great equalizer. In P. Lewis (Ed.), *Teachers, learners, and computers: Exploring relationships in CALL* (pp. 81–86). Nagoya, Japan: Japan Association for Language Teaching, Computer-Assisted Language Learning Special Interest Group.

Freire, P. (1970). *Pedagogy of the oppressed.* New York: Continuum.

Freire, P. (1973). *Education for critical consciousness.* New York: Continuum.

Freire, P. (1994). *Pedagogy of hope: Reliving pedagogy of the oppressed.* New York: Continuum.

Gee, J. P. (1990). *Social linguistics and literacies: Ideology in discourses.* Brighton, England: Falmer Press.

Gee, J. P. (2000). New people in new worlds: Networks, the new capitalism and schools. In B. Cope & M. Kalantzis (Eds.), *Multiliteracies: Literacy learning and the design of social futures* (pp. 43–68). London: Routledge.

Gibbs, W. W. (1995, August). Lost science in the Third World. *Scientific American,* 92–99.

Gieve, S. (1998). Comments on Dwight Atkinson's "A critical approach to critical thinking in TESOL": A reader reacts. *TESOL Quarterly, 32,* 123–129.

Hafernik, J. J., Messerschmitt, D. S., & Vandrick, S. (2002). *Ethical issues for ESL faculty: Social justice in practice.* Mahwah, NJ: Lawrence Erlbaum.

Hall, J. K., & Eggington, W. G. (Eds.). (2000). *The sociopolitics of English language teaching.* Clevedon, England: Multilingual Matters.

Hawisher, G. E., & Selfe, C. L. (1998). Reflections on computers and composition studies at the century's end. In I. Snyder (Ed.), *Page to screen: Taking literacy into the electronic era* (pp. 3–19). London: Routledge.

Hawisher, G. E., & Selfe, C. L. (2000a). Conclusion: Inventing postmodern identities—hybrid and transgressive literacy practices on the Web. In G. E. Hawisher & C. L. Selfe (Eds.), *Global literacies and the World-Wide Web* (pp. 277–289). London: Routledge.

Hawisher, G. E., & Selfe, C. L. (Eds.). (2000b). *Global literacies and the World-Wide Web.* London: Routledge.

Hawisher, G. E., & Selfe, C. L. (2000c). Introduction: Testing the claims. In G. E. Hawisher & C. L Selfe (Eds.), *Global literacies and the World-Wide Web* (pp. 1–18). London: Routledge.

Hawkins, M. R. (1998). Comments on Dwight Atkinson's "A critical approach to critical thinking in TESOL": Apprenticing nonnative speakers to new discourse communities. *TESOL Quarterly, 32,* 129–133.

Herring, S. C. (2000). Gender differences in CMC: Findings and implications. *CPSR Newsletter, 18*(1), 1–12. Retrieved February 4, 2003, from <http://www.cpsr.org/publications/newsletters/issues/2000/Winter2000/herring.html>

Horowitz, D. (1986). What professors actually require: Academic tasks for the ESL classroom. *TESOL Quarterly, 20,* 445–482.

Ioannou-Georgiou, S. (2002). Constructing meaning with virtual reality. *TESOL Journal, 11*(3), 21–26.

Ivanič, R., & Camps, D. (2001). I am how I sound: Voice as self-representation in L2 writing. *Journal of Second Language Writing, 10,* 3–33.

Ivanič, R., & Simpson, J. (1992). Who's who in academic writing? In N. Fairclough (Ed.), *Critical language awareness* (pp. 141–173). London: Longman.

Janangelo, J. (1991). Technopower and technooppression: Some abuses of power and control in computer-assisted writing environments. *Computers and Composition, 9,* 47–64.

Johnston, B. (1999). Putting critical pedagogy in its place: A personal account. *TESOL Quarterly, 33,* 557–565.

Kamhi-Stein, L. D. (2000). Looking to the future of TESOL teacher education: Web-based bulletin board discussions in a methods class. *TESOL Quarterly, 34,* 423–455.

Kamhi-Stein, L. D., Bezdikian, N., Gillis, E., Lee, S., Lemes, B., Micheson, M., & Tamaki, D. (2002). A project-based approach to interactive Web site design. *TESOL Journal, 11*(3), 9–15.

Kaplan, R. (2000). Foreword. In J. K. Hall & W. G. Eggington (Eds.), *The sociopolitics of English language teaching* (pp. vii–xiv). Clevedon, England: Multilingual Matters.

Kramsch, C., A'Ness, F., & Lam, W. S. E. (2000). Authenticity and authorship in the computer-mediated acquisition of L2 literacy. *Language Learning & Technology, 4*(2), 78–104. Available at <http://llt.msu.edu>

Kubota, R. (1998). Ideologies of English in Japan. *World Englishes, 17,* 295–306.

Kubota, R. (1999). Japanese culture constructed by discourses: Implications for applied linguistics research and ELT. *TESOL Quarterly, 33,* 9–35.

Kubota, R. (2001). Discursive construction of the images of U.S. classrooms. *TESOL Quarterly, 35,* 9–38.

Lam, W. S. E. (2000). L2 literacy and the design of the self: A case study of a teenager writing on the Internet. *TESOL Quarterly, 33,* 457–482.

Language Learning & Technology. Online serial available at <http://llt.msu.edu>

Lave, J., & Wenger, E. (1991). *Situated learning: Legitimate peripheral participation.* Cambridge: Cambridge University Press.

LoBianco, J. (2000). Multiliteracies and multilingualism. In B. Cope & M. Kalantzis (Eds.), *Multiliteracies: Literacy learning and the design of social futures* (pp. 92–105). London: Routledge.

Luke, A. (1996). Genres of power? Literacy education and the production of capital. In R. Hasan & G. Williams (Eds.), *Literacy in society* (pp. 308–338). London: Longman.

Luke, C. (2000). Cyber-schooling and technological change: Multiliteracies for new times. In B. Cope & M. Kalantzis (Eds.), *Multiliteracies: Literacy learning and the design of social futures* (pp. 69–91). London: Routledge.

Macedo, D. (2000). The colonialism of the English only movement. *Educational Researcher, 29* (3), 15–24.

Master, P. (1998). Positive and negative aspects of the dominance of English. *TESOL Quarterly, 32,* 716–725.

Matsuda, P. K. (2002). Negotiation of identity and power in a Japanese online discourse community. *Computers and Composition, 19,* 39–55.

McGarrell, H. M. (1998). The computer in English as a subsequent language writing: Roles and relationships. In P. Lewis (Ed.), *Teachers, learners, and computers: Exploring relationships in CALL* (pp. 137–146). Nagoya, Japan: Japan Association for Language Teaching, Computer-Assisted Language Learning Special Interest Group.

McKay, S. (1993). Examining L2 composition ideology: A look at literacy education. *Journal of Second Language Writing, 2*, 65–81.

Murray, D. E. (1999). Access to information technology: Considerations for language educators. *Prospect, 14*(3), 4–12.

Murray, D. E. (2000a). Changing technologies, changing literacy communities? *Language Learning & Technology, 4*(2), 43–58. Available at <http://llt.msu.edu>

Murray, D. E. (2000b). Protean communication: The language of computer-mediated communication. *TESOL Quarterly, 34*, 397–421.

Nunan, D. (1999). A foot in the world of ideas: Graduate study through the Internet. *Language Learning & Technology, 3*(1), 52–74. Available at <http://llt.msu.edu>

O'Donnell, T. G. (1996). Politics and ordinary language: A defense of expressivist rhetorics. *College English, 58*, 423–439.

Pally, M. (1997). Critical thinking in ESL: An argument for sustained content. *Journal of Second Language Writing, 6*, 293–311.

Pelgrum, W. J. (2001). Obstacles to the integration of ICT in education: Results from a worldwide educational assessment. *Computers and Education, 37*, 163–178.

Pennycook, A. (1989). The concept of method, interested knowledge, and the politics of language teaching. *TESOL Quarterly, 23*, 589–618.

Pennycook, A. (1994). *The cultural politics of English as an international language.* Harlow, England: Longman.

Pennycook, A. (1996). Borrowing others' words: Text, ownership, memory, and plagiarism. *TESOL Quarterly, 30*, 201–230.

Pennycook, A. (1997). Vulgar pragmatism, critical pragmatism, and EAP. *English for Specific Purposes, 19*, 253–269.

Pennycook, A. (1999) Introduction: Critical approaches to TESOL. *TESOL Quarterly, 33*, 329–348.

Pennycook, A. (2000). The social politics and the cultural politics of language classrooms. In J. K. Hall & W. G. Eggington (Eds.), *The sociopolitics of English language teaching* (pp. 89–103). Clevedon, England: Multilingual Matters.

Phillipson, R. (1992). *Linguistic imperialism.* Oxford: Oxford University Press.

Ramanathan, V. (1999). "English is here to stay": A critical look at institutional and educational practices in India. *TESOL Quarterly, 33*, 211–231.

Ramanathan, V., & Atkinson, D. (1999). Individualism, academic writing, and ESL writers. *Journal of Second Language Writing, 8,* 45–75.

Ramanathan, V., & Kaplan, R. (1996a). Audience and voice in current L1 composition texts: Some implications for ESL student writers. *Journal of Second Language Writing, 5,* 21–33.

Ramanathan, V., & Kaplan, R. (1996b). Some problematic "channels" in the teaching of critical thinking in current L1 composition textbooks: Implications for L2 student-writers. *Issues in Applied Linguistics, 7,* 225–249.

Reynolds, N. (1994). Graduate writers and portfolios: Issues of professionalism, authority, and resistance. In L. Black, D. A. Daiker, J. Sommers, & G. Stygall (Eds.), *New directions in portfolio assessment: Reflective practice, critical theory, and large-scale scoring* (pp. 201–209). Portsmouth, NH: Boynton/Cook.

Santos, T. (1992). Ideology in composition: L1 and ESL. *Journal of Second Language Writing, 1,* 1–15.

Santos, T. (2001). The place of politics in second language writing. In T. Silva & P. K. Matsuda (Eds.), *On second language writing* (pp. 173–190). Mahwah, NJ: Lawrence Erlbaum.

Scollon, R. (1995). Plagiarism and ideology: Identity in intercultural discourse. *Language in Society, 24,* 1–28.

Severino, C. (1993). The sociopolitical implications of response to second language and second dialect writing. *Journal of Second Language Writing, 2,* 181–201.

Shohamy, E. (1998). Critical language testing and beyond. *Studies in Education, 24,* 331–345.

Shor, I. (1992). *Empowering education: Critical teaching for social change.* Chicago: University of Chicago Press.

Shor, I. (1996). *When students have power: Negotiating authority in a critical pedagogy.* Chicago: University of Chicago Press.

Smith, J. (1997). Students' goals, gatekeeping, and some questions of ethics. *College English, 59,* 299–320.

Smoke, T. (1998). Critical multiculturalism as a means of promoting social activism and awareness. In T. Smoke (Ed.), *Adult ESL: Politics, pedagogy, and participation in classroom and community programs* (pp. 89–98). Mahwah, NJ: Lawrence Erlbaum.

Snyder, I. (Ed.). (1998). *Page to screen: Taking literacy into the electronic era.* London: Routledge.

Sotillo, S. M. (2002). Constructivist and collaborative learning in a wireless environment. *TESOL Journal, 11*(3), 16–20.

Stapleton, P. (2002). Critiquing voice as a viable pedagogical tool in L2 writing: Returning the spotlight to ideas. *Journal of Second Language Writing, 11,* 177–190.

Street, B. (1984). *Literacy in theory and practice:* Cambridge: Cambridge University Press.

Street, B. V. (1995). *Social literacies: Critical approaches to literacy in development, ethnography, and education.* London: Longman.

Sutherland-Smith, W. (2002). Integrating online discussion in an Australian intensive English language course. *TESOL Journal, 11*(3), 31–35.

Swales, J. M. (1990). *Genre analysis: English in academic and research settings.* New York: Cambridge University Press.

Swales, J. M. (1997). English as *Tyrannosaurus rex. World Englishes, 16,* 383–382.

Swales, J. M. (1998). *Other floors, other voices: A textography of a small university building.* Mahwah, NJ: Lawrence Erlbaum.

Swales, J. M., & Feak, C. B. (1994). *Academic writing for graduate students: Essential tasks and skills.* Ann Arbor: University of Michigan Press.

Swales, J. M., & Feak, C. B. (2000). *English in today's research world: A guide for writers.* Ann Arbor: University of Michigan Press.

Swanson, M. R. (1998). A view from both sides. In P. Lewis (Ed.), *Teachers, learners, and computers: Exploring relationships in CALL* (pp. 61–66). Nagoya, Japan: Japan Association for Language Teaching, Computer-Assisted Language Learning Special Interest Group.

Taylor, C., Jamieson, J., & Eignor, D. (2000). Trends in computer use among international students. *TESOL Quarterly, 34,* 575–585.

Thompkins, J. (1987). Me and my shadow. *New Literary History, 19,* 169–178.

Thompkins, J. (1990). Pedagogy of the distressed. *College English, 52,* 653–660.

Toff, M., & Curran, B. (1998). Interactive writing: Integrating computer skills into a process writing syllabus. In P. Lewis (Ed.), *Teachers, learners, and computers: Exploring relationships in CALL* (pp. 51–60). Nagoya, Japan: Japan Association for Language Teaching, Computer-Assisted Language Learning Special Interest Group.

Tollefson, J. W. (1995a). Introduction: Language policy, power, and inequality. In J. W. Tollefson (Ed.), *Power and inequality in language education* (pp. 1–8). Cambridge: Cambridge University Press.

Tollefson, J. W. (Ed.). (1995b). *Power and inequality in language education.* Cambridge: Cambridge University Press.

Tollefson, J. W. (2002). Introduction: Critical issues in educational language policy. In J. W. Tollefson (Ed.), *Language policies in education: Critical issues* (pp. 3–15). Mahwah, NJ: Lawrence Erlbaum.

Turkle, S. (1995). *Life on the screen: Identity in the age of the Internet.* New York: Simon and Schuster.

Vandrick, S. (1995). Privileged ESL university students. *TESOL Quarterly, 29,* 375–381.

Warschauer, M. (1999). *Electronic literacies: Language, culture, and power in online education.* Mahwah, NJ: Lawrence Erlbaum.

Warschauer, M. (2000). The changing global economy and the future of English teaching. *TESOL Quarterly, 34,* 511–535.

Warschauer, M., & Kern, R. (Eds.). (2000). *Network-based language teaching: Concepts and practice.* Cambridge: Cambridge University Press.

Wible, D., Kuo, C.-H., Chien, F., Liu, A., & Tsao, N.-L. (2001). A Web-based EFL writing environment: Integrating information for learners, teachers, and researchers. *Computers and Education, 37,* 297–315.

Zamel, V. (1996). Transcending boundaries: Complicating the scene of teaching language. *College ESL, 6*(2), 1–11.

Subject Index

assessment: accountability, 128;
accuracy and fairness, 114, 119–120;
alternative, 135–140, 141; analytic
scoring, 118; authenticity, 119,
129–131; bias, 119, 120; complexity
of, 120; conflicting roles of teachers,
136; constraints, 116, 141; by
construct, 130–131; context-sensitive,
123, 124, 128; criteria for, 118, 126,
128, 159–160; critiques of
psychometricians, 122–123; culture
of, 113; direct, 117, 121; ethics of,
131–134, 141; evaluation, 114; face
validity, 121; and genre familiarity,
134; high-stakes, 134; holistic (*see*
holistic scoring issues); indirect, 117,
121; informal, 128; and instruction,
136, 140; large-scale, 124, 128; liking,
128; local (*see* assessment, context-
sensitive); and L1 writing ability, 134;
and L2 language proficiency, 133;
meaningfulness, 119–120; meaning
of, 114; measurement, 114; measures,
122; objectivity, 120–123; and
pedagogy, 128; performance-based,
135–136; portfolio (*see* portfolio
assessment); purposes of, 115–116,
141; reliability, 122, 123 (*see also*
rater issues, reliability); rubrics, 118;
scoring problems, 117, 121 (*see also*
holistic scoring issues); self-
assessment, 140; single-sample
problem, 120; by skill, 130; social
and political aspects, 132–133;
source-based, 135–136; subjectivity,
120–121; by task, 130; and
technology, 142; terms, 114; test, 114;
validity, 122, 123, 127, 132;
washback, 116. *See also* rater issues

audience, 157, 158–170, 185;
arguments against, 168–170;
electronic, 163–168; expectations,
159–160 (*see also* contrastive
rhetoric, reader expectations; rater
issues); imagined, 157, 159–163;
peer, 157–158; real, 157, 159–163,
170, 180–182; teacher as, 159, 160,
170

beliefs, 8–11, 54–55, 96–97, 129, 141,
142, 186–187, 197, 199, 200, 206,
223, 224; sources of, 11–15

citation practices, 175–176. *See also*
textual borrowing
classroom perspectives, 43–52, 92–94,
134–140, 180–186, 218–224
context sensitivity, 199. *See also*
assessment, context-sensitive
contrastive rhetoric, 26–62; Chinese
counterfactuals, 28–29, 39; Chinese
essay, 37; classroom perspectives,
43–52; comparability of texts, 29, 40,
46, 47, 48; context sensitivity, 40;
critics' responses, 33–39; cultural
patterns, 30; deductive and inductive
styles, 34, 36, 37; defenders, 39–41;
discourse of, 53; ethnocentrism, 33;
expanded agenda, 39–41, 42;
extratextual influences, 30, 37,
41–42, 54; genre features, 47–48;
heteroglossia, 38, 39; ideological
implications, 42; influence of
schooling, 37, 38, 40, 53–54;
investigative pedagogical approach,
45–52; Kaplan's 1966 article, 27,
31–32; *ki-shoo-ten-ketsu*, 34, 36;
linguistic relativity, 29, 37; logical

Author Index

Italicized page numbers indicate pages in the end-of-chapter references and relevant readings lists.